New technology presents new problems.
*The New American Handbook
of Letter Writing* **offers solutions.**

This book will help you:

- Use e-mail courteously and responsibly

- Format—and personalize—computer-
generated forms

- Decide whether to send a message
conventionally or electronically
and more!

MARY A. DE VRIES is the author of more
than fifty books dealing with communication, including five books about letter writing. Several of her books are available in
Signet editions, including *The New American Three-Step Vocabulary Builder* and *The
New Robert's Rules of Order*, 2nd edition.

THE
NEW AMERICAN
HANDBOOK OF
LETTER WRITING

and Other Forms of Correspondence

SECOND EDITION

Mary A. De Vries

A SIGNET BOOK

SIGNET
Published by New American Library, a division of
Penguin Putnam Inc., 375 Hudson Street,
New York, New York 10014, U.S.A.
Penguin Books Ltd, 27 Wrights Lane,
London W8 5TZ, England
Penguin Books Australia Ltd, Ringwood,
Victoria, Australia
Penguin Books Canada Ltd, 10 Alcorn Avenue,
Toronto, Ontario, Canada M4V 3B2
Penguin Books (N.Z.) Ltd, 182–190 Wairau Road,
Auckland 10, New Zealand

Penguin Books Ltd, Registered Offices:
Harmondsworth, Middlesex, England

First published by Signet, an imprint of New American Library,
a division of Penguin Putnam Inc.

First Printing (Second Edition), January 2000
10 9 8 7 6 5 4 3 2 1

REGISTERED TRADEMARK—MARCA REGISTRADA

Printed in the United States of America

BOOKS ARE AVAILABLE AT QUANTITY DISCOUNTS WHEN USED TO PRO-
MOTE PRODUCTS OR SERVICES. FOR INFORMATION PLEASE WRITE TO
PREMIUM MARKETING DIVISION, PENGUIN PUTNAM INC., 375 HUDSON
STREET, NEW YORK, NEW YORK 10014.

CONTENTS

BUSINESS MODELS

SOCIAL MODELS

PREFACE

Let's get the bad news out of the way up front: A winning letter is no accident, and writing one isn't going to be easy for everyone. But using books like this one may ward off a few migraines, so you're on the right track.

I know people who used to have a major anxiety attack whenever they thought about composing an important letter. But they finally decided that career advancement would always be just out of reach if they didn't conquer the art of letter writing. So they worked at it, and now they're supercommunicators.

I'm not sure why you bought this book. You may want to sharpen all your letter-writing skills, or you may want to be certain that you don't embarrass yourself by using an out-of-date style. Or perhaps you just want to have several hundred models that you can imitate or use to stir your creative juices. Those are all legitimate reasons for buying a letter book and pursuing this topic further.

Incidentally, in case you hadn't noticed, this is a *handbook* about letter writing. Therefore, it's different from a straight model letter book in at least one respect: In addition to offering a large collection of models, it provides a variety of how-to information, such as:

- How to format a letter or memo
- How to adopt the right tone
- How to write great letter openings and closings
- How to know when to use a memo format and when to use a letter format
- How to address letters to men, women, companies, officials, and others
- How to sign a letter for someone else
- And much more, all with an abundance of examples

This revised edition has a lot of the useful material that was in the first edition, but it's been completely modernized to make it suitable for twenty-first-century correspondence. It also has some all-new information, such as:

- How to write, set up, and send an e-mail message
- How to make your letters to people in other countries more translation friendly
- How to avoid dangerous language that could get you in legal trouble
- How to write a bad-news message
- How to format a personal letter to family members and friends

The hundreds of model letters, memos, forms, invitations, and other types of correspondence in the previous edition have all been updated for this edition to be consistent with contemporary usage. But you'll find some new models, too, such as:

- A letter setting the record straight after someone has stolen your idea
- A letter aimed at lifting sagging employee morale
- A letter laying off someone because the company is going through bad times
- A letter to a sexual harasser telling the person to stop it
- A letter from a student telling his parents that he just dropped out of school

In this edition, all of the above has been arranged in six chapters:

1. **MESSAGE COMPOSITION** is loaded with practical tips for creating a successful message, whether it's a handwritten letter mailed to a friend, a typed or computer-prepared memo faxed to a business associate, or an e-mail message transmitted to a customer over the Internet.
2. **BUSINESS CORRESPONDENCE** zeros in on all the essential technical details about business mes-

sages—everything from proper formats to stationery selection to dictation do's and don'ts.

3. **BUSINESS MODELS** is a huge collection of realistic samples of business letters, memos, reports, proposals, invitations, and forms, with practical composition tips preceding each model.

4. **SOCIAL CORRESPONDENCE** focuses on all the important technical details about social or personal messages—everything from proper formats to stationery selection to hints about using commercial greeting cards.

5. **SOCIAL MODELS** is a large collection of realistic samples of social or personal letters and invitations, both formal and informal, with important composition tips preceding each model.

6. **THE REFERENCE SECTION** is an information-packed database full of valuable composition and formatting facts, including full-page examples of letter and memo formats, as well as envelope formats; instructions for writing and positioning the individual parts of letters and memos; an extensive list showing the correct forms of inside address, salutation, and complimentary close to use in business and social letters; and instructions, with examples, for writing proper signature lines.

When you finish reading this preface, take time to glance at the lists of business and social models in the front of the book. For convenience, strictly social or personal models are separated from business models. However, as you'll see when you get into the chapters, many of the business models can be used for personal business matters, such as a complaint about a household problem.

If you take a minute to browse through the lists of models, you'll become familiar with the major categories in which the models are arranged. But don't forget about the index. If you're searching for something very specific and you're not sure from the general categories in the lists of models where you might find it, look in the index. It refines general subjects much further.

The index is useful in another respect: Some overlap inevitably occurs among the models in the general categories. For example, a letter of apology may also be a letter of adjustment, or a letter of appreciation may also be a thank you letter. However, the index takes this into account and gives *all* page numbers for a particular type of letter.

I mentioned in the text that I have thousands of letters in my files, letters from others that I've saved over the years and many that friends and associates have given me to add to my collection. Naturally, I reviewed them before preparing this second revised edition. But if you're concerned that I may have duplicated one of your letters, don't worry. The models in this book are not copies of real letters. The actual letters gave me ideas, of course, but I created new models from scratch especially for the book.

The names that I used in the models are fictional, too, as you'll soon discover. I often borrowed words from nature and the environment and turned them into people-names, so you'll see letters addressed to characters such as *Mr. Crow, Mrs. Coffee,* and *Ms. Broomtail.*

The purpose of the models is to offer you a wide variety of messages that you can—and should—imitate. But we mustn't overlook the fact that successful communication is based on an understanding of *all* aspects of letter writing, from audience analysis to message composition to addressing and mailing. So don't short-change yourself by looking *only* at the models. Check out the handbook part of the book too. I don't want to give away the plot, so to speak, but you may even find a few surprises.

Message Composition

Most of us know that the old sticks-and-stones story—
the one suggesting that words can't hurt you—is false.
In truth, the wrong words can do a lot of damage, as
communication experts keep reminding us: Readers will
respond to you and your message favorably or unfavor-
ably, yes or no, depending on *what* you say and *how* you
say it.

Understandably, it makes some of us a little paranoid
to think that so much hinges on our words, even the
mere handful that we use in a typical message. But isn't
it a fact that every time you read a message, you form
a mental picture of the writer? The process is so automatic, though, that you may not even realize you're
doing it. Yet it happens, which means that other people
are doing unto us as we would do unto them.

But if you're a superskilled letter writer, you can relax,
because your readers probably picture you as intelligent, perceptive, sensitive, careful, knowledgeable, persuasive, understanding, reliable, and an all-around swell
person. On the other hand, if your communication skills
are weak or sloppy, your readers may simply see you
as a hapless bungler. However, if the hapless-bungler
characterization seems a bit unfair, it may help to know
that the image you create usually falls somewhere in
between *swell* and *hapless*.

For the sake of our image, then, most of us would like
to write winning letters or at least moderately decent
letters that don't make us look foolish. If you agree, the
next question—actually the *all-important* question—is
what constitutes a successful message? Think of it like a
great recipe for wonderfully decadent cheesecake. Both

1

the cheesecake and a successful message have not one but several crucial ingredients.

Let's start with the obvious: A message has to look good. Typos and other visual errors won't do much for your reputation as a careful professional. But the format you use also affects appearance. For example, it may signal that your company tends to be traditional and formal or modern and informal.

You're going to hate this, but one of the most important ingredients in a successful message is also one of the most troublesome—language. So you're not alone if you have trouble with grammar, word choice, and all the various technical details that can make or break a message. Unfortunately, it's not enough just to learn what's right or wrong. We have to be sensible, too, as this chapter makes clear.

Writing instructors, who can't resist turning everything into a rule, often recommend that writers follow the *golden rule of message composition:* Write unto others as you would have them write unto you. This philosophy applies to letter writing, too, and aside from the annoying fact that it's another rule, the comment has some merit. For instance, do you like people who:

- Get to the point?
- Present their facts logically?
- Sound friendly without being insincere?
- Use concrete, specific words?
- Know their subject?
- Avoid bias and prejudice?
- Understand your needs and interests?

I assume that you answered yes to each question, because these points and many others described in this book are all part of the mix that defines successful communication. Also, it doesn't matter what type of letters you write, because the main points of message composition apply to both social and business correspondence and both conventional and electronic messages.

Audience Analysis

Sometimes books like this focus too much on why or how someone prepares a message, and they overlook the person receiving the message. Yet people obviously prepare messages not only because they have something they want to say but also because they want to say it to someone—the reader.

When you misread an audience. I know what you're thinking: Audience analysis is automatic, so I shouldn't have to remind anyone that it's important to pay attention to the reader. Okay, perhaps reader evaluation *is* automatic, up to a point. But every day, writers—from homemakers to students to secretaries to corporate presidents—unwittingly offend someone by misreading the person, almost guaranteeing that they're going to trigger a negative response.

For example, a senior executive in a large company innocently started a letter to his professional counterpart in another firm like this:

Dear Chuck:

Our mutual friend Daisy Flowers recently let me know that you would like to have some information about our new Yankee Doodle gumdrop dispenser. . . .

The rest of the letter consisted of summary details about the dispenser, and it closed with an accommodating offer to demonstrate the machine at any time, day or night. Although the message said nothing unusual and certainly nothing provocative, Chuck shot back an indignant *no*, leaving the friendly, well-meaning writer baffled. What did he do wrong?

Was it a mistake to call Chuck by his first name in this initial contact? Did that sound too familiar? Probably not, since first names are common in informal social and business settings. Although it's bad form for a junior executive to be too familiar with a senior executive or for a younger person to be presumptuous with an older person, Chuck was supposedly the executive's counterpart, his professional equal. So what made Chuck respond so negatively?

Have you figured it out? The crime was not in using the recipient's first name in the initial contact; it was in assuming that the reader was a "Chuck" and not a "Charles." Bad assumption! The reader was in fact Charles Doyle Henderson II, who despised the name *Chuck* and considered it unfitting for his status and stature.

You may be saying that you would never have made such a dumb mistake, or you may think Chuck is so pompous that he deserves to be "chucked" at every opportunity. However, the writer wanted him to like the gumdrop dispenser, so whether or not Chuck (I mean *Charles*) was pompous, the writer needed to encourage a favorable response from him.

This Chuck-Charles dilemma should readily remind all complacent letter writers that smart people sometimes do dumb things. So what can you do to be ready for the Chucks who insist on being Charleses or for any other potential trap? The best insurance is to find out everything you possibly can about your readers.

Commonsense reader evaluation. If you know almost as much about a reader as you know about your favorite uncle, can you be 100 percent certain that you won't offend the reader? Probably not, although it will improve your odds. At some point, of course, you'll decide that you know as much as you'll ever know, and it's time then to pull out your favorite pen or crank up your trusty computer and begin composing.

But first, let's look a little further into this matter of using common sense. Assume that you're writing to Mindy Mink, and you know that she has a master's degree in business administration, is manager of a major department in a retail chain store, and earns $65,000 a year. You also know numerous other facts that we won't go into here.

Since you want to establish a friendly business association with Mindy, you may decide to break the ice on your first contact with an amusing anecdote. But then, just in time, you learn from a colleague that she tends to be all business. Common sense should tell you that this type of person may believe that humor has no place in business correspondence, so you would do well to drop the anecdote idea and simply write a friendly but straightforward letter.

Does the Mindy Mink scenario suggest that you should take a solemn vow always to be safely unamusing and forever dull? Certainly not. Sometimes dull is safe, of course, but the example means only that writers should be reasonably cautious and use common sense in approaching an unfamiliar audience. Above all, it means that the serious business of audience analysis involves much more than learning a few basics such as job title and salary.

For all of you who just decided that you hate letter writing, hold off changing careers a moment longer. There's no need to turn reader evaluation into a painful, dreaded ordeal every time you write a letter. Often you can just form a mental picture of your reader. For example, the reader may be a citizen of another country where informality and familiarity in correspondence are considered improper and disrespectful. You can therefore picture the reader as being formal and conservative. But when such an abbreviated mental image isn't sufficient, don't hesitate to compile a detailed list of reader characteristics. You may be very busy, but trust me, this step is *not* a waste of time.

The in-depth reader profile. I know, the topic of reader profiles sounds about as appealing as the subject of waste disposal. If it weren't so crucial, in fact, I'd suggest that you skip it. But that would be a huge mistake.

Perhaps it would stifle some yawns to know that many people in glamorous professions depend heavily on audience analysis. For example, we can learn a lot from the in-depth audience analysis done by advertising specialists. Have you ever wondered why some television commercials air only in certain parts of the country? Think about it: An advertiser spending hundreds of thousands of dollars would not be very happy if an agency targeted his or her homespun, folksy commercial for sophisticated Fifth Avenue shoppers in New York City—or vice versa. As a letter writer, you'll want to tailor your messages to specific readers in the same manner. Unfortunately, the only way to be certain that you're doing it properly is to dig deeper and develop, mentally or in writing, a detailed reader profile.

Developing a reader profile isn't as hard as you might think. But if you're still scratching your head at this point, a list of possible questions to ask may help. For example:

- What is the reader's age, sex, marital status, educational background, present job, and previous experience?
- Does the reader have a conservative or flamboyant life-style?
- Does the reader have subtle or overt prejudices, specific ideological or religious beliefs, or other significant traits?
- Does the reader live in a state, region, or country where customs and communication forms differ from yours?
- How does the reader like to be addressed—first name, nickname, last name with a professional or personal title such as *Dr., Mr., Ms.,* or *Mrs.*? See **REFERENCE SECTION: Forms of Address.**
- Does the reader tend to be sensitive and open or indifferent and closed?
- What characteristics does the reader admire in others?
- What characteristics does the reader dislike in others?
- What tends to motivate the reader to make positive decisions or to act on something—persuasive arguments, examples, tests, or other documentation?
- Is the reader an expert on the topic you intend to discuss?
- Does the reader have the authority to do what you want or to make the decision you want?

What should you do if you can't answer some of the questions? Be careful! If you're missing important facts, you obviously should avoid related remarks that could be construed as controversial or simply stupid.

The Right Tone

Did you know that the tone of your letters is as revealing as the tone of your voice? It's just much harder to create the right tone in a letter.

An offensive tone. Those of you who have *never* read a letter that makes the sender sound cold, angry, rude, or insincere stand up. If you stood up, I want you to take a lie-detector test because my files are full of such letters. Someone who writes "Let's get one thing straight" or "I thought I made myself clear about that" or "I can't understand what your problem is" must be having a very bad day. Or perhaps the writer is tactless and boorish all the time.

Then there's the sugary, syrupy, insincere message. Surely you've seen this type:

It's such a genuine pleasure to be writing to someone as brilliant and perceptive as you, and I mean that sincerely [*Not!*].

You're one of 50 million very, very special, discerning individuals [*Not!*] to receive this once-in-a-lifetime offer to purchase a real-life ant farm for $9,000.

It's hard to decide which extreme is the more offensive—cold and rude or gushy and insincere. Either way, I'm sure you'll agree that tone is a powerful force in any message. It can motivate a reader to like you and want to be your slave forever or to dislike you and pray that a million fleas will nest in your bed. Very simply, adopting a pleasing, conciliatory tone will do much more for you than using an abrasive, antagonistic tone.

Some letters aren't too gushy, and they're not cold or rude. They're simply too stuffy and formal, like a court paper. I guess certain people are impressed with the complex prose and stiff formality of legal documents—what they perceive as being very commanding and authoritative—but most domestic readers are not. Even international readers, who expect more reserve in correspondence, appreciate simple, clear comments.

The former manager of a nonprofit trade association once told me that he loved the sound of legal writing, and you could see this in his messages. But all of us in the office were such cowards that we never told him his letters sounded pompous and ridiculous:

> I am enclosing said document herewith and shall be honored to advise you further.

A pleasing tone. Fortunately, somewhere in between rude and gushy and between too much and too little formality is a friendly, sincere, sensitive tone:

> It was good to hear from you, Ken, and I'm looking forward to seeing you at dinner next month.

> Here's the report I promised to send you, Ms. Fishbein.

> Do let me know if you need additional information, Mr. Bellweather. We appreciate your interest.

> Thank you for letting me know that my second installment is past due.

Believe it or not, tone is so important that in many messages a sincere, appealing tone is *the* determining factor, the *only* way to get what you want. Even when other important factors are at work, a pleasing tone may be the one that tips the scales your way. In tough situations, for example, such as in converting an adversary to an ally or in motivating a foe to support you, tone is at the very least a highly advantageous tool.

How can I develop a pleasing tone in my messages, you ask? Easy. Among other things, be yourself—unless you're usually abrupt and rude; then try being someone else. For example, use a conversational tone and every-day language (but not slang) in most domestic messages (remember to use more formality and reserve in international messages):

No: Replying to yours of the 24th, we are pleased to enclose herewith the information you requested.

Yes: Here's the information you requested on April 24.

Use the active voice to strengthen your comments as well as to make them more conversational:

No: It is believed [*passive*] that prices will increase.

Yes: I believe [*active*] that prices will increase.

Use friendly (though not gushy) words generously:

No: I deeply appreciate your wonderfully kind and generous offer to assist me.

No: Please accept my eternal gratitude for your beautiful, unselfish assistance.

Yes: I *appreciate* your offer to help, Paul.

Yes: *Thank you* for offering to help, Paul.

Be specific without sounding demanding or threatening:

No: You *must* send us the booklets *without fail* by January 6.

Yes: Since class begins on January 7, please arrange for delivery of the booklets on or before January 6.

Watch out for innocent comments that may sound insulting:

We received your undated letter. [*Translation:* Dummy, you forgot to include the date.]

Also watch out for innocent remarks that may sound accusatory:

Your letter was sent to the wrong office and thus didn't arrive until today. [*Translation:* It's your fault that it's late, and I wish you stupid people would learn how to address your mail correctly.]

Beware of other innocent statements that may sound condescending:

After reconsideration, I'm sure you'll agree. [*Translation:* If you weren't so stupid, you would have understood the first time around, but I'm giving you a second chance.]

Avoid antagonistic words, but also avoid going to the other extreme:

No: You *claim* that you did not receive my check.
No: I am sick with grief and humiliation to learn that my check did not reach you.
Yes: Thank you for letting me know that the check I mailed on August 5 did not arrive.

When you goof. Do you take time to reread your letters before sending them? If you do, you'll save yourself some pounding headaches later. Many harsh words or jarring comments are unintentional, but somehow they slip into our messages, and we don't catch them the first time around. We know that the comments are unintentional because no one would deliberately offend customers or friends. That would be as bad as spitting on someone, and I trust not many of us do that.

For example, it doesn't make sense to wound an employee with criticism, because the criticism will create resentment, and the resentment may impair the person's productivity and interfere with his or her willingness to be cooperative. As you can see, it's a chain reaction. Moreover, why alienate a personal friend or business associate when life's lessons teach us that friends are much more helpful than enemies?

In spite of all your good efforts, though, what if you goof? Don't panic, but it may be necessary to write a letter of apology to maintain goodwill. Avoiding an unpleasant issue won't make it go away, and readers have more respect for people who frankly admit their mistakes or oversights. See **BUSINESS MODELS: Apologies** and **SOCIAL MODELS: Apologies.**

The *You* Approach

When to adopt the *you* approach. Readers like to think that a writer is talking directly to *them*—as people. There's nothing wrong with that, so your task is to think of the one who'll read your message as a real-life person, not a paper cutout. This is where the *you* approach comes in. This approach is so simple and natural that I'm always puzzled why more people don't use it. But some letter writers still cling to an old starched style that, mercifully, is slowly fading into the communication sunset:

No: It is hoped that the new library will be used as needed.

No: This writer hopes that the new library will be used as needed.

Yes: We hope that you will use the new library whenever you need it.

Yes: Feel free to use the new library whenever you need it.

We shouldn't forget that the point of view you take in your messages—how you address your readers—mirrors your attitude toward them. Although informality carried to the point of being overly familiar with a stranger isn't a good idea, extreme reserve or formality that's outdated, cold, and blatantly unfriendly is even worse.

In most domestic correspondence it's perfectly acceptable—even preferable—to refer to the reader as *you* and to refer to yourself as *I* or, if you're authorized to speak for others or for your company, as *we.* But this practice can't be applied universally. In international correspondence, for example, the first and second persons (*I* and *you*) aren't always the best choices. In certain countries, such as in Japan, the individual is secondary to the organization. In those cases *our/your company/firm/organization* is the better choice. See **International Correspondence.**

Advantages of the *you* approach. Do you ever *listen* to your letters? Try rereading your next letter out loud and listen to the way it sounds. Notice how letters written with a *you* approach sound more conversational, flow more easily, and give the impression that you identify with the reader:

No: The June issue of our community center newsletter may be of interest.

Yes: You may be interested in seeing the June issue of our community center newsletter.

No: It is hoped that the delay in shipping the merchandise will not be a serious inconvenience.

Yes: We sincerely hope that the delay in shipping your merchandise will not seriously inconvenience you.

No: Having considered all current applications for part-time summer employment, we regret to advise that your name has not been included among those selected.

Yes: I'm sorry that we won't be able to offer you part-time employment this summer.

In some cases, such as in the previous example about summer employment, the coldness of an impersonal approach is downright irritating. When a message has bad news (see **Bad-News Messages**), the offensiveness seems to be compounded. Therefore, if you're trying to achieve an appealing tone (see **The Right Tone**) that readers will respond to favorably, adopt the *you* approach as often as possible in your domestic correspondence.

Before all of this starts sounding too easy, we need to talk about exceptions to using the *you* approach, such as in international correspondence, mentioned earlier. Other material in which the *you* approach usually doesn't work well includes strictly formal documents, such as legal papers, formal reports, and formal invitations. The *you* approach is also a mistake if you want to avoid assigning blame or criticism. In cases of criticism, for example, such as in pointing out an error, you may want to avoid being direct: "*The* figures are incorrect" would sound less *personally* critical than "*Your* figures are incorrect."

The Effects of Stress

We all know that stress does scary things to people in both social and business environments. Whereas some people may chew on their nails in private and hide their hands while putting on a good front in public, others turn into a raging Godzilla wherever they are. But no matter how successfully you seem to be dealing with your stress, some of the anger and pressure you experience is still going to seep into the messages you write.

How stress affects messages. It's amazing how many ways stress can distort a message. It may appear as impatience, criticism, or almost anything else that's equally unproductive or rude. Whatever form it takes, it's usually hard to ignore. The problem is that releasing your stress in a letter won't justify the damage it will do to your (or your company's) image and your effectiveness as a communicator. Add to that the havoc wreaked on long-term personal and business relationships, and you may soon have a nasty little disaster on your hands.

Not to worry: The solution is much less complex than the problem. Very simply, don't send a message you write under stress until you've had a chance to rethink it. However, this suggestion may seem impractical to all you e-mailers (see **Electronic Mail**), because a common e-mail procedure is to key in the message and immediately send it before shutting down the computer or moving on to another task. In fact, one of the often-overlooked virtues of that old dinosaur known as paper mail is that writers are more likely to set aside a piece of paper, at least temporarily, and then reread it before popping it in an envelope.

Some people intentionally write but don't send emotional letters. They write them as a means to cool down. I know someone who writes a scathing letter whenever she's upset with another person. After she feels better, she tears it up. It's supposed to be a form of therapy, like kicking a chair. But it would make me too nervous. What if a well-meaning person took the letter and mailed it for you before you could tear it up?

Business letters you shouldn't write. A young secretary told me that she had once heroically rescued a biting letter from her boss's out box. He had written to a subordinate after a four-martini lunch that he had indulged in to escape his own boss's badgering. Later, at a much more peaceful time, the secretary confessed to him that she hadn't mailed the letter. The stars were apparently smiling on her that day because instead of firing the secretary, her boss thanked her profusely and also confessed, with much relief, that he had been desperately wishing he had never written the unpleasant letter:

Dear Milo:

I received your report concerning the new distribution plan for our western district and would like to clear up a couple things right now.

First, this plan is subject to my final approval after a six-month trial run—as you were told in the beginning. Until we know more about its long-term effectiveness, I think it was poor judgment on your part to send a copy of the report to the home office.

Second, you stated in your report that delays in transfers have been reduced, but you provided absolutely no evidence that this would be a long-term benefit. I can't go to the

board with such a statement unless I have something to
back it up.

In the future, please send all reports to me for approval of
content and routing instructions. In addition, be advised that
any statements concerning the success of the plan, or some
part of it, must be supported by full documentation.

Sincerely,

Henry Thistle

On a much less stressful day, Henry Thistle drafted a
more palatable replacement:

Dear Milo:

Thanks for the detailed report on our new distribution
plan. I certainly appreciate the work that you've put into
this project and have only a few thoughts to pass along
to you:

1. Since only two of the six months allotted as a trial run
   for our project have passed, perhaps we should withhold
   even preliminary judgment on its success at this time.
   Although the first two months look great, as you pointed
   out, I'd hate to disappoint the home office later if
   something unexpected happens. From now on, let's hold
   off on sending copies of your reports to the home
   office—just mail one copy to me as usual.

2. Your comments about the reduction in transfer delays
   sound very encouraging. Do you have any figures or
   other documentation you could send me to support your
   prediction that this will be a long-term benefit? I may
   need some ammunition when I meet with the board next
   month.

I'm looking forward to your next report and in the
meantime will be eager to see more information about the

reduction in transfer delays. Many thanks, Milo, for keeping me posted.

Regards,

Henry Thistle

Can you imagine how poor Milo would have felt if he had received the first letter? Although Milo apparently made a mistake in sending a copy of the report to the home office, the second letter made that point just as well as the first one without destroying his confidence and without ruining an otherwise good working relationship between Milo and Henry Thistle.

However, perhaps we should extend our sympathy to Henry Thistle. After all, something or someone was creating a huge amount of stress in his four-martini-lunch life. He apparently needed an outlet, and Milo's report conveniently arrived at the right time. If you take this situation—letter writer under stress and recipient available at the right (or wrong) time—and multiply it over and over, you have a fair picture of what's happening every hour in the business world.

Social letters you shouldn't write. What about the social world? It may seem that the strictness of form required for certain types of social correspondence, such as a formal dinner invitation, means that stress can't affect it. However, as you'll discover from the models in this book (see **SOCIAL CORRESPONDENCE**), regular social or personal notes and letters are subject to a writer's emotions just as much as business messages are. When e-mail is used, personal and social writers also run the same risk as business writers—the risk that someone other than the intended recipient will read the letter.

Notice in the next example how stress almost killed a friendship. A woman in Cleveland, Wanda Woodpecker, said that she once invited a friend from Chicago to spend the weekend with her. When she read the friend's reply, she couldn't decide whether to be hurt or angry:

Dear Wanda,

Thanks for asking me over, but I couldn't possibly come the weekend of the 12th or any other weekend this month. As you know, I'm swamped with tryouts for the Special Olympics and wouldn't dream of leaving the children in the lurch for anything in the world. We'll have to make it another time when I don't have anything more important on my calendar. But thanks anyway. See you later.

Love,

Pearl

It's understandable that Pearl was under pressure from her commitment to the Special Olympics and was no doubt feeling harried. Possibly she was a little annoyed with Wanda for dumping one more thing on her at that time. At any rate, she probably had little more than a minute to reply and didn't take time to choose her words carefully. That's too bad because Wanda concluded that she wouldn't be seeing her friend until Pearl had *nothing more important to do*. It's also too bad because Pearl could just as well have said something like this:

Dear Wanda,

I wish I could accept your invitation to visit the weekend of the 12th, but I have another commitment (tryouts for the Special Olympics), much to my regret. I would really love to see you—it's been much too long—and hope that we can meet here or there another time after the Olympics are over in September.

Thanks so much for asking, Wanda, and do keep in touch so that we can make definite plans later.

Love,

Pearl

The subtle effects of stress. It isn't necessarily an entire letter that goes sour when we're under stress. Sometimes the effect is barely perceptible. Possibly the strain we're under merely takes the edge off things and makes our comments sound a little more abrupt than usual, as though we're preoccupied with something else:

Under stress: Thanks for your letter of March 9.
Stress free: It was great to hear from you, Tom.

Under stress: I received your material today—thanks.
Stress free: The material you sent looks excellent, Marie. Thanks for sending it so promptly.

You don't have to be a card-carrying genius to reason that if stress affects communication adversely, even if only subtly, you should try to get rid of the stress, right? Okay, so none of us really knows how to do that. At the very least, though, you continually need to be alert to the damage it can cause in a message. Although it isn't always easy to see how stress has tainted a message, experience suggests that once you recognize the harm it does, you're more likely to watch for signs of it in your messages. Then you can decide if you should change any words or phrases or perhaps the tone of the entire letter (see **The Right Tone**).

Bad-News Messages

Would you rather receive bad news or deliver it? Most people would vote for the latter, although sending a negative message is hardly a joyful activity. Bad news in the business world usually applies to matters such as jobs, orders, requests, invitations, claims, or credit. Bad news in personal and social settings is more wide-ranging and could involve anything from declining a wedding invitation to telling someone that a friend or relative has died. For examples, refer to models throughout this book.

A high-risk message. Delivering bad news is risky. You may lose a good friend or customer if you don't phrase the message sensitively and provide some form of compensation or encouragement. Or you may lose something less tangible, such as general goodwill or confidence in you or your company. Therefore, it's not only the receiver who stands to lose something; if it's not handled properly, the bad news could create a no-win situation for everyone.

Buffers to soften the blow. Communication instructors regularly nag us to *get to the point* in a message. Usually, that's good advice, but it may not be the best strategy when you have to deliver bad news. If the first few words in a message bring terrible news, the reader may be so stunned and distressed that nothing you say after that will matter. Therefore, you may want to begin with a buffer or cushion—a more gentle preparatory phrase or statement to prime the reader for the coming blow.

Examples of opening buffers are compliments, expressions of gratitude, brief summaries of events leading up to the bad news, statements of policies that make the bad news necessary, and references to areas of common agreement:

> As usual, your work on the Raven account has been superb, Jean. Therefore, I'm happy as well as sorry to let you know that because the director has an interesting new assignment for you, she would like you to turn the Raven account over to other capable hands—those of Tom Barnacle.

> Thanks so much for your thoughtful letter recommending Edward Crow for the marketing slot. Although his résumé is impressive and we want to keep it in our active files, we'd like to find someone with a little more experience in this case.

> As you know, Adele, we've been eagerly waiting to launch the proposed *Executive Bulletin* this month, with you as our chief editor. However, it now appears that this schedule was a little premature.

We've considered your request for a salary increase, Ms. Redstart, and want you to know that we're very pleased with your first six months' work in the Training Department. Company policy, however, requires one year of employment before an employee's first salary review.

You're right, Sam. We all agree that the current rotation system has serious weaknesses. Since the board would prefer to keep the basic system intact, however, rather than drop it as you suggest, I'm wondering if you have any ideas for correcting the problems in the present system?

The last word. Since you don't want the receiver of bad news to go away complaining that you've ruined his or her life, all such messages—even those dealing with minor problems—should conclude with a thoughtful, preferably encouraging sentence or paragraph:

Although we have a no-refund policy on sale items, we're happy to offer you not only a full $50 credit for the turntable but also a free-shipping certificate for any replacement item that you select.

The no-buffer approach. As you can see from the preceding examples, cushioning bad news with a thoughtful opening statement works well in most situations, especially in personal situations, such as those affecting someone's livelihood or well being. But using a more direct, get-to-the-point approach may be better in certain other cases, such as in general policy announcements to employees or standard letters about merchandise availability:

Effective April 1 through September 1, store hours will be increased from a nine-to-five schedule to an eight-to-six schedule. All employees are therefore required to report to their supervisors an hour earlier during this period.

Catalog item #07632, a humidifier belt, is currently out of stock and will be shipped on or before November 18.

Even in this type of straightforward announcement or message, a slight softening or relaxation of the language wouldn't hurt:

Each year during our main shopping season of April 1 to September 1, store hours are increased from a nine-to-five schedule to an eight-to-six schedule. Therefore, we ask that all employees please check in an hour earlier during this period.

Thank you for your order for catalog number 07632, a humidifier belt. Although this item is currently out of stock, we expect a new supply shortly and look forward to shipping your order on or before November 18.

Words to avoid. Let's face it: Giving someone bad news is hard enough without making it worse by using threatening or frightening language. Whenever possible, therefore, avoid negative words such as these examples:

absurd	difficult	senseless
bleak	impossible	terrible
cannot	impractical	useless
claim	never	unwise
crisis	oppose	wasteful
demand	ruin	wrong

Word and Sentence Length

When more is not better. Show-offs love to use big, pretentious words, believing it reflects great intellect and high professional status. But the rest of us know better. More often, it reflects pomposity and lack of communication skills. Yet we also know that in some cases—in technical or specialized areas in particular—no short,

simple synonym is available or at least none that is as
familiar or fits as well in the discussion. Then a relatively
long, more complex word is a better choice.

Magazine *subscription*, for example, is a moderately
long word, but it's so commonplace and immediately
familiar to almost everyone that it wouldn't make
sense to search for a shorter, simpler substitute. Some
technical words such as *interface* are appropriate in
proper context (computer *interface*) but are pretentious in other cases (*interface* with a customer at
lunch). Therefore, although more is not always better,
writers need to use common sense in determining appropriate word length.

The same principle used for determining word size
applies to determining sentence length. We know that a
sentence with relatively few words is easier to read and
comprehend than a sentence with many more words. But
we also know that too many short sentences in succession will make a message seem choppy and difficult to
read. Therefore, some variety is acceptable and even
necessary.

International readers are a special case. They almost
always find it easier to translate and understand short,
simple words and sentences (see **International Correspondence**). Usually, the more syllables in a word, the
greater the translation and comprehension difficulty for
an international reader. Also, because much of the
phrasing changes in translation anyway, there's less need
to vary sentence length in an international message. So
a series of short sentences is just fine.

Pompous language. Even if you agree that more is not
always better, don't relax yet. Writers of both domestic
and international messages especially need to watch out
for words that may seem ordinary or unassuming but
are really unnecessarily pompous or complex—words
such as *commence* for "begin" or *modus operandi* for
"method." Although all writing needs some variety and
we shouldn't monotonously use the same term over and
over, most of the time short and simple language is preferred over long and complex language:

Pompous	*Unassuming*
per diem	a day
cognizant	aware
feedback	comments
obviate	do away with
sine qua non	essential
ascertain	learn
interface with	meet with
aggregation	total
endeavor	try
customary channels	usual way

Trite expressions. *Trite expressions* are overworked, old-fashioned, sometimes vague, and often wordy phrases that stretch out the length of a sentence. These stale expressions should be at the forefront of any writer's search-and-destroy editing mission:

Trite: This will *acknowledge receipt of* your letter.
Preferred: We *received* your letter.

Trite: After giving due consideration to each manuscript, we have made a selection.
Preferred: *After considering* each manuscript, we have made a selection.

Trite: *Allow me to express our appreciation for* your excellent suggestions.
Preferred: *Thank you* for your excellent suggestions.

Trite: We are below the estimate *at the present writing.*
Preferred: We are below the estimate *now.*

Trite: Please return the attached memo *at your convenience.*
Preferred: Please return the attached memo *by Tuesday, December 30, 200X.*

Trite: *Enclosed please find* our latest catalog.
Preferred: *Here is* our latest catalog.

Trite: I *have before me* your revised plan.
Preferred: *Thank you* for your revised plan.

Trite: *Please be advised that* the deadline is Wednesday, March 18, 200X.
Preferred: The deadline is Wednesday, March 18, 200X.

Trite: *Thanking you in advance for* any guidelines you may have.
Preferred: *I would appreciate* any guidelines you may have.

Trite: The disagreements are *too numerous to mention.*
Preferred: The disagreements are *numerous.*

Trite: Returns have been few *up to this writing.*
Preferred: Returns have been few *until now.*

Trite: *We regret to inform you* that this item is unavailable.
Preferred: *We are sorry* that this item is unavailable.

The rambling sentence. Did you know that using long, rambling sentences can easily double or triple the size of a message? That fact may not bother all writers, but it probably won't please a busy reader who has to trudge through all the excess verbiage to extract the gist of a message.

Business and social letters should be short messages of one or two pages—preferably one page that will fit on a computer screen if it's an e-mail message. Longer messages (three or more pages) often qualify as a report or proposal, and detailed comments might better be prepared as an attachment to a brief cover letter. In any case, if you want your letters to be relatively short, you'll need to pay close attention to word economy. See **Clarity and Conciseness**.

You may find it difficult to write economically at first—most people do—but that shouldn't discourage you. Tuck this thought in the back of your mind: Amateurs *write,* and professionals *rewrite.* So you'll be in good company if you have to rewrite your message many times while trying to convert dull, rambling sentences to clear, short comments:

> *No:* Ms. Lightfoot has contacted me regarding your request for her to serve on the cookie committee and has expressed sincere regret that she must decline your invitation to be a member of the committee this year.
>
> *Yes:* Ms. Lightfoot sincerely regrets that she won't be able to work on the cookie committee this year.

Paragraphing

How to handle long paragraphs. Most people hate to read long paragraphs, because it slows their reading and comprehension. Although no strict size rules exist for paragraphing, there are a number of things you can do to control the size of a paragraph.

Always examine your messages to see whether many paragraphs run more than eight to ten lines. If they do, divide them into two or more smaller paragraphs. Or if you have a long paragraph covering two or more points, you might assign each point to a separate paragraph. If a paragraph covering only one point is too long, you could simply divide it at a logical place and aim for a smooth transition from the first paragraph to the next. However, avoid dividing a paragraph (or sentence) just because it's long if dividing it will make the meaning less clear or will confuse the reader in some other way.

I have letters in my collection of samples that consist only of a single long paragraph. Not only does a letter with a single long paragraph look odd, but it's also more difficult to read. To add other paragraphs to a long one-paragraph letter, try including a brief introductory remark and a brief closing remark, thereby creating a three-paragraph letter.

Composing the opening paragraph. I hope we're all in agreement that most business messages and many social messages should be short and simple, get to the point as soon as possible, and end with a brief wrap-up. The openings and closings are especially important, and if they're long-winded, they can ruin a letter, no matter how short and simple the words and sentences are.

Have you noticed that experienced writers use many different types of openings? For example, they may use questions, tell an anecdote related to the point of the letter, quote someone important, or make an interesting statement. Often they simply begin with a thoughtful comment pertinent to the point of the letter:

No: In your letter of August 9 you asked about a special food grater that we carry. This would be our Greater Grater. I'm enclosing a booklet that describes this device and should give you the information you requested.

Yes: The information you requested about our Greater Grater is enclosed.

No: This morning I picked up a copy of our *Gazette,* and while reading it on the way to work, I noticed in the community section a list of recent appointments to the school board. Sure enough, halfway through the list I saw your name and realized that you had been appointed to the school board too. It was very gratifying to see your name on the list.

Yes: It was a pleasure to read in today's *Gazette* about your appointment to the school board.

If you want to add a warm, friendly touch, include the reader's name in the opening:

I appreciated your thoughtful message, Ned, and can assure you that I celebrated my birthday in style!

For sales or promotional letters, as well as many other business letters, you might try the newswriting technique of answering in the first paragraph as many of the questions *who, what, where, when,* and *why* as possible:

> We [*who*] would like to send you a free handcrafted crystal aardvark [*what*] as a special gift to introduce you to our important new Save the Aardvark Society [*why*]. This lovely masterpiece will be sent to you from our Cincinnati headquarters [*where*] the moment we receive the enclosed certificate with your signature [*when*].

Writing the closing paragraph. If you've never thought about a letter's closing, do yourself a big favor and start thinking about it now. Closings are very important not only in bringing your message to a sensible conclusion but also in influencing people to respond or act in a certain way.

You'll find that the best closings have certain qualities: They're courteous and simple, and they use positive words and suggestions. Other factors may also be important, such as including a deadline if time is significant. But there are some qualities that are undesirable, such as giving a reader too many choices. For example, avoid suggesting more than one date, action, or response. Especially, one should *never*—this is critical—use a closing to start a new conversation:

> *No:* You may mail your order now, or telephone us, or send for our catalog.
> *Yes:* Mail your order today!

> *No:* Perhaps I can be of help. If you let me know, in fact, I could look into another matter for you as well: a new recording of barnyard sounds. I think this would be at the top of the charts overnight. Here's my plan: . . .
> *Yes:* If I can be of further help, do let me know.

Using the reader's name with a pleasant phrase is common—and a good idea—in closings as well as in openings:

Thanks for your thoughtful note, Julie. I'm really looking forward to seeing you at the carnival.

Clarity and Conciseness

It sounds easy—be clear and concise. Surely everyone can do that, right? Then why, you ask, are misunderstandings and even lawsuits so common in both the social and business worlds? The culprit is often faulty communication. *We* know what we mean (usually), but we don't make our meanings clear to *others*. I'm sure that there are language purists who always say precisely what they mean, but the rest of us are shamefully vague much of the time.

Factors that contribute to clarity. We know that specific, concrete words are clearer than general expressions. For example, if you were discussing attendance at a meeting of the Eggbeater Society of America, and you knew that three hundred of fifteen hundred members were present, you could accurately state that *20 percent of the membership was present.* A reader would be able to form a much clearer picture of attendance that way than if you merely said that the meeting had a *fair* or *poor turnout.*

But what if precise facts and figures are unavailable or if they're not as essential? For example, if you were talking about the popularity of Aunt Frieda's raisin buns at a potluck church social, you might have to (or want to) generalize and state only that *many* people requested a copy of her recipe. In that situation, specific numbers wouldn't be as important to the reader, unless of course the reader was Aunt Frieda.

Although word choice is especially important (see **Word Choice** and **Fuzzy language**), it's not the only factor that's important. Brevity also contributes to clarity, and most of us have discovered that a long, rambling commentary is much harder to follow than a short, to-the-point discussion. (See **Word and Sentence Length** and **Wordiness**.) The style and format of a message may also add to or detract from its readability. See **A Personal Style** and **REFERENCE SECTION: Letter Formats** and **Memo Formats**.

Fuzzy language. Let's get it over with and all plead guilty up front to using vague adjectives and adverbs. Under threat of a fine and imprisonment, perhaps we ought to be forced to underline every adjective and adverb in our drafts and then be required to substitute something specific for each vague word:

No: She's a *good* typist.
Yes: She's a *fast* and *accurate* typist.

No: Your investment should increase *significantly* next year.
Yes: Your investment should increase by *11 percent* next year.

No: Why don't you come for a visit *some* weekend in June?
Yes: Why don't you come for a visit the weekend of *June 20–21*?

No: The new procedure is *very successful.*
Yes: The new procedure *has reduced overhead costs by 15 percent.*

No: He visits *infrequently.*
Yes: He visits only *once a year.*

Wordiness. Some forms of wordiness are easy to spot whereas others are not. For example, are you aware when someone uses a combination or repetition of two synonyms, such as *first* and *foremost, prompt* and *speedy, refuse* and *decline*? Do you notice when the modifier in some wordy expressions, such as *final* conclusion, creates a redundancy? But the repetition or use of words that mean the same thing may not be the problem. Someone may simply use more words than he or she needs to or should use.

Remember, though, that the number of words you use will affect the tone and style of your message. So it isn't always desirable to pare a message to the bone, because it may then sound too abrupt and formal. For example, many writers nowadays intentionally adopt a friendly, conversational style that requires more words than a very lean, terse, formal style. As you can see, the writing style in this book leans in that direction. But the long versions in the following list are too wordy for most, if not all, situations:

Wordy	*Concise*
a great deal of	much
are of the opinion that	think that
at a later date	later
based on/due to the fact that	because
in order to	to
in the course of	during
in the event that	if
it is clear that	clearly
it would not be unreasonable to assume	I assume
month of January	January
subsequent to	after
the bulk of	most
with the exception of	except

We also need to remember that vague and wordy language increases the cost of correspondence. For example, a rambling and unnecessarily wordy three- or four-page letter takes more time to prepare and usually costs more to mail or fax than a succinct one-page letter. As you can see, it's costly and wasteful to perpetuate bad letter-writing habits. In fact, it would cost much less to take more time initially learning how to edit wordy letter drafts until being clear and concise becomes second nature.

Word Choice

You might be surprised how many words are used incorrectly in letter writing by people with several college degrees and those holding high offices. We hear similar errors on television and radio newscasts, too, and regularly see them in newspapers.

Commonly misused words. I used to work with someone who continually said *infer* when she meant *imply*. *Imply* means to suggest by inference or association. *Infer* means to reach a conclusion from facts or circumstances:

He didn't mean to *imply* by his remarks that the company is dishonest.

We might *infer* from the discussion that the trend will continue.

Like most people, I've been guilty of poor word choice on more than one occasion. For example, I used to use *assure,* which means to give confidence or make certain, when I should have said *insure* or *ensure. Assure* should be used *only* in reference to persons:

I can *assure* you that we will not abandon our principles.

Insure or *ensure,* which also means to make certain, is used in reference to things. As everyone knows, *insure* also means to guard against loss:

Those steps will *insure/ensure* that the program will succeed.

Please *insure* the package for $50.

Many people write *balance* when they mean *remainder. Balance* means a degree of equality and also means the amount in a bookkeeping account. *Remainder,* or what is left, is used in all other instances:

> We need to *balance* the budget.

> What is the *balance* in the rent account?

> Let's spend the *remainder* of the day shopping.

People often refer to someone's *reaction* to something or someone when they really mean *response. Reaction* is a response to stimuli. *Response* means an answer or a reply:

> He had a bad *reaction* to the flu vaccination.

> We're waiting for their *response* to my proposal.

Two of the most misused words are *which* and *that. That* should be used in restrictive or essential clauses. Because the clause is essential, it *cannot* be omitted and therefore should *not* be set off by commas. *Which* should be used in nonrestrictive or nonessential clauses. Because the clause is not essential, it *can* be omitted and therefore *should* be set off by commas:

> The car *that has a crushed fender* [essential to indicate *which* car] belongs to Doug.

> Cars, *which I prefer over trains* [not essential to main point of sentence], are America's foremost means of transportation.

I can hear some of you asking, who cares? Ah, but here's the catch: To those who are fortunate enough to know correct word usage, our misuse signals to them our carelessness, lack of professionalism, and ignorance.

In spite of all I just said, word choice refers to more than making the right selection between two similar terms. The discussion in **The Right Tone**, for example, mentions the pitfall of choosing antagonistic words. **Word and Sentence Length** suggests substitutions for long, complex, pretentious words. **Clarity and Conciseness** compares the use of fuzzy and concrete terms.

Negative words. This is a red-alert subject, because some of the most damaging words are those with negative connotations. Negative words, such as the examples in **Bad-News Messages**, can also have an adverse impact in messages other than the bad-news variety. Using words such as *inferior,* for example, might insult someone by suggesting something unflattering about a person or a person's work. Some negative words stir up feelings of apprehension (*fault*), dissatisfaction (*unhappy*), or anger (*deplore*). When certain negative words, such as *irresponsible,* are directed at a person, they become fighting words that are almost guaranteed to trigger or fuel a quarrel.

Defamatory words. The subject of defamation is an issue that we all ought to think about much more than we do. We know that some words, when used in certain contexts, cast others in an unfavorable or even injurious light. But we don't always realize that such words might get us in serious legal trouble. So if you use words such as *cheat, extort, incompetent,* or *unethical* to describe someone or someone's work to others, don't be surprised if you need to hire an attorney.

Biased words. Another topic that should catch everyone's attention, in a different way, is nondiscriminatory communication. Three categories—sexism, bias toward the handicapped, and racial or ethnic discrimination— are so easily mishandled that they give even expert letter writers cause for concern.

First sexism: Follow these tips if you want to avoid sexism in your messages:

- Use asexual words: *salesperson,* not *salesman.*
- Use parallel references: *Mr.* Snow and *Ms.* Winters, not *Mr.* Snow and Tina.
- Use professional rather than personal emphasis: Penny Pruett, a *competent* assistant, not an *attractive* assistant.

- Refer to women as adults: the *men* and *women,* not the *men* and *girls.*
- Use a neutral reference to spouses: the guests and *spouses,* not the guests and *wives.*
- Omit gender emphasis: the service representative, not the *woman* service representative.
- Use a neutral reference point: *his* and *her* or *their,* not *his.*

Follow these tips to avoid handicap bias in your messages:

- Avoid undue emphasis: Don Davis, *who is a quadriplegic veteran,* not the *quadriplegic veteran* Don Davis.
- Rephrase humiliating, demeaning comments: *speech and hearing impaired, disabled,* or *challenged,* not *deaf and dumb.*
- Avoid remarks that stereotype people: *He has excellent hearing,* not *He has developed excellent hearing because he's blind.*
- Avoid undue attention to a disability: the *guest of honor,* not the *blind guest of honor.*

Finally, follow these tips to avoid social or ethnic bias in your messages:

- Avoid white-nonwhite classifications: *Mexican-Americans,* not *nonwhites.*
- Avoid undue emphasis on race or ethnic background: the *English instructor,* not the *black English instructor.*
- Avoid humiliating words: the *Puerto Rican* workers, not the *disadvantaged* workers.
- Avoid reverse implications—remarks that suggest the opposite about a racial or ethnic group: Jose is a *hardworking* employee, not an *unusually hardworking* employee, which might suggest to some that most people in his racial or ethnic group tend not to be hardworking.
- Avoid stereotyping: *Some people* are shrewd businesspersons, not *Jews* are shrewd businesspersons.

Since old habits die hard, letter writers need to be continually on guard for the unintentional slurs and lingering stereotypes that offend various groups and individuals.

A Personal Style

Style variations. If we were talking about fashion, such as the cut of a suit or dress, everyone would know immediately what the word *style* means. In letter writing, *style* refers to the cut of your message, so to speak. In matters of writing, *style* is a small word with a big meaning. Broadly, it encompasses *everything* that characterizes the way you say something and the appearance of your written material. Your style, therefore, may be very different from the style of others you know. If we generalize, it's easy to picture widely differing styles. For example:

- Some writers have a cumbersome, laborious, long-winded, wordy style; others have a clear, readable, succinct style.
- Some writers punctuate heavily and use excessive capitalization of terms; others use very little punctuation and capitalize only official names and titles.
- Some writers use long, complex, pretentious language; others use short, simple words and sentences.
- Some writers generalize everything and qualify every statement with *usually, normally,* or *generally*; others make firm, confident, specific statements.
- Some writers use a tone that's cold and formal; others use a tone that's warm and conversational.

All of these things or any other aspect of your writing reflects your personal or business style. To get a better impression of the factors that influence your style, refer to the previous sections in this chapter, the discussion of formats in **BUSINESS CORRESPONDENCE**, and the following topics in the **REFERENCE SECTION: Letter Formats, Memo Formats, Parts of a Letter, Parts of a**

Memo, Forms of Address, Letter Salutations, Complimentary Closes, and **Signature Lines.**

Developing a different style. If you've ever reread your own letters and thought they sounded dreadful, you may have decided that you need to develop a different style, such as a more relaxed, conversational style. Since you already have a style of some sort, good or bad, much of the material in this book can be used as a cross-check against your present style. It may help you decide if your present style is up to date, appropriate for your business or social situation, accurate, and so on. To a point, you can simply decide what suits you and imitate it.

Perhaps your present letter-writing style is technically correct, but you want to have a style that especially sounds and looks like *you* or one that more closely matches your preferences. Some things, such as minimal or heavy capitalization and punctuation, can easily be adapted to suit your preferences. But other things, such as correct word usage, can't always be changed: Sometimes a word is simply right or wrong in specific contexts.

Something that should make all of us sit up and take notice is the undeniable fact that our letters often make not only a first impression but also a lasting impression on our readers. E. B. White (author of the famed *Elements of Style*) once said that all writers, by the way they use language, reveal something of their spirit, their habits, their capacities, and their biases. How's that for a good reason to work seriously on developing a winning style?

International Correspondence

Different rules for international messages. Are you sitting down? The fact that there are different rules for international messages is the good news. The bad news is that different rules may also apply within a particular country or within a certain region of a country. The only way to deal with that nuisance is to study each country or region and tailor your messages to fit the expectations and customs of the particular area. If you don't and you unwittingly say the wrong thing, the blunder may offend the reader.

General guidelines. Follow these general guidelines in *all* countries:

- Use the same spelling and capitalization style that you use in domestic communication.
- Use the same conventional or e-mail format that you use in your domestic messages.
- Choose precise, clear language (*never* trendy words, jargon, cliches, slang, or idioms) that will make sense when translated literally by the international reader.
- Watch for grammatical problems, such as misplaced words or punctuation, that will cause translating nightmares for the reader.
- Use short words, sentences, and paragraphs to help the reader easily translate the message.
- Use more punctuation than you might use in domestic messages (but *not* misplaced punctuation), such as a comma after a short introductory word or phrase, to guide the reader through each sentence and paragraph and to help him or her avoid misreading something.
- Spell out all abbreviations on first use and put the abbreviated form in parentheses after the spelled-out version.
- Be strictly consistent in spelling, capitalization, punctuation, and other matters to avoid confusing the reader with unexplained changes in style.
- Use greater reserve and formality than you would use in a casual domestic message.
- Avoid a pushy, bold tone, especially if you're a woman writer.

Guidelines for individual countries. Follow these country- or area-specific guidelines in *individual* countries or regions:

- Use the accepted business language of the individual country or area, which often is English.

- Have your business cards printed on the reverse side in the reader's (non-English) language, avoiding abbreviations and symbols that the reader may not understand.
- Use the personal and professional titles common in the particular country or area, such as *Miss* (*Señorita*) or *Mrs.* (*Señora*), not *Ms.,* in Mexico (*Ms.* is rarely used outside the United States).
- Follow the style of the particular country or region or the person's preferred arrangement of first, middle, and last names, such as that in Asian countries where the family name is traditionally stated first, as in *Yam Mun Hoh, Mr. Yam.*
- Avoid topics, such as meat eating, sex, or politics, that may be forbidden in the particular country or area because of religious, political, economic, or other customs.
- Be careful not to suggest a personal meeting or telephone conference on a day that is a holiday or holy day in the particular country or region.
- Follow individual practices in the reader's country for the conduct of business, as for example the taboo in some Asian countries against conducting business in the first letter or meeting.
- Follow individual practices in the reader's country regarding references to individuals or their companies, as for example the preference in Japan to refer to a person's company (*your* company) rather than to the individual (*you*).
- Compliment the reader, such as by mentioning something or some place that you admire in the reader's country.
- Look for some way to show respect, such as by including a popular phrase stated in the reader's language, even if English is the accepted business language in that country or region.

Converting domestic phrasing to international phrasing. Notice the difference in sentence length, clarity, and complexity in these examples of the same comment directed to both a domestic reader and an international reader. Don't worry about your comments to an international reader sounding too simple. People who don't speak English and therefore have to translate letters written in English will love "simple":

Domestic: No, we certainly didn't intend to send you Jon White's personnel file, and I can't imagine how it got mixed in with the Wind Tunnel Report. My apologies for the confusion, Jeff.

International: No, the Jon White file is not part of our Wind Tunnel Report. The file was sent to you by mistake. We meant to send only the report. Please excuse our error, Mr. Balustro.

Domestic: Thanks, Don, for sending us your impressive new space-saving tool holder for our consideration in regard to advertising it in our monthly catalog. I'll let you know what our ad people say as soon as I hear.

International: Thank you, Mr. Sjandara, for sending us your company's new space-saving tool holder. We agree that it is very useful. Therefore, I have sent it to our Advertising Department for further evaluation. I will call you immediately when I learn if it can be advertised in our catalog.

Domestic: We're looking for new items to offer our customers and would like to know more about your electronic products and accessories, particularly your new Business Edition Instant Camera and the Ultra Alkaline Batteries.

International: Surefire Electronics wants to offer its customers more electronic products and accessories. We are especially interested in cameras and batteries. Therefore, we would like to know more about two of your company's products. Would you please tell us about the Business Edition Instant Camera and the Ultra Alkaline Batteries?

Electronic Mail

Who uses e-mail? This is for all e-mailers: Did you know that not everyone likes e-mail or wants to use it? I know, you can't believe it. Did you also know that some people don't even own a computer (horrors!), and some who do own one don't turn it on every day to receive e-mail?

Although personal use of e-mail is increasing, most heavy-volume e-mail use occurs in businesses that not only use computers but have them turned on all the time. Even there, however, some businesspeople believe that if senders or receivers will need paper file copies, why not just print a paper copy to begin with and fax it or mail it conventionally? Also, those who want a message to appear formal or prestigious should use conventional paper letterhead, not e-mail.

Network communications. Whether letter writers prefer paper or electronic mail, many use e-mail at least some of the time. In business, they may zap messages back and forth over a local area network of physically connected computers, or they may send messages through an Internet connection.

For all non-Internet readers, the *Internet* is that mysterious, intangible, worldwide collection of interconnected computer networks that enables people to send messages from one computer to another over the telephone lines. This process therefore requires that both the sender and receiver have a properly equipped computer and software capable of handling e-mail. There's obviously a lot more to it than that, but you get the idea.

How to prepare e-mail. The thought of preparing e-mail is usually intimidating to newcomers, but it's not as terrifying as you might think. Also, the procedure for typing and sending a message is the same whether you're directly connected to the Internet, whether you subscribe to a network service (like America Online) that connects you to the Internet and also provides access to other information, or whether your computer is physically linked to other computers in a local business network.

When you're ready to send a message, you should follow the specific prompts (instructions) of your particular software, which will tell you where to type the recipient's name, e-mail address, and other heading material, such as a subject line:

From: Dennis Orange <dorange@oze.com>

To: Barry Silver <bsilver@ggh.com>

Subject: Third Quarter Income Statement

Date: October 9, 200X

For the rest of the message (the body), you should follow the same general rules for composing and formatting any other letter or memo as described throughout this book. (See the model of an e-mail message in the **REFERENCE SECTION**.) Since e-mail begins with memo-style headings and omits the salutation, use the reader's name in the first paragraph to make the message sound more personal:

Barry, I have the figures you requested. Call me (ext. 2000) when you return from New York, and we can set up a date to discuss them.

Composing and setting up an e-mail message is the hard part or at least the most time-consuming part. Sending the message is comparatively quick and simple. In fact, I've never met an e-mailer who didn't love the fact that electronic transmission is easy and instantaneous. But there's a downside too. It tempts some people to send messages they really don't need to send, even though we're all busy enough without having to read unnecessary letters waiting in our computer. It's also a minus when the ease of transmission tempts e-mailers to become chatty and rambling or to transmit too quickly, before they've had a chance to review what they just wrote.

Instantaneous transmission quickly loses its appeal when too much haste speeds a hurtful or insensitive message into the waiting arms of the recipient's computer. As if that isn't worrisome enough, remember that in spite of passwords and other security measures, privacy is less than guaranteed in e-mail. If the transmission is misdirected and reaches someone else, your message won't be safely sealed inside an envelope. It may be hanging out there on someone else's computer screen for the rest of the world to read. Even if it correctly reaches the intended reader, how can you be certain that others at the reader's home or office won't have access to it as well?

However, if you can live with those drawbacks, e-mail may become the new love of your life. If it is, here are more tips for preparing electronic messages, many of which also summarize the tenets of Internet etiquette (known by e-mailers as *netiquette*):

- Use correct grammar, spelling, capitalization, and punctuation, the same as you would use in a paper letter or memo.
- Follow the other guidelines in this chapter about tone, word choice, and so on.
- Avoid wasting other people's time by thoughtlessly speeding numerous messages to a general list that includes people who don't want or need them (a process called *spamming*).
- Avoid attaching long files that may take the recipient a long time to download.
- Use emotion, such as humor or sarcasm, discriminately, especially in business messages, and be certain that it will be appreciated and understood (see the forthcoming examples of smileys).
- Use abbreviations (see the forthcoming list) sparingly, too, and send recipients a list of any abbreviations or smileys that you use.

- Never use the immediacy of e-mail to transmit messages composed when you're tired or angry.
- Be careful not to initiate any hastily prepared, potentially offensive or inflammatory comments (called *flaming*) that could trigger hostile, rapid-fire exchanges, and don't speed back a hasty but ill-conceived response to someone else's provocative message.
- Don't use e-mail to send bad-news messages (use conventional mail or a personal telephone call or visit).
- Avoid commenting about other people if the comments would embarrass you should others, in addition to the intended reader, retrieve the message.
- Always preview what you've typed before transmitting it during a conversational exchange.
- Avoid the use of all capital letters, which in e-mail is the equivalent of shouting.
- Use single-subject messages that fit on one computer screen.
- Precede your comments with a brief, descriptive subject line.
- Use lists, short paragraphs, and other formatting options that are easy to read on a computer screen.
- Never publicly circulate or post another person's message to you without that person's permission.
- Always forward messages you receive in error either to the intended recipient or back to the sender, and include an explanatory cover letter.

What to do when a reader hates e-mail. Believe it or not, some people view computers disdainfully. These people will remind you that one can't curl up in bed with a computer the way that one can get comfy with a good book or a notepad and pencil. So if you know that someone doesn't share your fascination with computers and e-mail, give the person a break.

Rather than shove your e-mail down a nontechnical throat, print a paper copy of your letter or pen the person a note (yes, people still do that). Then fax it or put it in an envelope and leave it in your out box or drop it in one of those big blue boxes you still see on street

corners. You'll survive the trauma of sending an occasional conventional message, and the recipients will
adore you for your deep compassion and understanding.

When it's okay to use smileys. That friendly sounding
word *smileys* refers to something known more formally
as *emoticons,* a name for conversational shorthand used
in e-mail—short, funny little symbols used to indicate
emotion in a message. You're probably familiar with the
original smiley face *:-)* expression, although it may not
look like a smiling face (eyes, nose, and mouth) if you
don't tilt your head to the left. In any case, this type of
shorthand is considered unprofessional in business e-
mail and should be used only in personal messages.

Two types of symbols are common, and both are
meant to indicate emotion or an attitude that isn't obvious from words alone. The *smiley,* just mentioned, is
formed with characters such as parentheses or asterisks,
as in the characters *:-&* for tongue-tied. The *nonsmiley*
consists of small letters that stand for the first letter of
each word describing the emotion or attitude, as in the
symbol *<i>* for irony.

Not everyone uses precisely the same symbol for a
particular emotion, so it's helpful to a reader if you enclose a list of the symbols you'll be using in your messages to that person. The following are examples of
smileys and nonsmileys (many of the recent books about
computers and e-mail have detailed lists):

Grin	<g>
Just kidding	<jk>
Lips are sealed	:-#
Not funny	:/
Oops!	:-*
Sigh	<s>
Surprised	:-o
Tongue in cheek	:-J

Other e-mail shorthand. Yes, there's more. As anyone
with a computer soon learns, we live in an age of shortcuts. Unlike the smiley and nonsmiley symbols, some
conversational shorthand—again, for personal letters

only—has nothing to do with emotion or attitude. It's merely a lazy way of writing common expressions, such as *BTW* for "by the way":

As a matter of fact	AAMOF
Bye for now	BFN
Face-to-face	F2F
Fill in the blank	FITB
Ha, ha, only kidding	HHOK
In any case	IAC
On the other hand	OTOH
See you later	CUL
Thanks	TNX
Yes, I understand	YIU

Contemporary messaging has prompted a simple admonition that you'll probably hear over and over until you're sick of it: Although electronic communication has provided us with a powerful new tool, it has also created a special need to use this tool courteously and responsibly. In case that sounds like a statement of the obvious, it is. But keep in mind that the child in all of us sometimes forgets basic manners when we have a new toy to play with. We need to be sent to our rooms now and then to rethink our behavior. For kids of all ages, therefore—both e-mail junkies using e-mail for fun and businesspeople using it for results—it's important to use this new toy respectfully and judiciously. CUL.

Business Correspondence

Many moons ago business correspondence largely consisted of the traditional typed letter. (Does anyone remember manual or electric typewriters?) Letters were prepared on business letterhead, and the Western Union telegram was used for rapid transmission. Now you can zap a message around the world by e-mail in far less time than it would take to carry it to a mailbox. Nevertheless, people still type or, with a computer, print out and conventionally mail traditional letters. The letters even look about the same as they used to look, so at least one thing—format—hasn't changed very much.

Format

This matter of *format* may not be your favorite subject, but I can't think of any way to avoid it in a book about writing letters. It would be like avoiding the topic of trees in a book about vegetation. So let's just get it out of the way.

Basic formats. In this book, *format* refers to the arrangement or layout of the parts of a letter, memo, or other type of message on a page. If you let your computer format your letters for you (my software keeps nagging me to help), this subject may not seem relevant to you. If you want to devise your own format, though, notice that the **REFERENCE SECTION** illustrates three common business-letter formats—block, traditional, and simplified—and three common memo formats—note, standard, and e-mail. The **REFERENCE SECTION** also includes a traditional envelope format and the optical-character-reader (OCR) format required by the U.S. Postal Service for fast machine reading and sorting.

Parts of letters. As you can see by this subhead, the information in this chapter tends to be a little technical, which is a nice way of saying that it may be slightly dull. But the fact that technical matters are important means that a deftly composed message isn't enough by itself. The overall letter also has to be set up properly and look attractive on a page or computer screen.

No need to memorize the next list, but here's a preview of the parts of a letter described in the **REFERENCE SECTION**. They're listed in the order in which they should appear in the letter.

Date
Personal or confidential notation
Attention line
Inside address
Salutation
Subject line
Body
Complimentary close
Signature
Reference initials
Enclosure notation
Filename notation
Delivery notation
Copy notation
Postscript
Continuation page

The **REFERENCE SECTION** also discusses some important related information that we won't get into here. But just to give you an idea, the information about signature lines deals with pesky questions such as whether the title *Ms.* should be placed in parentheses preceding a name. I have letters in my files in which *Ms.* is used in the signature line, though it should *not* be

included except in international correspondence or unless the writer's gender isn't clear without it: (*Ms.*)
T. H. Farmer.

If you've ever missent a letter or later realized that
you used the wrong title for someone, you know that
two of the most important parts of a letter are the inside
address and the salutation. Therefore, the **REFER-
ENCE SECTION** lists the correct forms of address to
use in correspondence.

Also covered there are sticky problems such as how
to address a husband and wife together when only the
wife has a doctor's degree and—very important—who to
mention first. One alternative, sometimes used in social-
business correspondence, is to place both names on one
line: *Dr. Lela and Mr. Orrin Hamburger.* Another possibility, more common in regular business messages, is to
stack the two names on separate lines. As you can see,
in both styles the person with the highest-ranking title
is listed first:

Dr. Lela Hamburger
Mr. Orrin Hamburger
1500 Main Street
Princeton, NJ 08540

Parts of memos. Some people love memos because
they're a little easier to set up than letters are. But others hate them because they look less dignified and too
informal. However, with the rise of e-mail, we'll all be
seeing a lot more of the memo format, so we'd better
get used to it.

Notice that the parts of a traditional memo, also listed
in the **REFERENCE SECTION**, are somewhat different
from the parts of a letter. In most formats, a letter has
an inside address, a salutation, a complimentary close,
and a signature line. A memo, however, begins with a
heading consisting of various guide words: *Date, To,
From, Subject,* and so on. Following that is the memo
body but no complimentary close or signature block.
After that, though, a memo has the same type of concluding reference information used in a letter: reference

initials, enclosure notation, filename notation, delivery notation, copy notation, and postscript.

Like a letter, a memo also may have a continuation page with the same type of heading as that used on a letter's continuation page.

Importance of format. Making an argument about the importance of format isn't as hard as you might think. Granted, the various details about formatting a message are somewhat tedious and boring, and many organizations already have an established format that all employees are required to follow. But the appearance of a letter is *so* important—remember, first impressions count—that you can never know too much about proper formatting. Perhaps your company's established format violates some long-standing rule about letter setup and you can impress your boss by pointing this out—tactfully, of course.

Think for a moment about the letters you receive. Have you ever received one that just didn't look right? If so, you're probably well aware that improper spacing and incorrect positioning of the elements of a letter can ruin the letter's appearance. In fact, a poor letter format can create a bad impression before the recipient reads even the first word. Each time that I see an ugly format, I can't stop myself from visualizing the person who created it. Believe me, it's *not* a pretty picture. It can't be said too many times: First impressions count.

Common sense, therefore, tells us that an attractive format is very important if you want to convince a reader that you're a neat, careful, accurate professional. But a pleasing format is useful in another, even more practical sense. It tells the reader whether you or your company tends to be traditional, conservative, modern, efficient, and so on.

Someone who uses a block format, for example, and especially a simplified format (see the sample formats in the **REFERENCE SECTION**), appears to be an efficient, contemporary individual. Someone who uses a traditional format appears to be more conservative. So you can make a statement about yourself or your company with the format you choose.

Choosing a format. Like many others, I started out using a traditional format. That was the most common format in the days when typewriters were the only game in town. But the traditional format wasn't efficient enough for me—too much time-consuming indenting and tab setting—so I switched to the more modern and more easily set up block format. If ever I'm in even more of a hurry, I'll probably switch to the even easier to set up simplified format, which omits the salutation and complimentary close.

But don't let me influence you. Unless your company has a firm policy about format, the one you choose is up to you, and you probably already know what you like. Whatever saves time and looks modern appeals to many businesspeople, whereas something that looks more traditional or conservative is important to others, such as to bankers or lawyers. In general, your business or profession, your personal tastes, and any company requirements will all play a part in your choice.

Business Stationery

Let's assume that unless you're starting a new company, your organization already has standard business letterhead, matching envelopes, and possibly memo letterhead or at least some type of "From the Desk of" notes. You probably have business cards, too, that you can swiftly stuff into the hands of unsuspecting people before they realize what's coming. (I wonder why we assume that every man, woman, dog, and cat in the universe needs one of our cards.)

However, even though you may already have all this stationery, nothing is forever, and companies like to update their stationery from time to time. Therefore, it's worth knowing something about choosing the right stationery for you or your company.

Letterhead stationery. I assume that most of us take our stationery for granted and that no one is losing sleep over matters such as paper grade or weight, even though paper experts know that both factors are important. But overall appearance is something else: We all want our stationery to look good enough to impress the dickens out of others.

As far as the technical details are concerned, if you've ever ordered stationery for yourself or your company, you'll know that you can choose economy-, standard-, or premium-grade paper to fit the intended use. For example, standard letterhead (8½ by 11 inches and usually 20- or 24-pound weight) may be a high-grade sulfite bond or a 25, 50, 75, or 100 percent cotton-content paper, usually in a white or pastel color.

But before you put out a lot of extra money for cotton-content paper, look at some of the high-quality bonds. Many of the bond papers look as expensive as the usually higher-cost cotton papers. (*Reminder:* Paper for continuation pages, used when letters run over one page, should be of the same type and quality as the letterhead paper.)

When executives write social-business letters, such as a letter thanking a business associate for a gift, they sometimes use Monarch (nothing to do with butterflies), or executive-size, paper. It's about 7 by 10 inches and may have either a smooth or textured finish, as preferred. The envelopes for executive stationery (3⅞ by 7½) are somewhat smaller than the regular No. 10 (4⅛ by 9⅛ inches) or No. 9 (3⅞ by 8⅞ inches) envelopes used with standard letterhead. An even smaller envelope is the No. 6¾ (3⅝ by 6¾), often used for notes, invoices, and other smaller-size material.

Regardless of size—and sizes may vary depending on the manufacturer—envelopes used with letterhead should be consistent in color and grade with the letterhead paper. The style and color of any printing that appears on the envelopes should also match that of the letterhead.

Papers differ in more ways than I have room to mention. Watermarked paper, for example, has a translucent mark or design that's visible when the paper is held up to the light. Some papers are brighter and smoother than others, and since that type of paper is less likely to curl and jam in a machine, it's often preferred for computer printers and copy machines. Next time you're paging through an office-supply catalog, notice the ads for paper. You'll see that paper manufacturers and office suppliers usually indicate whether a particular paper is suitable for printing, copying, or other uses.

Misuse of business stationery. We all know that some employees use company supplies for personal matters—not you or me, of course—and business letterhead is one of those misused supplies. Although business letterhead is suitable for most business purposes, it obviously shouldn't be used for noncompany business. Therefore, one should *not* use company letterhead to write to someone about a personal lawsuit or to solicit donations for a personal club or charity.

Letterhead design. It may make you dizzy to visit printers and view their sample letterheads, but otherwise, the experience is worthwhile. It will be immediately clear that the design of letterhead varies widely according to the type of business. A lawyer might have a conservative printed or engraved name-and-address heading, whereas a toy manufacturer might have a supermodern three- or four-color letterhead with a catchy product symbol or with the company logo (symbol). Today, almost anything goes as long as the design is appropriate for the particular profession or business. (*Note:* Family crests are used only on stationery for strictly social purposes.)

Have you ever seen engraved business stationery? Not likely, although some top executives still use it. Engraving was once a much more common process used to produce type and designs on fine letterhead stationery. However, because of the high cost of engraving, most stationery is printed nowadays, sometimes in shiny raised letters (created by a process called *thermography*) that resemble engraving. (*Reminder:* Executives who have their names printed or engraved at the top left or right of the letterhead, beneath the company name, should not repeat their names in the usual position of the typed signature line at the bottom of the letter.)

Memo stationery. What do you think of when you hear the word *memo*? In some companies the memo is becoming almost synonymous with the e-mail message. You e-mailers know all about that. However, it may surprise you to know that conventional paper memos, especially interoffice memos, are still widely used for a variety of informal purposes: to send a note to a business colleague, to order supplies, to send brief messages to friends and associates on business committees, and so on. In those cases, memo stationery might follow the example of the business letterhead—same paper, same size, same logo, and so on.

Office-supply stores have a variety of commercial memo forms, and printers can print your company's name, address, and logo on virtually any style form, including computer forms. Also, with the right equipment, you can design and print almost any type of letterhead in-house. Nevertheless, the sale of commercial memo forms is still big business.

Business cards. Have you ever met a businessperson who didn't use business cards? Perhaps, but the words "Let me give you my card" are among the most often repeated in business. Nowadays, when I see someone digging around in his or her pocket or wallet, I just hold out my hand because I know a card is coming. I keep hoping for money, but it's always a card.

Most of the cards, which may be in either a shiny- or matte-finish card stock (heavier than ordinary paper), are about 3½ by 2 inches in the single-card style. Fold-over cards are double-size cards folded once to resemble the single size. Although you may use a larger card size, and possibly should if a lot of advertising copy must go on it, recipients like something that will fit in a wallet or a file of other standard-size cards.

You can design and print business cards in-house, the same as memo or letter stationery, or order them from a printer. Shopping malls, mail centers, and other places even have machines about the size of an ATM that you can use to produce your own instant cards.

Most cards for executives are printed, with or without raised letters, in black on a white or pastel card stock.

Other employees, such as sales personnel, may have cards with two or more colors. Many companies want their business cards to match their other stationery in type style, colors used, and so on.

For details about social cards, see **SOCIAL CORRE-SPONDENCE: Social and Personal Stationery.**

Arrangement of the data. The next question is how to arrange the information on a card. In a way, you're on your own, because you won't find any firm rules about arranging the data on a business card. However, certain patterns seem more prevalent than others do. For example, high-level executives often put the person's name in the middle of the card and the job title, company name, address, and telephone/fax/e-mail number in the lower left and right corners. But any other arrangement that's clear is just as acceptable.

Below the executive level, people often put the company name in the center of the card and the person's name, title, department, address, and telephone/fax/e-mail number in the lower left and right corners. Again, any other arrangement that's clear is also acceptable. Or you may want an entirely different arrangement of data, possibly to provide room for listing office hours or other information. That's fine too.

However, regardless of the layout of data that you prefer, always spell out *Company* or abbreviate it *Co.* according to the way the name is officially registered. Also, omit titles such as *Mr., Mrs., Ms.,* or *Dr.* (*M.D.* would follow the name), unless you need a title to clarify gender, as in *Mr. Leslie Peppercorn.*

For ideas, you may have computer software with sample business card formats. Otherwise, you'll find that printers have many examples.

Business cards and gifts. It's almost an understatement to say that gift giving is a common practice in business. Although executives often enclose business cards with gifts, some authorities frown on this practice. Gift giving, even in business, is supposed to be a *social* gesture, and according to strict etiquette, you should enclose a *social* card (formally called a *visiting card*). See **SOCIAL CORRESPONDENCE: Social and Personal Stationery**.

But here's the problem: Social cards aren't used as much nowadays. So what should you do? If you don't have a social card, don't worry about it. You can personalize your business card, or make it less businessy, by drawing a light line through your name with pen and ink (but without completely obliterating it so that others can still read it). Then write a personal note on the front or, if you need more room, on the back and *sign* the note, preferably with your first name only. See? There's a solution for everything.

Methods of Production

You won't find any big surprises here: The most familiar means of producing business letters are by handwriting, typewriter, and computer. If additional copies are needed, the most familiar means of duplicating the letters are by computer, printing press, and photocopier. Fax, as you probably know, is more often referred to as a method of transmission rather than production or duplication.

Handwriting. I know people who would cringe at the idea of handwriting *business* messages. They would argue emphatically that handwriting is for *personal* correspondence, that it has no place in business correspondence, and that business letters and memos should *always* be prepared by computer or typewriter so that they look businesslike and professional.

Okay, but what about all those quickie gems we receive on little rainbow-colored, self-sticking notes or those hastily penned "From the Desk of" messages? It's unlikely that anyone would take time to type such messages, at least not the self-adhesive notes. Also, many *informal* business memo formats are designed especially for handwritten messages. Although I'm sure that none of us would want to decipher several pages of someone else's handwriting, some would nevertheless argue that it makes perfect sense to pen *very brief,* informal messages rather than go to the time and cost of producing a regular letter or memo.

Computer preparation. It's official: The computer is the vehicle of choice for preparing business messages, although the basic, but less versatile, electronic typewriter is also used in many small firms and at least in part in larger corporations. Speed, ease of editing, and ability to merge new facts into stock letters are a few of the advantages of using a computer, as devoted users well know. Also, letters can be formatted in advance and the format stored in the computer, so that you don't have to reset paragraph indention, margin settings, and so on with each new letter. To be fair, though, high-end electronic typewriters also have many of the timesaving editing and formatting features of computers.

As you know, the world changed dramatically with the opening of the Internet to businesses across the globe, and since then, e-mail (discussed in **MESSAGE COMPOSITION**) has become an especially important tool. So computer-prepared messages include memo-style e-mail messages as well as the traditional paper memos and letters.

Fax transmission. You've probably noticed that fax machines have been multiplying like rabbits. They're everywhere, and users can't imagine life without them. However, since independent fax machines have no keyboard for preparing messages, you have to prepare a letter or other document elsewhere, such as by typewriter or computer, and then take it to the fax machine for transmission. A handy alternative is to use computer equipment and software that's set up for sending faxes directly from the computer.

If you're interested in the technical process, fax transmission has traditionally involved creating signals that will travel over the telephone lines. For example, once a document is inside a machine, the copy (both words and graphics) is scanned and converted to signals that will travel over the telephone lines to another fax machine. The other machine then reconverts the information and spits it out in paper form.

But you can bypass the direct telephone connection if you have an Internet-enabled fax. With this capability, you can dial an e-mail address instead of a telephone fax number and send your fax to someone's e-mail address. As you can see, everything is interconnected nowadays (fax machines, computers, telephones, and whatnot), thanks in part to the Internet.

Mailing Guidelines

Most of us worry much more about handling outgoing than incoming mail because there's so much more to do with the outgoing mail. Nowadays we have to make an additional decision: how to *send* a message—conventionally or electronically.

Some of you may primarily use e-mail, fax, and other means of rapid transmission for your correspondence, but let's face it: Most organizations send some of their correspondence—often a lot of it—through the U.S. Postal Service. They also use private delivery companies, especially for overnight express service when neither fax nor e-mail is appropriate. (Detailed mailing guidelines are available from the private companies, and the Postal Service publishes and sells subscriptions to its *Domestic Mail Manual* and *International Mail Manual.*)

Electronic mail. E-mail aficionados think that e-mail preparation is one of the easiest tasks in the world. If you're a devoted e-mailer, I'm sure that you'll agree with that assessment. The rest of us can take comfort in the fact that the software and electronic network being used will take each of us by the hand and gently guide us through the mystery of e-mail preparation.

Did you read the preceding chapter, **MESSAGE COMPOSITION**? If you didn't, this might be a good time to do so. The section **Electronic Mail** offers many practical do's and don't's for preparing and sending electronic messages. The discussion also includes special guidelines such as when and how to use e-mail shorthand (abbreviations and *smileys*—symbols representing emotions).

The e-mail process is fairly simple. For example, as explained in the previous chapter, your e-mail software will tell you where to type specific data, such as the intended recipient's name and e-mail address. After you've filled in this introductory data, and before you press the key to transmit, you'll be returning to more familiar territory. I say "more familiar" because you should compose and set up the body of an e-mail message the same as the body of a conventional paper memo. See the material on memos and the sample formats in the **REFERENCE SECTION**.

Let's say that you've composed and formatted your message, and you're congratulating yourself, as well you should if it's your first message. But before you hit the key to send your masterpiece off into cyberspace—that intangible realm where electronic messages travel—remember to use your spell-check program *and* to proofread your message manually for errors and other problems. Longtime e-mailers can benefit from that advice too. If composition, not transmission, is your concern, refer to the topics in the preceding chapter (word choice, tone, word and sentence length, and so on).

What if you're still more comfortable with paper copies? If so, you can relax, because it's easy to print a paper copy of any e-mail message you send or receive and file it in the paper files. But it's up to you. After you're more at home with e-mail, you may decide to dispense with paper. If so, you can edit the messages you prepare directly on screen and immediately send them from your computer. Similarly, you can also read any incoming messages on your computer screen, without printing a paper copy of them.

But you'll probably want to save your outgoing and incoming e-mail messages. So where do you file the copies if you decide to kick the paper habit? In your computer, of course, while crossing your fingers that your system won't crash one day and eat up all your electronic files. (Wary users back up everything on removable disks.)

Conventional mail. Conventional mail is another world, almost another galaxy, although many of the same procedures are important in both conventional and electronic mail. For example, before mailing a paper message you would proofread it the same as an electronic message and check that all errors have been corrected. With a paper letter, you would also check to be certain that the letter has been signed (I receive about one unsigned letter a month) and that enclosures are attached.

Forgetting to enclose the enclosures seems to be a problem that busy people share. I can't begin to tell you how often I've had to let someone know that an enclosure wasn't enclosed. But if you can solve that problem, or if it isn't a problem for you, the next question is how to assemble and enclose the material.

A logical way to arrange paper enclosures is to put the items in the order mentioned by the enclosure notation at the bottom of the letter. If you have various odd-size enclosures, put the large ones behind the letter and the small ones in front of it. Place coins in a separate small envelope or tape them to a card.

So much for assembling the items. How should you attach them together, or shouldn't you attach them? This brings us to a discussion of two mortal enemies—metering/stamping machines and paper clips. The clips jam the machines, and the machines—in retaliation, no doubt—chew up the envelopes and their contents. Since paper clips damage the postal equipment and the equipment then damages the mail, we have no choice but to staple loose items to the letter or fold and tuck them, without paper clips or staples, inside the first fold of the letter.

What, you ask, should I do if I *must* use paper clips? Easy. If it's essential to use paper clips, you clearly have to outsmart the equipment. One way to do this is to put the letter in the envelope upside down, with the paper clip away from the postage area where it might jam the postal equipment. Or if you have large enclosures, you might want to send them in another envelope apart from your letter. But you probably will still have to deal with the paper clip dilemma if there's more than one page.

Envelopes. I'm certain that even you die-hard e-mailers send some material in conventional envelopes now and then, so this subject shouldn't be obsolete just yet. Whatever you're sending, you'll either be typing or, with your computer, printing the address directly on an envelope or a mailing label. As always, proofreading is mandatory, and you'll want to compare the address on the envelope with the inside address on the letter to be certain that the information is the same. See the models in the **REFERENCE SECTION** for the correct placement of data.

Choosing the right envelope won't drain anyone's brainpower. You can mail your standard letterheads in either a No. 10 (most common) or No. 9 envelope. See the discussion of envelope sizes in **Letterhead stationery**.

However, folding and inserting your mail in the envelope isn't quite as easy, if you want to do it right. First fold the letter in thirds, with the second fold leaving an edge of ¼ inch showing at the top. Then insert the letter in the envelope so that this small protruding edge is visible before you seal the envelope (again, if you use paper clips, put it all in upside down). If you use a window envelope, fold the letter so that the address panel faces the outside.

If you follow these guidelines, the reader can pull out the letter by grasping the small edge, open the letter, and start reading without twisting or turning it. Readers adore people who know how to fold and insert letters so they don't have to struggle with them.

Mailroom economy. If you're so loaded (financially, that is) that you don't care about saving money, you can skip this section. But I've never heard of a business that doesn't want to save money. In fact, businesses want to reduce their expenses every bit as much as most of us want to reduce our household budgets. So here are a few ideas for cutting mailroom costs:

- Combine mailings to the same person and send bulky material by third-class postal mail or in reduced form, such as by microfilm.
- Consider whether a telephone call, fax, or e-mail message would be less expensive than a conventional letter.

- Be certain that you really need special services or rapid delivery, such as special delivery or overnight express, before using it. Overnight delivery, for example, won't help if the letter will arrive over the weekend when offices are closed and the intended recipient is away.

- Ask yourself how much protection a valuable or important document really needs. For example, does it have a significant monetary value? For some letters with important documents attached, certified mail may be as useful as registered mail. (Registered mail is appropriate for items of monetary value and is insured for an appropriate amount.)

- Send mass mailings at a lower-cost bulk rate (ask for details at your local post office), unless first-class delivery is essential because of time constraints or another reason.

- Clean up mailing lists periodically to eliminate postage-wasting obsolete addresses and to update others.

- Remember that the wrong equipment or improperly functioning equipment can soon waste a substantial amount of money. Accurate postal scales and metering equipment encourage distribution accuracy and eliminate wasted paper and postage.

- Subscribe to the free newsletter *Memo to Mailers* (National Customer Support Center, U.S. Postal Service, 6060 Primacy Parkway, Ste. 201, Memphis, TN 38188-0001) for further information on mailing and mailroom economy.

Dictated Letters

Dictation isn't what it used to be. Nowadays it's so easy to prepare letters by computer that some executives prefer to type and send many of their own messages rather than dictate them. Others like to compose a draft by computer and give it or a disk to a typist for final preparation and mailing.

Some businesspeople, however, predict that an accelerating pace of activity and the need to save time will push executives back to voice dictation and away from their laptops and desktops. *Never,* you say? I'm skeptical, too, so let's wait for the verdict about this.

Corrections. The nice thing about drafting a letter by computer, or even longhand, is that you can edit and revise the draft as much as you like before transmitting it or giving it to a typist for completion. But when you dictate a letter by machine, you may need to rely on a transcriber to correct and polish your message (unless you ask for a copy that you can rework before it's sent). If you're uneasy about letting someone else polish your messages, you'll need to become very adept at dictating a sufficiently polished message. If only minor corrections are needed, the transcriber can easily handle such routine changes.

I don't know if practice makes perfect, but proficiency certainly increases with practice. In the beginning you may not like the letters you compose by voice, but with time and practice you'll learn how to *say* what you want to *see* on paper or on screen.

Dictation tips. Unless you're already an expert at talking to a machine, some of the following tips may help improve your dictation. Giving sufficient instructions (format, number of copies, and so on) and speaking clearly at an even pace are essential. Otherwise, the transcriber may misunderstand or completely miss part of your message. Therefore, you need to avoid abrupt or extreme changes in the level of your voice and talk directly (but not too closely) into the speaker or mouthpiece at a slow enough pace to avoid slurring words. (*Suggestion:* Do your dictation before you order several cocktails for lunch. One transcriber told me that she can *hear* it if a dictator has been drinking.)

You'll want to practice voice control for another reason: People who dictate letters use voice inflection to indicate punctuation. A pause, for example, may indicate the end of a sentence and hence the need for a period, or it may signal the need for a comma within a sentence. But be certain to specify if you want any special punctuation, such as an exclamation point after a sentence or a colon preceding a list.

Transcribers may be good at their jobs, but they don't have crystal balls. It's necessary, therefore, to alert a transcriber if you want a change in format, such as a series of points to be typed as a numbered list and indented, with one blank space above and below the list. It's also important to spell out proper names, even familiar ones (*Browne* with an *e*), as well as unusual terms (*docucarrier*) and acronyms (*ACRL*). You should also provide any other essential information that you have readily available, such as ZIP codes, so that the transcriber won't have to waste time searching for it.

Unless the transcriber knows your preferred style, remember to specify what you want. For example, do you want symbols, such as %, or words, such as *percent?* In fact, you should clarify anything that could be misunderstood or unfamiliar to the transcriber, including letters of the alphabet that sound the same, such as *v* and *d*: "*v* as in *victory*" or "*d* as in *dog*."

Forms

Although it's an exaggeration to say that there's a form for every task in business, perhaps there should be. As we're often reminded, time is money, and forms do save time.

The word *form* is one of those big umbrella terms that's used in a variety of contexts. For example, a fill-in employment application is a form, but so is a repetitive standard message that's written and formatted like a regular letter. Specifically, then, you can design a form for a particular application, such as a dental-appointment reminder, merchandise requisition, or fax-transmittal cover sheet; generally, you can create it for a particular business or profession, such as a consignment house, medical facility, or credit-reporting bureau. In other words, you can handle nearly anything that's repetitive or standard as a form, and you can make a form suitable for virtually any type of business or profession.

Characteristics of a form. Does your job require that you write essentially the same words over and over? Some such messages are ideally suited for a standard message or at least a standard format. Perhaps the message will have blank spaces where you fill in certain facts. Many standard messages, such as payment reminders (see the illustration **Forget Something???**), are designed as fill-in forms.

People who do a lot of fill-in work on forms love computers, because computer software makes fill-in work easy. Also, you can store stock clauses, sentences, paragraphs, and even complete letters in the computer so that repetitive information doesn't have to be retyped each time a new message is sent. Some programs consist entirely of already prepared, complete forms (letters, requisitions, legal documents, collection notices, sched-

Forget Something???

Yes, your payment is past due.
Won't you take a moment to mail
your check today?

Invoice No. _____
*Date Due*_____
*Amount*_____

TO: _____
_____
_____

Blue Sky Industrial Park
Belmont, CA 94002

ules, and so on) to which you need add only names, addresses, or various other individual facts.

Setting up a forms program. If you've fallen madly in love with the simplicity and timesaving feature of forms, why not expand your use of them? To begin a forms program, simply start collecting letters and other standardized material that you receive (that's how this book began) and make extra copies of repetitive items that you send to others. Also copy samples from books such as this one or from software programs. Then rewrite the forms to suit your own business activity, separating the standardized versions into logical categories (applications, appointments, orders, and so on). This may sound overly simple, but it's really all you need to do.

Although you can store stock phrases, clauses, sentences, paragraphs, or entire letters in your computer, you may need large quantities of a particular letter or other form—too much to print the copies with your desktop printer. In this case, if your company doesn't have a large computer and printer, you may want to have a printing establishment run off a large supply of your standard forms, such as your appointment cards or order acknowledgments. For example, retail companies frequently send printed form letters such as this:

Dear Customer:

Due to an unanticipated delay from our supplier, the items on your recent order have been back-ordered. However, we will ship them as soon as a new supply is available.

Thank you for your patience. We hope this delay will not seriously inconvenience you.

Sincerely,

Order Service Department
The Gremlin Corporation

Personalizing forms. We know that when you print out multiple form letters by computer or send them electronically, each one *looks* as though it's an individually prepared letter or e-mail message. But when you have a large number of copies printed by printing press, the various copies may unfortunately look more like form letters than individual, original letters. To give such printed letters a more personal appearance, you might try using good quality paper, signing each letter individually, and sending each one by first-class mail.

In spite of all you do, however, a form letter printed by printing press may always look like a form letter printed by printing press. What should you do if it's important that it look like an original, individually prepared letter? You probably already know the answer: If a letter has to look original, *don't* use a printed form letter. Instead, prepare the letter individually and print out each copy with your computer or send each one by e-mail.

What can I say? Forms may save enormous amounts of time and money, but as much as we may appreciate the ease and simplicity of using them, we have to accept the fact that the easy way isn't always the best way. It's a lot like life, isn't it?

Business Models

Are you busy during your workday? If you're not, tell me how to get a job like yours. Everyone I know is looking for shortcuts: how to do something in less time but still do it well. The pressure to work faster is one reason that busy people like models—something they can imitate.

Does this mean that if you use models you'll never again have to compose another letter? No, let's not get crazy. Although model letters are widely used for routine matters and even some things that are not so routine, there are limits. Some matters involve circumstances so unique that you have to compose a letter specifically discussing the unusual situation and using just the right language and tone for it.

Perhaps you've designed artificial wings for penguins, have opened a flight school for them, and now want to sell the graduates to a film studio. I think we can agree that it's not likely you'll find another letter already written about this subject. However, it's not far-fetched to say that other sales letters may suggest the right tone and writing style to use. Some may also illustrate the appropriate steps to take in developing a persuasive message, such as how to hook the reader in the first paragraph.

Fortunately, many business messages are fairly standard, and you can usually find a similar letter in your files or in a letter book such as this one. Now and then you can even use most of the letter as is, changing only individual facts, such as names and dates. But either way, the idea behind the models in this book is to give you something to imitate, in full or in part.

A large collection of several hundred models sounds

great, doesn't it? But it's less than great if you can't quickly find the ones you need. Therefore, the models in this book are organized in major categories, such as *adjustments, apologies, proposals,* and *transmittals.* That arrangement should help you locate a particular type of letter more easily.

Some overlap among the categories is unavoidable, however, which means that a particular model could be in one of several groups. A letter of *adjustment,* for instance, might also be a letter of *explanation* or *apology,* or it could be an *acknowledgment* of a problem or a reply to a *complaint.* So if at first you don't see exactly the letter you want in the forthcoming models, check the full list of business models in the front of the book, or look in the index at the end of the book.

As you read the models, keep in mind that most are written in the casual, conversational style of today's domestic correspondence. To make them suitable for an international reader, you would have to adjust your writing style. For example, in addition to using short sentences and paragraphs, you would need to use very precise, straightforward English—no idioms, such as *take one's time*; no cliches, such as *bite the bullet*; no contractions, such as *she'll*; or any other hard-to-translate expressions. For more tips, reread the discussion **International Correspondence** in **MESSAGE COMPOSITION**.

Okay, you now know how the models are written and organized. The next question is whether *you* would prefer to maintain the collection in a computer file, in a paper file, or in both. Computer, you say? In that case, if you have a scanner, you can scan as many models as desired into your computer. Or you may decide to type suitable models as you need them and, each time, save them in a computer file for future use.

Don't worry. I haven't forgotten those of you who are more at home with paper files (I'm not willing to give up mine either). You can simply photocopy the models that you want, or each time that you imitate one in preparing correspondence, you can make an extra copy. Then you can place the copies—organized by category—in your own file folders or in an indexed three-ring binder where you can quickly retrieve them. For information about form letters and stock paragraphs, see **BUSINESS CORRESPONDENCE: Forms**.

Acknowledgments

Let's start with something easy that we all do: acknowledge things that people ask or send us. If we didn't acknowledge such things, the sender would have no way of knowing if the object or message reached us, if we liked or hated it, or if he or she should call or write to find out what's going on. If you've ever waited and waited for an acknowledgment, you'll know how annoying it is to send something and be met with silence.

If you're wondering *what* should be acknowledged, simply let common sense guide you. For example, gifts and most original messages should be acknowledged. (An *original letter* means a letter that a person composed especially for you.) So you would acknowledge an *original letter* from someone who wrote to give you information that you had requested for a report you're writing about a new talking rain gauge. But you wouldn't acknowledge a mass-mailing *form letter* that you received from the Rodents Society of America soliciting a donation.

You'll be happy to know that most acknowledgments, such as one confirming the receipt of information you requested, are easy to compose. But when you acknowledge something and *additionally* provide information, you'll have to give it more thought—possibly even do some research.

One thing we can't escape is the fact that all letters, even simple acknowledgments, create a first and sometimes lasting impression of writers and their companies (reread the introductory paragraphs about this in **MESSAGE COMPOSITION**). Therefore, to make that first impression a good one, you should promptly send your thanks and let the person know that you received what he or she sent. If you're the sender, you should promptly send any information that someone requested.

Fill-in form. Do you need to track or monitor the receipt of materials you send someone? If you do, don't hold your breath waiting for the person to tell you what you want to know. Instead, enclose a fill-in acknowledgment form that the recipient can quickly complete and return to you. If your company doesn't have a standard form, you can easily make up one to suit your needs:

> PLEASE COMPLETE AND RETURN THIS FORM IN THE ENCLOSED POSTAGE-PAID ENVELOPE. THANK YOU FOR YOUR COOPERATION.
>
> Date:_____
>
> We hereby acknowledge receipt of the following materials from_____ :
>
> ( )_____
> ( )_____
> ( )_____
> ( )_____
>
> Signature_____
> Company_____
> Address_____
> _____

In employer's absence. Everyone—staff and management alike—should already know how, or else should learn how, to acknowledge correspondence and other material properly. So let's assume that you've acknowledged dozens or even hundreds of messages, gifts, and other items. But have you ever acknowledged something for someone else, such as for your boss? When their employers are traveling, assistants, secretaries, and other office personnel usually acknowledge any correspondence that isn't forwarded to the traveler. In most cases, this type of acknowledgment should include an offer to help in the meantime:

Dear Ms. Cologne:

Since Mr. Antrim will be away from the office until August 5, I'm sending you the report that you requested. As soon as he returns, I'll ask him if he has any additional material that might interest you. In the meantime, I hope that the enclosed report will be useful.

If I can do anything further to help until Mr. Antrim returns, please let me know.

Sincerely,

Information received. When you were the sender, some people may have left you dangling forever, keeping you guessing about whether they ever received what you sent. Others, though, may have acknowledged it promptly. I just hope that you know more who fit the latter description than the former. Either way, most of us agree that anyone who *promptly* sends us something we need deserves not only an acknowledgment but also a note of thanks. Of course, thanks are always due when someone personally sends you something, even if it's a little late in arriving:

Dear Jody:

Thanks very much for sending the price list and distribution schedule that I requested. They'll both be a big help when I'm working on our budget.

I really appreciate your quick response, Jody. The information is just what I need.

Regards,

Remittance with overpayment. As you know, people don't have time to acknowledge the receipt of routine payments, such as someone's monthly rent check. The usual assumption is that your canceled check is your receipt. Only when something nonroutine happens is it necessary to respond. An error in payment requiring a

refund, for example, may make it necessary to acknowledge the payment *and* explain why a refund is being
sent. If the check doesn't have a remittance slip where
you can explain why a refund is due, or if your company
doesn't have another routine means of responding, such
as using a fill-in form, you'll have to compose a basic
acknowledgment letter:

Dear Mr. Warlock:

Thank you for your payment of our April 16, 200X, invoice
number OC-65732. We note, however, an overpayment.
The amount due is $473.20, whereas your check total is
$493.20. Therefore, our check refunding the overpayment of
$20.00 is enclosed.

We appreciate the opportunity to handle your roofing repairs
and hope that you'll call on us again when we can be of
further service.

Sincerely,

Request for proposal. Let's say that you want to acknowledge a request and promise to do something later.
That's fine, but try to include a firm or at least an ap-
proximate date for the something that you'll do later.
For example, if someone asks you to prepare a proposal,
you may not want to say no, but you also may have a
good reason for avoiding a firm commitment at the time
of writing. As you reply, keep in mind that readers hate
to be left hanging without any idea of what you plan to
do or when you plan to do it:

Dear Mr. T'ang :

Thank you for requesting our proposal to service your two
Laundromats on Adams Place and Charter Road. We
appreciate the opportunity to describe our service program
and will submit a proposal on October 2, 200X.

Sincerely,

Telephone call. Are you someone who handles everything by telephone? Even if you're inclined to grab the phone whenever anything comes up, it's still a good idea to have a written record of decisions, agreements, and so on. If you want to acknowledge or confirm in writing certain business that was transacted by telephone, repeat the date and any decisions made, including agreements reached during your conversation:

Dear Mr. Culpepper:

This will confirm our telephone conversation of May 7, 200X, in which we agreed that your last shipment of pinto beans contained two empty cartons. I appreciate your offer to replace the two cartons this week and will be expecting the shipment by truck freight on or before May 17, 200X.

Thanks very much for your help.

Sincerely,

Verbal invitation. We mustn't forget about face-to-face conversations either. After all, not all requests are made by telephone or in writing. In general, you should treat a verbal request or offer the same as one made by letter. Therefore, if you're chatting at the water cooler and someone invites you to join a committee, you should follow up your on-the-spot comments with a written acknowledgment, confirming any important facts or discussion:

Dear Wendy:

Thanks again for asking me to serve on the Finance Committee this year. As I indicated yesterday, I expect to have a limited travel schedule and should be able to participate actively.

I'll look forward to seeing you at the meeting next month.

Regards,

Adjustments

Problems and adjustments are a little like lovers in a love-hate relationship who need each other to survive. If we didn't have problems, we wouldn't need adjustments, or at least we wouldn't need as many. But the only problem-free world I've found exists in the pages of science fiction novels. In the real world, complaints and adjustments are daily fare.

Although the circumstances surrounding an adjustment may cause tempers to flare and stubborn streaks to blossom, the situation may not be all bad. The bright side is that the occasion may also give you an opportunity to discover and correct problems and, generally, to strengthen your business relationships.

In some situations, though, it may seem irresistible to imply or say—perhaps correctly—that you're right and the reader is wrong. But you'll probably regret doing it. Tact and sensitivity are almost mandatory in making adjustments. Also, if someone is unhappy, it's important to correct the situation promptly to avoid losing a customer or friend or having the company's (or your) image damaged.

Agreeing to replace merchandise. At best, it's frustrating to order something and eagerly await its arrival only to discover that when it finally does arrive, the blankety-blank thing doesn't work. Many companies ask customers to return a defective product and then offer them a replacement, refund, or credit. But no matter what type of adjustment your company makes, if the company is at fault or the product is defective, it's important to offer sincere apologies and try to make an adjustment that will satisfy the customer:

Dear Ms. Artichoke:

We were very sorry to learn that your new Clean-All Vacuum recently damaged your favorite linen draperies. Thank you for returning the machine so promptly.

Since the product is still under warranty, a replacement model of the same style and price is enclosed. Although we haven't yet determined the cause of the problem, this replacement Clean-All has been carefully inspected to ensure that a similar problem will not happen again.

We sincerely regret the delay and inconvenience this has caused you but hope that you'll now be pleased with your new Clean-All.

Thank you for your patience.

Cordially,

Billing error. It shouldn't surprise anyone that in a credit society, credit card billing errors are not uncommon. Letters about billing errors with charge accounts are generally handled the same as errors with other types of purchases. In all such cases, it will help the reader if you include a subject line in your letter (it's not necessary to use the word *Subject* in the line). Include the name of the holder of the card, the issuer's name, and the account number:

Ladies and Gentlemen:

BELLA F. WORMWOOD
WONDERCARD ACCOUNT 111-222-333-444

Your February statement to Ms. Wormwood shows a charge of $220 for a flight from Little Rock to Phoenix. However, the reservation for this flight was canceled by telephone and a follow-up letter sent on January 6, 200X.

I'd appreciate it if you would send me a corrected statement showing that Ms. Wormwood's account has been credited for the full amount of the returned ticket.

Thank you.

Sincerely,

Extension of time. As you know, not all adjustments involve merchandise or money. Life is a little more complicated than that. In business it's often necessary to adjust schedules and other plans to deal with changing conditions:

Dear Mr. Piroshki:

Thank you for granting a three-week extension for me to complete my study of the effect of sea biscuits on the world economy. I appreciate your interest in this important project.

I expect to mail the results of my study to you on November 17, 200X. In the meantime, please accept my apology for any inconvenience this delay may cause.

Sincerely,

Newspaper correction. We all make mistakes, right? We also see them every day in books, magazines, and newspapers. When you're requesting a correction or adjustment in printed material but don't know the name of the person to whom you should mail the request, select an appropriate title. *Dear Business Editor,* for instance, will direct your letter to someone in the business area of a newspaper or magazine better than a nonspecific title such as *Dear Sir* or *Madam*:

Dear Business Editor:

We noticed an error in the business section of the August 2, 200X, edition of your newspaper. The article "Surrey with a Dome on Top" should have stated that Modern Carriages, Inc., *leases,* not sells, pleasure carriages to resorts and tour groups.

We would appreciate it if you could print a correction in your next edition. Thank you.

Sincerely,

Refusing credit adjustment. Some of us have learned the hard way that certain things may seem obvious to us but apparently are not at all clear to our clients or customers. To maintain good relations, it may be necessary to point out even simple details. However, the trick is to do this without implying that the reader is a dummy who should have known something. Otherwise you may not have the individual as a client or customer for very long:

Dear Ms. Fleahopper:

Thank you for asking about an adjustment in your company's copier maintenance policy, which was recently revised to reflect a reduction in the number of machines covered.

The amount that you paid for the original agreement ($1,579) covered the period from January 21, 200X, through January 20, 200X. Since this policy was revised to be effective January 21, 200X, you were covered for the full period under the previous policy; therefore, no credit is due.

If you have any question about your coverage, don't hesitate to call. We appreciate your business and look forward to serving you for another year.

Sincerely,

Refusing to replace merchandise. You probably won't be able to make all the adjustments that people request, and then you'll need to explain your refusals with tact and consideration. If you can offer an alternative—anything, even a suggestion for the future—it will make your refusal seem less harsh:

Dear Mr. Flaxseed:

We were very sorry to learn that you were not satisfied with the trousers purchased during our Merry Christmas sale. Unfortunately, our store policy prevents us from accepting returns or making refunds on sale merchandise. Although we can't offer a refund on the sale items, we do have many other trousers available at regular price. Any of them could be returned unworn.

We sincerely regret that you're unhappy with your purchase and hope that your next selection at our store will be much more satisfactory.

Cordially,

Request for instructions. You've probably seen the claims forms that some companies enclose with certain merchandise—forms to be completed and enclosed with damaged or unsatisfactory merchandise that must be returned. If no such forms or instructions are included when you receive an order, and if something is damaged, call the number provided by the seller. If your company needs a written record, write to report the problem and ask for instructions:

Ladies and Gentlemen:

Upon unpacking the Mylar shades purchased from you on March 20, 200X, and delivered to our office on April 9, 200X, we discovered that two of the shades were badly scratched. I'd appreciate receiving your instructions for returning the merchandise and your estimated delivery date for replacements. A copy of our original order is enclosed.

Thank you very much.

Sincerely,

Announcements

Hardly a day passes that we don't *hear* or *read* one or more announcements. For some people, hardly a day passes that they don't *make* one or more announcements. Whether you write certain announcements yourself or whether specialists in your company do this probably depends on the size and makeup of your firm. In either case, one of several formats is possible: letter, memo, press release, bulletin, card, brochure, invitation, and so on.

If you need huge quantities of the announcement, you may have them printed. But if you need only a limited number, you may prepare the material by computer and print out the required number of copies in-house. For example, you may use a formal, printed invitation for the announcement of a business opening. You may use a press release to make a timely announcement of an upcoming conference. You may use a memo or letter format for other announcements that are primarily factual, informative messages for employees.

Formal meeting notice. For legal reasons, organizations are fussy about certain meeting announcements. Mostly, though, the concern is over details such as the date of the meeting and who calls it, not over questions such as deciding whether to use a letter or printed card format. For example, announcements of stockholders' meetings, board of directors' meetings, and association annual meetings would follow the requirements specified in the organization's bylaws. Often the notice itself is sent on printed slips or cards:

NOTICE

ANNUAL MEETING OF THE
U.S. VAMPIRE SOCIETY, INC.

The Annual Meeting of the members of the U.S. Vampire Society, Inc. will be held at 1:30 p.m. on Friday, June 7, 200X, in the Black Room, Hillsdale Manor, 212 Moonlight Drive, Erie, Pennsylvania 16505.

Count Limburg

Secretary

Informal meeting notice. Details provided in announcing informal or unofficial meetings are much less of a

worry since they don't involve legal requirements specified in bylaws or other documents. Although a large convention is typically announced by press release, radio
and television spots, and a printed program packet, a
small in-house meeting is commonly announced by telephone, fax, e-mail, or conventional interoffice memo:

TO: All Department Heads

MARCH MEETING

The next meeting of department heads will be on Monday,
March 9, from 10 a.m. until 3 p.m. in the Conference
Room. Lunch will be provided in the Executive Dining
Room.

I'll mail the agenda for the meeting on February 28.
Therefore, please send any items to be included to Phil
Partridge in the Business Office by February 25.

Also, I'd appreciate hearing from you right away if you're
unable to attend. Thanks very much.

Job promotion. Companies like to make a big deal out
of high-level promotions. At the very least, you would
probably announce the promotion of a top executive to
the press by press release and to other employees by
bulletin or memo. You might announce lower-level appointments, such as departmental appointments, by letter or memo. Common objectives in the latter case are
to notify employees of the newcomer's arrival, to help
employees become acquainted with the person, and to
motivate everyone to work together effectively:

TO: Members of the Research Department

ASSISTANT DIRECTOR APPOINTMENT

It's a pleasure to announce the appointment of George
Ipswich as assistant director in our Research Department. He
will fill the position left open by Joanna Dalrymple, who
recently moved to Atlanta.

George, who has worked in market research for more than a decade, is familiar with all stages of activity in our department, having once handled each major function from questionnaire development to product testing. His solid background and full understanding of our varied needs and problems make him exceptionally well qualified to handle the challenges that characterize his position.

I know that George will welcome your full cooperation and consideration as he assumes his new duties. We all wish him much success.

New address. When you relocate your business, you obviously don't want to keep it a secret. You want to let clients or customers know where you are as soon as possible, and you can do this by letter, postcard, newspaper notice, and so on. The following announcement could be printed on a card or as a form letter (omit the salutation and complimentary close if you prefer the look of a printed notice rather than a letter):

Dear Customer:

We moved!

As of Monday, April 1, 200X, the Best Corporation in America will be located in our new facilities at 2121 Powder Grove, Hartford, CT 06104. The toll-free telephone number for this new location is 800-555-7022.

Call us today! We guarantee that you'll be even more satisfied with the high quality and fast service you'll receive from the skilled representatives at our new address.

Sincerely,

New business. Ditto when you have a new business: You want to let prospective clients or customers know about it as soon as possible. To announce the opening of new offices, professional persons and other businesses may use printed or engraved cards, with matching envelopes. The size of the cards may vary (printers have lots of samples) but must meet the minimum postal requirements of 3½ by 5 inches:

William Buckhill

Attorney at Law

announces the opening

of law offices

at 14 Roanoke Avenue
Atlantic City, New Jersey 08411

Wednesday, May 16, 200X

New policy. Most of us know firsthand that things don't stand still for long in the business world. Nearly all businesses change policies or procedures from time to time, and they typically announce such changes by letter to clients and customers and by memo to in-house personnel:

Dear Ms. Wishley:

We're happy to announce that beginning July 1, 200X, the Happy Hikers Manufacturing Company will offer preferred customers like you the choice of a full refund or credit on any order placed with us.

If you're dissatisfied with a shipment, whatever the reason, all you need to do is return it, and we'll credit your account or forward your refund promptly—no questions asked. Next week our representative Arthur Appleseed will call you with more details about the savings and convenience that this new policy will provide for you.

We want you to know how much we appreciate all of the orders you've placed with us in the past, and we're eager to help you any way we can in the future.

Cordially,

Price increase. No one who's reasonably sane likes bad news. It helps, then, when it doesn't sound so bad, when the action appears justified, and when you seem to be as concerned as ever about the recipient's welfare:

Dear Mr. Finchley:

Although we've been able to maintain constant pricing for many years, we find that because of an increase in our transportation costs, we must unfortunately make a small increase in the price of our future line of wood and steel filing cabinets. These new prices, shown on the enclosed price list, will go into effect on September 5, 200X, and will apply to all orders received after that date.

We appreciate having you as a customer and hope that we'll continue to be able to fill your needs in the months ahead.

Sincerely,

Apologies

Two words will get you through many bad times in the business world: *I'm sorry*. There's something disarming about people who apologize openly. The most recent spat that I overheard completely dissolved when those two words entered the conversation. The angry antagonist simply melted, saying, "Oh, that's all right. We all make mistakes. Don't worry about it."

The person who erred easily won that round. Although this may not seem fair, look at it this way: One person got off the hook, and the other cooled down in time to stop himself from ruining a successful business relationship. Also, he was correct in saying that we all make mistakes, which makes it very hard to justify attacking someone for doing the same thing that we're all guilty of doing.

In business, too much is at stake for someone to throw it away merely because he or she would rather go to the dentist than say "I'm sorry." Although these words won't come easily to everyone, it's well worth adding them to your vocabulary.

Delayed reply. We already know that correspondence should be acknowledged promptly by someone else in the office when you're away. See **Acknowledgments: In employer's absence.** But if something happens to prevent that, the acknowledgment will have to wait till you return. If that happens, add a word of apology for your tardy response:

Dear Tim:

Please forgive my delay in responding to your inquiry about the budget. I've been away on business, and my assistant had to accompany me this time, so the mail has been late in reaching me.

As you pointed out, time is short, so I'm looking forward to finishing the project. Also, I know that you're looking forward to having me finish it too. I've met with the supervisors at our two plants and believe I have enough information to complete the budget by April 1. But I'll call you next week to discuss various items in more detail so that I'll have an opportunity to incorporate any suggestions you may have.

Please accept my apologies if this late reply to your letter has caused you any concern.

Best regards,

Delayed shipment. When shipments are going to be delayed, as they often are, the usual procedure is to notify the person, department, or company placing the order. Large firms may use standard postcards or form letters to report the delay. The forms may be printed with a general message, such as "The item(s) you ordered has been back-ordered." Or they may have blank spaces where you can merge certain facts by computer. Either a letter or memo format may be used:

TO: Purchasing Department

YOUR ORDER NO. 16100

We're sorry to let you know that the four cases of #7 clamps that you ordered on October 25 are temporarily out of stock. However, they've been back-ordered and will be shipped promptly on or before December 1.

We regret any inconvenience this delay may cause. If there's any way that we can be of help in the meantime, please let us know.

Financial error. Have you noticed that when people make mistakes in handling money, they can't resist pointing out that computers and other machines make mistakes too? That's okay if a customer wants to do that, and in fact, it's probably true. But a company representative shouldn't make excuses. If your company is responsible for a mistake, it should be standard policy to admit it promptly, correct it, *and apologize.* If an error affects a large number of people, you may want to use a form letter such as this:

Dear Customer:

We sincerely regret that due to a processing error, the electronic debit for your May payment was transferred from your account on April 14 rather than on April 24.

Upon discovering this action on April 17, we immediately issued a credit for the amount of the April 14 debit. The statement you receive from your bank will show the initial debit and the transaction on April 17 that in effect canceled the early withdrawal.

Please accept our apologies for any inconvenience or embarrassment that this processing error may have caused. If you incurred an overdraft charge as a result of the early debit, please submit a copy of your bank statement reflecting the charge, and we'll be happy to reimburse you.

It has been our good fortune to have you as a customer,
and because we value your business so highly, we're taking
immediate steps to ensure that potential errors of this
nature are avoided in the future.

With sincere good wishes,

Misunderstanding. We're often told that part of the
so-called spice of life is that people don't always want
the same things or hold the same beliefs. That's all very
nice, but the downside is that these differences often
lead to disagreements, and when communication is ineffective, misunderstandings result. Sometimes they occur
even when the communication channel is wide open. Although a misunderstanding isn't a great crime, it can
cause serious problems in a working relationship if it
isn't rectified. As always, if you're even partially at fault,
the most reliable response is to admit it and apologize:

Dear Eddy:

Yes, I did rewrite selected portions of the Stonecraft report.
It didn't occur to me that the wording couldn't be changed,
and I do apologize for altering the copy.

In the future I'll be certain to ask for clarification when the
instructions state "careful and thorough editing." From your
November 9 letter, I've concluded that this means only
corrections in grammar and punctuation as well as
consistency in style, but without any rephrasing, whether or
not it may be needed. I'm sorry that I misunderstood the
instructions and would be glad to erase any rewriting that I
did, leaving other editorial work intact.

I appreciate learning about this from you and can assure
you that I'll clarify and follow all instructions to the letter
next time around.

Sincerely,

Not fully responsible. It's no secret that you can apologize and express regret about some problem *without* ac-

cepting responsibility for it. I don't want to encourage any bad habits, but the truth is that businesspeople do this all the time. However, the blame must truly fall elsewhere, or you should always be willing to accept responsibility. Another possibility is that both parties share the blame for something. In either case, it's important to write a tactful letter that doesn't bluntly say "It's your fault, don't blame me":

Dear Ms. Whitecastle:

I'm so sorry that you were kept waiting at my office on July 7. I know how busy you are and realize that you don't have an hour to waste waiting for someone.

When I took the call from someone in your office last week, I was asked if 10:30 a.m. on Thursday would be convenient. The time and day were fine, so I confirmed the appointment on the spot since my assistant was on vacation that week. Apparently, though, the caller intended to say Tuesday, an easy slip in the confusion of a busy day. I just regret that I didn't telephone your office later to reconfirm the time and date. The day would have been clarified then, no doubt.

Please accept my apologies for missing our appointment. I hope it won't prevent you from arranging another meeting. Now that my assistant has returned, I'm confident we'll get it right this time.

Best wishes,

Policy restriction. You shouldn't have to apologize for your company's policy just because it doesn't appeal to someone else. However, if the policy—even a good one—causes dissatisfaction to a client or customer, it's important to show sensitivity and concern that you're unable to help. In other words, you're not being critical of the policy; you're simply sorry that it, like most regulations in life, can't be all things to all people:

Dear Mr. Rootcanal:

Although we wish that we could make use of your excellent educational background and job experience, for certain positions it's company policy to promote from within our organization whenever possible. Therefore, the supervisory position you mentioned will be filled by a candidate from our word processing pool.

We certainly appreciate the interest you've shown in our company and suggest that you contact our personnel office to discuss other positions that may be available and of interest to you. In the meantime, we'll keep your name on file in case our policy should change in the future.

Thank you very much for contacting us. I wish you much success in finding a challenging and rewarding position.

Sincerely,

Poor service. You've probably noticed the brief, fill-in or checklist forms that car dealers, motels, and other businesses sometimes provide to customers for them to use in reporting problems they encountered while dealing with the organization. If a customer reports that service was unsatisfactory—or worse—you should immediately send a thoughtful letter of apology and an assurance that the problem is being corrected:

Dear Ms. Popsicle:

Thank you for sending us your comments on our service report card. We appreciate your letting us know that your instructions were not followed concerning the use of 20w/50 rather than 15w/40 motor oil.

This problem of using another grade of oil has been brought to the attention of our Service Department. Although our service personnel normally follow a customer's preference or explain why this should not be done, it seems that the mechanics were understaffed that day, and apparently, this oversight occurred as a result. However, you're quite right in pointing out this problem to us, and we want you to feel free to return at your convenience to have the oil changed to the grade of your choice without charge.

Please accept our sincere apologies and our assurance that we have taken steps to be certain that you receive the best service possible in the future.

Sincerely yours,

Appointments

For some people, a day at the office is an endless succession of meetings. Sound familiar? Various personnel may set up the appointments by letter or make the plans by telephone. In the latter case, they're often confirmed by memo or letter (when time permits).

An appointment letter, or a response to one, may be the first thing that a prospective client or customer sees from your company, and as I keep saying, first impressions count. To make a favorable impression, therefore, it's important that a message be clear, accurate, and courteous. Since appointment letters include details such as time, place, and date, they have to be precise too. They also should be sent in time for the recipient to be able to respond and comply with the suggested arrangements.

If you're asking for an appointment, state why you want it; suggest a time, place, and date; and ask for confirmation. If you're responding to a request, repeat the details and, if necessary, suggest an alternative or politely say no.

Acceptance of request. Everyone in a hurry, take note: The initial acceptance of a request for an appointment can be *very* brief. But also notice that the following one-sentence acceptance nevertheless mentions the key facts:

Dear Mr. Ferret:

I'll be happy to meet you in your office on Friday, December 10, at 2 o'clock to discuss our investment program.

Cordially,

Arrangements. Some businesspeople travel so much that they almost live in motels. Others keep their out-of-town business to a minimum. In both cases, when the arrangements must be made in advance, either a telephone call (confirmed by letter) or a letter such as the following example can be used to set up appointments. Let the reader know if you want a reply by fax, telephone, or other means:

Dear Mr. Camelback:

Richard Waterbug, vice president of production at Constructive Toys for Toddlers, will be in Chicago on Tuesday, March 19, and would like to arrange a tour of your plant while he's there.

Would it be possible for him to visit your facilities sometime during the morning on Tuesday? I'd appreciate it if you could let us know by telephone (212-555-6000) or fax (212-555-6100) what time would be convenient for you.

Thank you very much.

Sincerely,

Cancellation. Not many people make it through life without having to cancel appointments now and then. To do this, briefly state why you're not able to keep the appointment and apologize for any inconvenience caused by the cancellation. If you still want to meet sometime, but don't know when, you can simply say that you'll set up a new appointment later:

Dear Mr. Reindeer:

I'm very sorry to let you know that I'll be unable to keep our February 11 appointment to discuss the patent. Our warehouse has been backlogged recently, and I'll have to help out temporarily. Since at present it isn't clear when I'll finish, I'll have my assistant set up a new appointment with you in a couple weeks.

My apologies for any inconvenience this may cause you, Mr. Reindeer. But I'll look forward to meeting with you very soon.

Cordially,

Change of plans. In general, to change the time, date, or place of an appointment, follow the same procedure just described for a cancellation. Refer to the original plans and state the proposed alternative. Also, apologize for having to make a change, and ask if the new time is convenient:

Dear Roxie:

An unexpected complication in my travel schedule is going to prevent me from meeting you on Friday, September 16. However, I'm free on Tuesday, September 20. Would it be convenient for you to meet me then in my office at our West Avenue building about 1:30 p.m.?

I'm sorry that I can't keep our original date, but please let me know if Tuesday is satisfactory for you.

Thanks very much, Roxie. I'm looking forward to seeing you soon.

Regards,

Confirmation. Another easy one. To confirm an appointment, repeat the time, date, and place. Also, try to sound pleased to be meeting the person. Even an assistant replying for someone else should say something nice to give the message a pleasant tone:

Dear Mrs. Goldfinch:

Last week Ms. Gadfly suggested that you meet with her Thursday morning, June 6, to discuss your new duties at the Gooseberry Salon. This is just a note to let you know that she's looking forward to seeing you in her office at 10:30 a.m.

Sincerely,

Postponement. Question: Do you *really* want to see Mr. X who is requesting an appointment with you? The alternatives are to say yes or no or to refuse an appointment now but leave the door open for a later meeting. It's inconsiderate, though, to give the impression that you'll see someone later if you have no intention of doing so:

Dear Ms. Betelgeuse:

Thanks for letting Ms. Hammertoe know that your store is now stocking a full line of computer supplies. As much as she would like to see them, I'm sorry that, because of previous commitments, she won't be free for several weeks.

If you'd like to telephone me at 555-1217 after May 29, I'll check to see how her schedule looks at that time.

Sincerely,

Refusal. Have you ever met someone who stubbornly wouldn't take no for an answer? Since it's possible that you may need the person or the person's product or service in the future, it's never wise to be insulting or to toss the person out of your office, however tempting that might be. This is a time to practice restraint and, firmly but nicely, say no—again:

Dear Mr. Boxcar:

Thank you for letting us know that you'll be available next Monday morning and would like to discuss your temporary help service with Ms. Hamstring.

As Ms. Hamstring has previously indicated, we're very pleased with our present arrangements for temporary help and definitely will not consider any other services in the foreseeable future. Therefore, she asked me to let you know that a meeting would not be helpful to either of you at this time.

We appreciate your interest, however, and thank you for writing.

Sincerely,

Appreciation

When someone does something that's nice or beneficial to you, you don't say "Yeah, okay, whatever." Presumably, you show appreciation. It's good public relations as well as common courtesy to do so. Very simply, people like to be appreciated, and letters that positively influence the feelings and attitudes of others are critically important.

Since letters of appreciation are usually brief and easy to compose, there's really no excuse for not sending them freely. In fact, you can use any logical occasion: the receipt of an important contract, an order from a customer, or lunch with a business associate.

The tone of this type of letter should sound warm and genuine. If it's too gushy, though, it will sound insincere. Generally, be natural, explain why you appreciate what was done, offer to reciprocate (if appropriate), and encourage the person to contribute further (if appropriate). Throughout, use lots of friendly words, such as *appreciate, generous, special, thank you,* and *wonderful.*

Company tour. How many of you have toured someone else's company or guided others through your company? Quite a few, I assume, because this is a common
practice. For example, to provide the best possible service for a client, you may want to arrange a get-
acquainted tour of the client's facilities. Even though this
is to the client's advantage, too, one or more persons at
the client's facilities will nevertheless have to take time
away from their other duties to greet you and assist you
in the tour. This is your cue to express appreciation for
their time and effort on your behalf:

Dear Ms. Sundance:

Thank you very much for arranging such an informative tour
of your institute. I'm confident that I have a much better
understanding of your work and that this will help us to
represent your organization more successfully in the future.

I sincerely appreciate your time and thoughtful attention,
Ms. Sundance, and hope that you'll be able to visit our
facilities in Denver on your next trip west.

Cordially,

Group effort. We hear a lot of grumbling about the
conflicts between management and everyone else in a company. Some of these conflicts are very real too. But then
a noteworthy occasion comes along and helps us to put our
complaints aside, at least for a while. Sometimes an entire
office or department does something so special that it earns
the genuine appreciation of its employer, and management
decides to praise everyone in a letter. In such cases, you
wouldn't have to send each employee an individual letter.
A form letter would do. However, the letter should sound
sincere and not only give well-deserved praise but also
motivate the employees to contribute further:

TO: Members of the Mail Room Staff

The Board of Directors wants to thank every one in the
Mail Room for the outstanding job that was done in

holding the line on mailing expenses in spite of recent rate increases. Without your dedication to increasing the efficiency in procedures and ever seeking new cost-cutting measures, we could never have stayed within our budget.

We're all impressed by your serious efforts on behalf of the company and want to extend our appreciation to each one of you. The loyalty you've demonstrated during the past year merits the highest commendation, and this tribute will be recorded permanently in each of your personnel records. We're truly proud of you and sincerely thank you for your selfless and generous contributions.

Cordially,

Helpful suggestion. Not everyone likes to take advice—of course, you and I are the exception—but many suggestions are valid and very helpful. In addition, here's another opportunity to cement productive working relations by showing appreciation:

Dear Arn:

The branch manager at the Ocelot Satellite Corporation just called and would like to see me next week! Since he mentioned your name, it's clear that the call was a result of your letter to him suggesting that we get together.

Thanks ever so much, Arn. I really appreciate your effort and hope I can be of help to you someday.

Best regards,

Overnight hospitality. Has a business associate in another city ever invited you to stay overnight during a business trip? It happens, and such thoughtful gestures deserve a warm, personal expression of appreciation whether or not you accept. If you do accept, of course, you should promptly send a letter of appreciation after the visit:

Dear Maddie:

Thanks for a delightful evening with you and Joe. I certainly enjoyed visiting with both of you in your lovely home, and dinner was a very special treat for me. You must give me a chance to reciprocate the next time you're in Albuquerque.

My best to Joe and the children.

Cordially,

Personal favor. I suspect this will sound like an understatement: Businesspeople frequently exchange favors. It's part of the working relationship, even more so when the two individuals are friends as well as coworkers. Either way, an expression of appreciation for a favor should be automatic:

Dear Tina:

What would I do without you? I really appreciated your help in closing the downtown offices. I knew we had to be out because our lease had expired, but until you climbed on board, I had serious doubts about making it. But thanks to you, we were out on time, and I can now relax in our new quarters.

If ever I can reciprocate, Tina, do let me know.

Best wishes,

Sympathy message. When you receive expressions of sympathy from coworkers and from business associates outside the firm and they contain a personal message (as opposed to a printed message alone), send an acknowledgment to the writer and express appreciation for his or her thoughtful message. But keep it short—about one to three sentences:

Dear Mr. Rediform:

Thank you for your thoughtful expression of sympathy and offer of assistance following the accident. Your kind words were very comforting, and I appreciate knowing that I can call on you if the need should arise.

Sincerely,

Collection

This is not a pleasant subject, especially to anyone who has been the target of collection efforts. But it's a fact of life that people and companies don't always pay their bills on time—or at all.

Since the unpaid bills of customers and clients can amount to huge sums of money, creditors have no choice but to take steps to collect as much as possible. Collection efforts begin in the creditor's firm, usually in the credit or accounting department of a large firm. Small organizations without specialized departments or offices must handle this matter in their general offices.

Here's the way it usually works: A series of letters or forms are sent, beginning with friendly, sometimes humorous reminders and becoming increasingly stern. The final message is really an announcement that the matter is being turned over to a collection agency or an attorney. Since the objective is to collect, each message must give the customer a chance to pay, such as providing additional time or offering an installment plan. Each message also must provide a reason or incentive to pay, such as to protect the person's credit rating.

Specialists often compose collection letters because the tone, language, emphasis, timing, and legal implications are all critical in relation not only to the debtor's economic circumstances but also to his or her psychological state of mind. To put it mildly, people in debt are often under tremendous stress, and they can become angry and stubborn as well as frightened. In fact, you could easily make people so angry that they would rationalize not paying at all, even when they're later able to do so.

In addition, it's not helpful for a company to gain the

reputation of being an unfair tyrant. Goodwill and a favorable image in the business world are important. Also, since some delinquent accounts may eventually become paying customers, it's necessary to maintain their goodwill. In general then, something is terribly wrong when one starts to look upon the customer only as the enemy. Collection, therefore, must be handled objectively and unemotionally.

1. Friendly reminder. Let's be fair. A late payment may be simply an oversight, so the first notice should be casual and friendly. It should suggest that the customer may already have sent the payment, and in fact, the payment and the reminder sometimes do cross in the mail. For this initial reminder, you can use a short letter or a standard fill-in commercial form (if your firm doesn't already have its own reminder forms):

Dear Ms. Merrymaker:

Oops! Did you forget something? We all do that, so I thought I'd remind you that your payment of $291.79 would be very much appreciated.

If your check to the Valentine Press is already in the mail, please disregard this notice and accept our thanks. If you haven't sent your payment, won't you take a moment to mail it today?

Cordially,

2. Firm reminder. When the friendly reminder doesn't prompt a payment, you can assume that something is amiss, especially if the account is sixty or ninety days past due. It's time, then, to issue a stronger reminder. Although the language shouldn't be harsh—perhaps the person had an accident and isn't up and around yet—it should make clear that you're concerned:

Dear Ms. Merrymaker:

More than sixty days have passed, and we're concerned that your payment of $291.79 has not yet reached the Valentine Press.

We've checked our records and believe that the amount is correct. Since we haven't heard from you, we assume that your records agree with ours. Therefore, before this unpaid balance affects your credit standing, won't you send us your check today or let us hear from you right away if there's a problem that we should know about?

Your cooperation will be very much appreciated, Ms. Merrymaker. Thank you.

Sincerely,

3. Discussion letter. A series of collection letters commonly includes a discussion letter (Can we talk?). This message tries to entice the customer at least to communicate and bring out in the open what the problem is so that the creditor can help work out a mutually satisfactory solution:

Dear Ms. Merrymaker:

We were hoping to hear from you in response to our last letter concerning your past-due account of $291.79. But even though the Valentine Press has mailed several statements and letters, there has been no word in return.

Perhaps you're having problems that make it difficult for you to pay the entire amount all at once. If this is the case, I'd like you to feel free to tell me about it—in confidence, of course. I'm sure that we can set up an easy payment plan appropriate for your circumstances.

Please let me hear from you right away, Ms. Merrymaker. It's very important that this matter be resolved without further delay.

Sincerely,

4. Special appeal. Things are getting serious now. When the discussion letter fails and the account is three or four months past due, it's time to make a special appeal. Depending on the account, the amount due, and so on, you might appeal to something such as the customer's fairness or self-interest. Whereas you might space the first couple letters thirty days apart, by now it's time to begin making contact every ten days to two weeks:

Dear Ms. Merrymaker:

We're at a loss to understand why we've had no word from you regarding your long past due amount of $291.79. For several months we've been writing to you about this matter and must know your intentions immediately. Although we'd like to work with you if you're experiencing unexpected financial difficulties, it's impossible for us to help until we know your situation.

Please send us something today. I'm sure you'll understand that the Valentine Press is unable to continue to maintain your account under the present conditions. Therefore, if we don't hear from you by telephone or mail at once, we'll have no choice but to pursue other collection procedures.

Sincerely,

5. Announcement of other action. By now frustration is obviously setting in. After sending four letters without any response, it's time to announce that other action will be taken unless the customer takes advantage of this one last chance—by a clear deadline—to make payment:

Dear Ms. Merrymaker:

I was disappointed that you didn't reply to my letter of April 1, because we now must take other action to collect the balance of your past-due account of $291.79.

I regret to let you know that if we don't receive your payment by April 15, you'll next hear from the Dragonfly Collection Agency. We sincerely hope that you'll take this final opportunity to avoid further damage to your credit standing and to avoid the additional costs you may incur if legal action is taken.

Just send your check to the Valentine Press by April 15, and the matter will be resolved before we take this serious step.

Sincerely,

Agency arrangements: Time's up. When even the threat of outside action does not elicit so much as a telephone call from the debtor, you'll probably transfer the account to an attorney or, more likely, to a collection agency:

Ladies and Gentlemen:

The Valentine Press would like to engage your services in collecting the past-due account of Ms. Merrillee Merrymaker amounting to $291.79. To help you evaluate our preliminary requests for payment, I'm enclosing copies of our correspondence to Ms. Merrymaker and a data sheet showing transactions pertaining to the past-due account.

Since Ms. Merrymaker was a reliable customer of the Valentine Press for many years preceding this incident, we would appreciate it if you could extend every opportunity to her to return her account to its former status.

If we can provide any other information, please let us know. Thank you for your help.

Sincerely,

Agency notice to customer. Collection agencies and attorneys move swiftly to begin collection efforts. Although this is a very specialized area and is usually handled by experts, an initial announcement might read like this:

Dear Ms. Merrymaker:

The Dragonfly Collection Agency has been authorized by the Valentine Press to collect from you the long past due amount of $291.79. It's our understanding that you have not responded to any previous claims for payment, and we're therefore prepared to seek immediate collection.

This letter should serve as official notice to you that unless you contact us within ten days from the date of this letter to make satisfactory arrangements for payment in full or by installment, we will initiate collection proceedings.

Yours very truly,

Complaints

If you didn't receive what you ordered or were promised, you have a right to complain, and you probably will. I would. Surprisingly, the person you contact may not cringe at your telephone call or letter. Companies are often eager to learn about defective products, poor service, or the unsatisfactory behavior of their employees. It's one way to discover how products, services, and actions are being received and what needs to be done to improve them.

Your letter of complaint should provide all details concerning the problem you experienced—"Your toaster is a heap of junk" isn't helpful to a company—and indicate what type of action or adjustment you expect. You may be furious or at least annoyed, but the tone and language you use should be reasonable and unemotional. If you rant and rave, the reader may decide that you and your letter should be dismissed as irrational and unreasonable.

Discourteous caller. It's hard to know why people are rude, but not everyone has a winning personality, and some people seem to be totally inept when it comes to human relations. Most of the time it's not worth your time or effort to complain about a rude employee in another company. But if you're uncomfortable about having the person handle some aspect of your business, you should contact the organization and make your concerns known to someone in authority:

Dear Mr. Dumfries:

One of your insurance representatives, Cecil Locoweed,
called us today to recommend that we increase our business
coverage. The conversation was most unsatisfactory, and
we're requesting that another representative be assigned to
our account.

Although the need for additional coverage may be
necessary, we objected to Mr. Locoweed's attitude and
insistence that we make an on-the-spot decision. When we
stated that we would need full details before making such a
commitment, he suggested that if we were smart, we would
increase our coverage, and if we weren't, we wouldn't
increase it. We're not accustomed to dealing with such rude
and unprofessional behavior and expect to have something
as important as insurance coverage handled by someone
who is emotionally mature and responsible.

We were always pleased with the assistance your company
personnel provided previously and would like to continue on
that basis. Please let us know if you can appoint another
representative to review our policy and discuss our needs
with us at an appropriate time.

Thank you.

Sincerely,

Misunderstanding about bill. Money will always be the
cause of many complaints. Count on it. One thing that
especially irritates people is being billed for more than
they expected. If you were quoted less than the amount
on a bill you receive, call or send a letter right away:

Dear Mr. Drumbeat:

I'm returning your invoice 61395 because it includes a
charge that was not mentioned in your telephone quote of
September 2, 200X.

Our company needed an air-conditioning duct cleaned and repaired. During our telephone conversation, you quoted a total cost of $28 an hour and an estimated completion time of two hours. The bill, however, states that work was charged for one service repairperson at $28 an hour and one trainee at $14 an hour, each working two hours.

We did not agree to pay more than $28 an hour and had no need for a trainee in any case. Even if we had agreed to pay an additional $14 an hour, there was room for only one person to work, and the trainee merely stood nearby and observed. In view of your firm quote of September 2 and our acceptance of those terms, we're requesting that you send a corrected invoice of $56 ($28 an hour for two hours).

The work, incidentally, was satisfactory, and we'll be happy to send you our payment as soon as we receive the corrected invoice. Thanks very much.

Sincerely,

Misunderstanding about instructions. When someone misinterprets or overlooks your comments or instructions, you may get something you didn't bargain for. If time won't permit having the person redo the work, you'll probably be angry and inclined to let the person know. However tempting that may be, you may need the person's cooperation later, so tact is in order. Even if you're positive that you'll never need to work with the individual again, a person who loses control soon gets the reputation of being an irrational hothead. So being Mr. or Ms. Calm-Cool-and-Collected is usually the wisest approach:

Dear Bernie:

I received your research material for the special education issue of our newsletter, but I'm afraid that we can't use it.

If you'll refer to my memo of August 18, you'll see that I requested a comparison of test-score ranking for all schools in the state *each year* during the past ten years. Your statistics compare the ranking ten years ago with the current year. The intent of the article on testing was to produce a curve for our school, showing the progression each year, compared to the state average, again for each year.

With the deadline upon us, we'll have to scrap this idea, since there isn't time to collect new figures for the other years. I know that you put in a lot of hours on this, and I'm sorry that your time was wasted. Next time, you may want to reread my instructions an extra time before proceeding to be certain that you're right on target.

If ever you have any questions about an assignment, don't hesitate to ask. Some of my instructions may be unclear, and I'll be happy to explain anything that puzzles you.

Regards,

Theft of idea. Assume that you've been developing a great idea, and you mention it to a couple coworkers. Before you can present the idea to your boss, however, you learn that one of the coworkers has already presented your idea as his own. It had never occurred to you that someone might steal your idea—your car, perhaps, but not something intangible like an idea. So what should you do, short of strangle the thief? You can obviously express your displeasure to the thief at an opportune moment, but first you need to straighten out this matter with your boss. Your letter should state that the idea was yours, how and when you developed it, and so on. In the scenario just described, you would also state that you had mentioned it to the coworker thief:

Dear Ms. Grapevine:

I read with interest your memo relating a suggestion given to you by Henry Puma about expanding our product survey next year to include educational institutions. Since this is an idea I've been researching and developing since last

October, I was surprised to see the suggestion attributed to
Henry.

Although I briefly mentioned my idea to Nancy Cascade and
Henry Puma at lunch on Monday, I didn't have the full
details of my study ready. Therefore, Henry no doubt had
no supporting data to present to you along with my idea.
But I expect to have full details ready for you next week.

The data have already been entered into my computer, and
my tabulations are nearly finished. When you read my
report next week, you'll be pleased to see that the results
of my long-term study completely support the benefits of
including educational institutions in future surveys.

I'm looking forward to presenting my report to you next
week and, in the meantime, will be happy to answer any
questions you may have.

Thanks very much for your interest, Ms. Grapevine.

Cordially,

Unreliable supplier. Businesspeople who have to deal
with undependable suppliers must have sky-high stress
levels. Companies that depend on deliveries to operate
can be seriously handicapped when suppliers are unreliable. Late deliveries make it impossible to fill orders for
customers on time, and that may mean lost income:

Dear Mr. Cartouche:

For the fourth time in the past two months customers have
told us that they can no longer wait for the supplies they
had ordered. This has been a result of late deliveries from
your warehouse.

Under the circumstances, we must cancel our recent
purchase orders no. Z851901 and no. Z861999, both
contingent on delivery by March 1, 200X. In each case,
delivery is already several weeks late, and customers have
in turn canceled their orders with us.

We hope that these delivery problems will be solved very shortly. The loss of customers is very serious to us, and we depend heavily on a regular and reliable source of supply to serve our community.

Sincerely,

Unsatisfactory performance. Most of us assume that people or companies hired to do a job are supposed to provide reasonable quality work or meet industry standards. But it doesn't always work out that way. Therefore, if performance is substandard, you have a right to speak out. In fact, it would be unfair to let the persons involved continue without realizing your concern. Although you might like to tell the people what you *really* think, unleashing your wrath on them probably won't motivate them to work any harder to please you. They may even dislike you so much that the opposite will occur. Constructive criticism, therefore, is much more likely to help both sides:

Dear Mr. Mukluk:

I've completed the personnel review forms that you sent last week and am returning them with this letter.

You'll notice that all reviews are satisfactory except one. Several months ago, when we were shorthanded, you suggested that we use Hugo Edelweiss, who then transferred from the File Center to our Bookkeeping Department. Although he had previously worked as a bookkeeper for another firm and was eager to return to that work, we found his overall background in this area to be insufficient for our needs.

Other employees have complained that they've had to devote excessive time to helping him find errors that he made and in training him to undertake tasks that would be routine to an experienced bookkeeper. We require fast and accurate work, and in that respect, Mr. Edelweiss doesn't meet the performance standards of our department.

I'm recommending that he be transferred back to the File Center as soon as possible. Although his work isn't satisfactory for our purposes, he may have other abilities that qualify him for other duties or positions.

I'd appreciate it if you would call this week to discuss the qualifications for a replacement. Thanks very much.

Sincerely,

Unsatisfactory product. Some products just don't work well, and it's not unheard of to get a lemon even from a reliable company. Because this happens, companies are used to handling these problems. So if something is wrong, you might ask for repairs, a replacement, or a refund, or you might decide never again to deal with the company. But if in general you like the supplier and the merchandise, you'll probably try to get the problem resolved while continuing to use the company's products:

Dear Ms. Paradiddle:

I'm sorry to let you know that our model KT-100 copier installed two months ago has not met our expectations. Although your service representative has been here seven times to make adjustments, the machine is still not working properly. The paper jams continually, often tearing on one corner, and it's not providing the quality copies that were shown to us during a demonstration on another KT-100 in your store.

Since your service personnel have been unable to correct the problems, we must conclude that the machine is defective. Although we'd like to arrange for a replacement, we're reluctant to install another KT-100 with the prospect of the same problems. Therefore, I'd appreciate a telephone call from you this week to discuss the options available to us. We'd like to solve the problem without delay, however. It's important to our business to have a copier available and working properly, so your immediate attention will be greatly appreciated.

Thanks for your help and cooperation. I'll look forward to hearing from you shortly.

Sincerely,

Unsatisfactory service. We all know that businesses depend on other businesses for a great variety of outside services, from deliveries to janitorial help. Since one thing usually impacts on another, customers and clients will eventually be affected, and that can mean loss of business and income. Sometimes the impact is more subtle, though. Perhaps you can't point specifically to a loss of customers or income, but the unsatisfactory service tends to make your company look bad in the eyes of its public. Since image is always a major concern to professional people and business organizations, that alone would be a big problem:

Dear Mrs. Firedrake:

We'd like to alert you to a problem with the janitorial service that you provide for Two Penny Decorating Consultants. The physical appearance of our offices and showroom is crucial to our type of business, and any deficiency immediately causes our customers to question our decorating capabilities.

During the past month we've opened the offices each morning to find furniture and samples moved for cleaning but not returned to their proper positions, creating an unattractive layout that customers find haphazard and unappealing. Tabletops have not always been cleaned, and soiled rags used in cleaning on occasion have been left hanging on the arm of a chair in the customer-seating area. Almost every morning something greets us—and our customers—that is very unattractive and certainly not what a customer expects of a qualified decorator.

Since the visual effect of a shoddy cleaning job will discourage our customers, we need to solve this problem without delay. Therefore, I'd appreciate it if you would telephone me at 555-1271 this week to discuss a rapid solution. I'm confident that we can resolve the problem without discontinuing your service.

Thanks very much for your help and cooperation.

Sincerely,

Credit

Try to find a person or firm that doesn't buy on credit or borrow to finance projects and new ventures. You won't find many. Today's business community and society at large are both strongly credit oriented. The amount and variety of credit correspondence generated as a result are staggering. Although much of it is routine, the same as in other types of correspondence, one aspect is more pronounced—confidentiality.

Would you want your private financial needs revealed to everyone else? Hardly. Therefore, credit information is protected from the curious eyes of the general public. Although the adequacy of this protection may be something of a joke, considering how easy it is to find out whatever you want to know about someone, letters pertaining to credit must nevertheless be treated as private and confidential. Whatever privacy results from that effort is better than nothing.

Creditors and debtors may be adversaries in one sense, but they also have a mutually beneficial relationship. One is at a loss without the other. This close link propels both sides into an ongoing circle of contacts.

Tact and consideration are paramount, which sometimes tests everyone's patience, especially since a lot of rejection and denial are involved. Honesty and accuracy are at the top of the list too. Because the very future of individuals and companies may depend on the way that credit matters are handled, a mistake—or mistruth—could cost someone a great deal.

Alternative. Businesses can't afford to slam the door on everyone who doesn't qualify for immediate credit.

But to some people who are trying to get credit, it may seem that businesses do exactly that. In any case, to prevent prospective customers from going elsewhere, companies may send a friendly refusal letter that urges the applicant to handle transactions with cash for the time being and then reapply later:

Dear Ms. Acropolis:

Thank you for letting us know about your interest in our computer tables.

As much as we would like to extend credit to your firm, an investigation of the references you supplied indicates occasional payment problems. It's our policy in such cases to ship merchandise COD or by advance cash payment. Perhaps you would like to place orders now on this basis and apply for credit privileges again in another six months.

We appreciate your thinking of us, and I hope that we'll have an opportunity to provide the computer furniture you need.

Sincerely,

Collection resolution. Who hasn't had cash-flow problems at some time? Okay, so some of you haven't, but believe me, it's not unusual. If it happens and borrowers can't meet current obligations, they should immediately contact the creditor organization. One of the best ways to protect one's credit is to be up front about a problem. If you can also offer to make payments on an outstanding balance until it's possible to pay the balance due in full, that's even better:

Dear Mr. Foxtail:

I received your letter of October 7 concerning my past-due account of $2,140.95 and would like to propose a resolution to this matter.

We've been experiencing difficulties in our cash flow due to our own collection problems, so I fully understand and appreciate your position. We're working daily to improve this situation, but until it improves, I'd like to send you $214.10 per month for a period of ten months to fulfill our obligation.

I'm enclosing the first check for $214.10 today, and if this proposal is acceptable to you, our next check will follow one month from this date. Should we be successful in our collection efforts in the coming months, I'll be most happy to pay the entire balance due at once.

Please let me know if you'd like me to proceed as described here. Thank you so much for your patience and understanding.

Sincerely,

Denial. Organizations obviously can't freely hand out credit without following *some* rules and regulations. For example, a credit check following the receipt of an application may turn up something unfavorable. However, a poor credit record may not be the problem. Perhaps the applicant doesn't have enough income to qualify for certain credit terms. In any case, the credit denial, which is usually straightforward, should include a standard clause about discrimination. Since both state and federal regulations apply in matters of equal opportunity, you should examine your own state statutes for any additional requirements of credit and lending institutions:

Dear Mr. Widdershins:

After careful consideration of your application for a Viking Supercard account, we regretfully must let you know that we're unable to grant your request at this time.

Our decision is based in whole or in part on information (or lack thereof) contained in a credit report obtained from Cactus Credit Records, 1176 Oceanside Avenue, San Francisco, CA 94118, 415-555-7178.

Sincerely,

Boyd Province
Credit Manager

The Federal Equal Credit Opportunity Act prohibits creditors from discriminating against credit applicants on the basis of race, color, religion, national origin, sex, marital status, age (providing that the applicant has the capacity to enter into a binding contract); because all or part of the applicant's income derives from any public assistance program; or because the applicant has in good faith exercised any rights under the Consumer Credit Protection Act. The federal agency that administers compliance with this law concerning this bank is the Federal Deposit Insurance Corporation, 25 Ecker Street, San Francisco, CA 94105.

Denial explanation. If a lender said no to your application for credit, would you want to know why? Most of us would. When people ask why, creditors should respond with an accurate and honest report. Also, the letter should repeat the notice about regulations against discrimination and any applicable state regulations:

Dear Mr. Widdershins:

Thank you for your letter of January 16, 200X, requesting more information about our recent decision concerning your application for a Viking Supercard account.

The terms as stated in your acceptance certificate (copy enclosed) were that card issuance was subject to the approval requirements of the Viking Bank. Our criteria allowed for no more than five revolving lines of credit with a balance. The credit report we received from Cactus Credit Reports, 1176 Oceanside Avenue, San Francisco, CA 94118, 415-555-7178, showed that you have nine such accounts.

I hope this information has answered your question. But if I can be of further help, please let me know.

Sincerely,

Boyd Province
Credit Manager

The Federal Equal Credit Opportunity Act prohibits creditors from discriminating against credit applicants on the basis of race, color, religion, national origin, sex, marital status, age (providing that the applicant has the capacity to enter into a binding contract); because all or part of the applicant's income derives from any public assistance program; or because the applicant has in good faith exercised any rights under the Consumer Credit Protection Act. The federal agency that administers compliance with this law concerning this bank is the Federal Deposit Insurance Corporation, 25 Ecker Street, San Francisco, CA 94105.

Information. I assume that you have credit cards and possibly a mortgage, car loan, or other types of credit. If that's the case, you can easily see that an enormous amount of credit is being provided every day throughout the country. This also means that such a huge amount of credit information is being exchanged that credit bureaus and large organizations have to use standard request and reply forms. However, now and then you may receive a letter request from another organization without a form enclosed for you to use in responding. If so, you'll also have to reply by letter. As always, the facts you offer should be clear and reliable, whether they're positive or negative, and the information should be sent in confidence:

Dear Mrs. Seaweed:

We're happy to send you, in confidence, the credit information that you requested about the Sundew Corporation.

Our relationship with Sundew has been excellent. They've paid all of our invoices within thirty days throughout the seven years of our association. Most of their purchases have ranged between $6,000 and $8,000 a month.

Based on our own satisfaction with the Sundew Corporation, I believe that the organization is completely reliable and creditworthy.

Sincerely,

Offer. If you or your company has a good credit rating and has previously used credit with a particular organization, don't be surprised if you're invited to borrow again. Or perhaps you're the one sending such an invitation to someone else. If so, as a means of protection, your letter should state that final approval of all loans is subject to a regular credit check:

Dear Ms. Larkspur:

Thank you very much for choosing Forthright Lenders for your financial needs. We appreciate the responsible way that you've handled your account with us, and we want you to remember that we're always here when you need money. We like doing business with you, and we'd like to continue to serve your needs.

Because you're one of our preferred customers, and because of your excellent credit rating, we have $2,500 available for you, subject only to normal credit requirements.

We hope you already know that doing business with Forthright Lenders is a comfortable and enjoyable experience. After all, we're your friends and neighbors, and we want you to have the money you need to use however you wish. So if extra cash would come in handy, call me today.

We appreciate your business, and I hope that we may continue to be of service to you when you need money, now or in the future.

Sincerely,

Statement reminder. If you or your company has a line of credit exceeding a certain amount, you may be asked to keep an up-to-date financial statement on file with the creditor. This practice is fairly common. Most people, though, need to be reminded to file a current statement:

Dear Customer:

In a recent review of our files, we found that we do not have a current financial statement from you. This type of information is required for lines of credit of $5,000 or more.

We're enclosing a standard form for you to complete and would appreciate it if you would return it to us in the enclosed envelope, provided for your convenience. For us to review your file for renewal of your line of credit, we'll need the completed form on or before April 1, 200X. But if you've already sent a recent statement to another department of our bank, please let us know, and we'll make a note for our files.

If you have any questions, or if we can help you in any way, please don't hesitate to write or call. We're looking forward to hearing from you soon.

Sincerely,

Employees

You won't find many categories bigger than *employees* in a letter-writing book. For some reason, though, this surprises many readers. Perhaps that's because we assume that letter writing refers to communication with clients or customers and others *outside* the firm. Yet there's an endless flurry of messages that never leave a company.

Much of the discussion about or among employees takes place in person or over the telephone. But conventional written correspondence or e-mail is necessary in many cases. The memo format is commonly used for in-house correspondence, both paper and electronic, although the letter format is used too. Some of the correspondence is copies of outgoing letters also sent to co-workers to keep them informed of activity.

Within a particular building, the messages may be faxed, sent by e-mail, or placed in interoffice envelopes and hand delivered. Written communication also occurs between one building and another, one department and another, or one facility and a remote facility.

Mass communications—form letters to all employees—are useful to announce policy changes, motivate employees, and build goodwill in the workforce. Even though telephone and other oral messages are common, some things are best put in writing to ensure that orders and decisions are not forgotten later.

Company pride. Even when things are going well, employees become complacent and need a pep talk every so often to stir up their enthusiasm for the company. Perhaps a letter of commendation from someone in authority, such as the organization's president or director, will do the trick. However, writers sometimes forget that to arouse enthusiasm in others, they have to sound enthusiastic themselves. Letters that sound like a big yawn won't do. Also, even though the letter will probably be prepared as a form letter or memo, it should *sound* personal:

Dear Employees:

I just received some exciting news for all of us at Azimuth Department Stores. The City Council has announced that our store will receive an award for having the most outstanding display during the holiday season!

When I recall how hard all of you worked, staying after hours for nearly a week, to set up our special World Peace display, I'm not surprised that we received top honors. But the award belongs to all of you. After all, *you* selected the theme, *you* designed the display, and *you* put it all together.

What more can I say? You're all wonderful, and I'm very proud and happy to be part of such a talented and dedicated team. A sincere, heartfelt thanks to all of you!

Cordially,

Giving advice. Where do you go if you need advice about something at work? Probably to someone in the company that you trust or like, right? Coworkers frequently turn to one another for advice, but it's a two-way street. In other words, sooner or later you'll be asked to *give* advice to someone else. If that happens, it's important to be as serious about the request as you would want someone else to be in giving advice to you:

Dear Jess:

It was great to hear about your plans to install office partitions on the third floor. This is an excellent way to avoid costly room additions and still create functional private offices.

The four basic sizes you proposed would be sufficient for the staff that would occupy the new quarters, and neutral colors would be perfect for the small areas. My only suggestion concerns soundproofing. With so many offices and computers, a quiet working environment may be hard to achieve without acoustical panels.

I'd recommend installing partitions made of sound-absorbing material with additional sound-absorbing acoustical wall panels (hung like a picture) behind noisy machines. These panels can double as bulletin boards or display centers. Over time, increased worker productivity in a quieter working environment will more than pay for the extra cost of soundproofing.

Your overall plan sounds excellent, Jess, and I wish you much success with the conversion process. In the meantime, if I can be of help, just let me know.

Best regards,

In-house invitation. So you want to have an office party. I doubt that you'll want to send invitations that make it sound like an off-putting formal affair. No problem. You don't need printed or engraved formal invitations to invite employees to an office party. A letter or memo format is appropriate for such informal notices or invitations. However, the copy should nevertheless mention all pertinent facts: time, date, place, if refreshments or meals are to be provided, the number to call for confirmation (if desired), and so on:

TO: Personnel Department Employees

FROM: Walter Penobscot, Jr., Director

RETIREMENT PARTY—HERB SANDSPUR

A retirement party for Herb Sandspur will be given on Friday, November 7, 200X, at 4:30 p.m., in the Conference Room. As you know, Herb is leaving the company after twenty years in our department.

Next month Herb will be honored by the Board of Directors with a special achievement award. But for our party, I'd like to invite each of you to donate $2 so that we can send him on his way with a token of our affection and appreciation for all his good work in the Personnel Department. You can leave your donation with my assistant in Room 218.

I hope that each of you will attend the party for Herb. I've reserved the Conference Room from 4:30 until 6:30 p.m. on the seventh and have made arrangements for nonalcoholic beverages, cocktails, and hors d'oeuvres to be served. Please call me at extension 6314 by Monday, November 3, to let me know if you'll be able to come. Hope you can join us.

Layoff. Layoffs and firings are difficult matters to deal with, to say the least. Even mere mention of the word *layoff* or *firing* causes many hearts to skip a beat. It's best to get right to the point after a gentle opening phrase or sentence, and the entire letter should be written as sensitively as possible:

Dear Ms. Perilla:

As you may know, for several months the Razorbill Trucking Company has been experiencing an especially difficult period while product strikes have remained unresolved. We had hoped to keep all our employees at work during this period, but without goods to transport, we realize that this won't be possible.

I deeply regret, therefore, that we'll be unable to continue your employment after June 1, 200X. Although we all hope this layoff will be temporary, we can't commit ourselves to a resumption of normal activity until the major strikes are settled. But we've been very pleased with your work and will promptly notify you of any changes in this status.

If you have any questions, feel free to call me at 555-8400. In the meantime, please accept my best wishes for your future.

Sincerely,

Morale. When things aren't going well in a company, department, or office, employee morale often takes a nosedive. Before it sinks so low that productivity suffers and before employees start looking for other jobs, management must think of something to do or say to lift everyone's spirit:

Dear Rick:

Now that we've all had a chance to digest Edgewater's recently announced plans for reorganization, I want to give you my thoughts from a departmental perspective. Mostly, I want to pass along the good news that has somehow been lost in the reorganization shuffle.

Although you've probably heard rumors of massive layoffs resulting from the reorganization, the reality is that the restructuring will make many jobs even more essential and more secure. It's true, of course, that our department will be merged with the Customer Relations Department, and three people must be relocated. Notice that I said *relocated,* not let go. In fact, management is making every effort to keep layoffs to a minimum.

The best news is that the reorganization is expected to make Edgewater highly competitive and very profitable in the coming years and even in the near future. As profits rise, the company will once again hire (or rehire) more employees. Salary increases will become not just a hope but a certainty—and I'm happy to report that people like you, who are already on board and working with us in the reorganization, will be first in line!

My view, therefore, is that the reorganization is *good news* for everyone in our department, even for the three people who will be moved to exciting new assignments in other areas. Considering that all of us will have a rewarding future at Edgewater, I hope that I can count on you to stay with us and reap the benefits of a stronger, more profitable company.

Best regards,

Resignation. People resign for different reasons: age, more money, dissatisfaction with the present job, and so on. Because future employers will likely check your record with the company, it makes sense to leave on good terms, even if you're unhappy about something or angry with someone. If you're planning to resign, therefore, don't give anyone a chance to say that you left over some unresolved conflict. Simply state that a new opportunity has come up, or that you feel it's important to search for one, and express appreciation in some way. For example, you might mention someone's help or the useful experience you gained while working for the company:

Dear Ms. Kiwi:

I'm submitting my resignation as assistant manager effective July 24, 200X. I recently discovered an outside opportunity that will enable me to make greater use of my educational background and special abilities in investment research.

I greatly appreciated your help and guidance during my four years with the Pennyroyal Corporation and am pleased that I had an opportunity to work for such a fine organization.

Sincerely,

Salary increase. Some lucky people get a raise about every year. Others never get one unless they ask for it, and even then, not everyone who asks for a raise gets it. If you're the person who has to break this news to an employee, you've probably discovered that saying no can be a lot harder than saying yes. Since you don't want to discourage the employee, you need to offer some type of encouragement in spite of the monetary refusal:

Dear Ms. Frisbee:

I appreciated seeing the progress report you sent last week. Thank you very much. It's clear that you've made excellent progress since joining our firm six months ago.

Although I'm impressed with your performance record and am very pleased that you're eager to make further contributions, company policy prevents me from considering a salary increase for you until the end of your first year of employment. At that time, your record will be automatically evaluated by our review board, and you'll be notified of any decisions concerning a salary increase.

I know that you spent a lot of time preparing the report, so I'm placing it in your file where the board will be certain to see it during their review. In the meantime, many thanks for doing such fine work, Ms. Frisbee.

With all good wishes,

Sexual harassment. One of the dreaded problems in a company is sexual harassment. You hope it never happens to you, but what if it does, or what if you sense that it may be waiting around the corner? If a situation gets out of hand, you'll presumably report your case to the appropriate person in authority. But well before that happens, before the situation becomes hostile, what if you simply want to write a letter to the harasser? What should you say? Although every situation is different, and you may want to discuss your situation with an attorney, a minister, or other person, here is one possibility for a firm but reasonably friendly letter to a harassing coworker:

Dear Harry:

I want to let you know how much I enjoy my job in the studio, but I have one problem that you can solve.

Your increasing personal attention has become disturbing to me, and I'm very uncomfortable with some of your jokes and other comments. Since I have every intention of avoiding personal or romantic relationships with coworkers, this overly friendly attention must stop immediately.

I'm certain that we can work together without any improper personal involvement, and I'm hopeful that you'll agree so it won't be necessary for me to take this matter to anyone else.

Sincerely,

Welcome. Don't you feel sorry for new employees? They're like little puppies lost in the wilderness. But you can make it easier for them by being friendly and helpful. For example, as a friendly gesture, you might send a welcome letter. It would help to build goodwill and good working relations by making the employee feel at home and enthusiastic about the new position:

Dear Randi:

It's a pleasure to welcome you to the Sales Department. With your excellent background in promotional writing, I'm certain that you'll find numerous opportunities to use your talent in our department.

Soon you'll meet the other members of our group, and I know they'll be happy to greet you. We all work hard, but most important, we work *together* and enjoy a special sense of fellowship.

By all means, stop at my office whenever you have a question or something to discuss. I'm looking forward to working with you and am eager to help you get acquainted with your coworkers and our department.

Best regards,

Explanations

Kids aren't the only ones who keep asking us why this or that is true: Dad, why doesn't Gramma have any teeth? Why can't I paint a picture of Fluffy on the front door?

At work, you may think that it's enough merely to say yes or no if you're authorized to make a decision, that others shouldn't question your motivation or reasoning. Up to a point, that may even be true. But taking that position ignores the fact that people respond more positively and work better when they know *why* they should do something or *why* they may not do something.

For example, in matters of refusing proposals, contracts, promotions, and salary increases, people are entitled to know why their efforts and ideas don't merit acceptance and therefore what, if anything, they can or should do to reverse that situation. Sensitive matters, particularly with outsiders, are usually best addressed in a letter format, but routine explanations to in-house personnel may be sent as memos.

Late delivery. Unless you have superhuman patience, you know how annoying it is to wait and wait for a delivery. Therefore, when customers are expecting supplies from you by a certain date, you need to be particularly considerate in explaining the reason for any delay and in expressing regret about the inconvenience the delay is causing. Nevertheless, depending on your policy, you may be unable to offer the customer any form of compensation, such as a refund or discount. In that case, it will also be necessary to make that fact clear as gently as possible:

Dear Ms. Colander:

We were very sorry to learn that the solid state insect killer you ordered didn't arrive in time for your Fourth of July office picnic. Your order apparently arrived just as our supply was exhausted, and it was necessary to wait until a new shipment arrived. Unfortunately, our supplier's deliveries were running late, and this in turn affected our shipments to customers.

Although our company has no policy to provide a discount under these circumstances, you may return the item unused for either a refund or a credit toward another purchase. I'm enclosing a copy of our catalog so that you can consider other needs you may have when you make your choice.

We very much regret any inconvenience that you've experienced and hope that we'll have an opportunity to serve you again.

Sincerely,

Oversight. A popular saying is that professionals check things twice. Wouldn't it be nice if everyone did that? We might not have to deal with so many errors and oversights. But let's be honest: Busy people forget things and make mistakes. In fact, we all forget things and make mistakes. Therefore, when someone points out an oversight, the only thing to do is to apologize, explain the reason, and offer to make amends:

Dear Mr. Dugong:

Thank you for letting us know that your golf course
sprinkler was delivered without the wheel base. I've asked
our Shipping Department to send a base by United Parcel
Service today.

I know that you had requested the sprinkler by August 9 to
prepare for an upcoming tournament, and we regret the
oversight in sending a sprinkler without a base. Ordinarily,
our sprinklers are sent with a step spike, and our shipping
clerk must have removed the spike from your carton but
forgot to insert the wheel base. To ensure that this doesn't
happen again, we're changing our procedure to be certain
that orders are double-checked for type of base before
shipping.

We hope that your wheel base will arrive soon and that the
delay has not seriously inconvenienced you. Please accept
our apologies as well as our good wishes for your next
tournament.

Cordially,

Policy change. As you know, companies often announce new policies or policy changes by interoffice
memo. The message is distributed to all employees or
to those who are affected by the policy. When it's a
matter of general company policy, the memo should
come from someone in authority, such as the president
or a general manager:

TO: All Department Managers

FROM: Drew Notchback
          Vice President and General Manager

COMPUTER DISKETTE SECURITY

Last week there were three reported cases of missing
diskettes and more than ten cases in the past month.
Fortunately, the diskettes did not contain sensitive material

and were apparently lost or misplaced due to carelessness. Nevertheless, this situation should alert us to the possibility of loss or theft of confidential information.

Although our company has a workable security code system for our hard disks, not all diskette files have locks, and not all of those with locks remain secured by the user. Previously, we left it up to each department to establish and monitor security. However, the continuing loss of diskettes and possible adverse consequences indicate that we need a general company policy.

Hereafter, please instruct all employees in your department that only *locking* diskette files may be used. Any files without locks should be taken to the Purchasing Department immediately and exchanged for locking files. Furthermore, all files must remain locked at all times except during active use.

Users will be held accountable for any missing diskettes. In addition, as a departmental manager, it will be your responsibility to determine any such loss, to arrange for the replacement of data, and to reprimand the user or take other appropriate action.

We regret the need to impose more stringent measures but believe that preventive measures will help us to avoid a serious or unfortunate incident in the future. The board will greatly appreciate your cooperation in implementing this change in policy.

If you have any questions or recommendations, please feel free to contact me at any time. I sincerely appreciate your help and interest.

Promotion denied. The next model suggests one of those good news–bad news situations. The bad news is that almost any refusal may cause disappointment. The good news is that your language and tone can soften the blow. So if you have to say no to an employee, start with a thank you or acknowledgment of the employee's contributions, honestly explain your reasons for the refusal, and mention any later change in circumstances that might in turn cause a change in your position:

Dear Mr. Druid:

Thank you for sending me such an impressive account of your contribution in the Biosynthesis Lab.

I know it took a great deal of time, planning, and effort to increase productivity by 20 percent. The timesaving steps you recommended have certainly paid off, and we're delighted with your initiative and willingness to assume additional responsibility.

Although I value your contribution and recognize fully that the entire organization benefits from the contributions of dependable employees such as you, I'm sorry that we can't grant the promotion you requested at this time. Another outstanding candidate for the assistant director position has been with our organization for many more years and has the extensive experience that seniority usually provides.

I hope that you won't be discouraged by this decision, because in time there will definitely be other positions available that may appeal to you and will be even more suitable. You may be certain that I'll remember your interest and noteworthy accomplishments and will make every effort to see that appropriate measures are taken to make use of your abilities.

In the meantime, Mr. Druid, please accept my thanks and deep admiration for all your good work.

With best wishes,

Scheduling problem. How do you feel about deadlines? If that was a huge groan I heard, I understand. One of the hardest tasks in any organization is scheduling work to meet deadlines while still maintaining priorities and the requirements of daily operations. The hard truth is that it doesn't always work well, and you may need the cooperation of other in-house personnel, offices, or departments or even that of outside organizations. Fortunately, if you explain your problem, most people will be happy to work with you:

TO: Laurie Haboob

FROM: Mike Epaulet

TIME-WORK STUDY REPORT

While I was reading your memo stating that you'd like the time-work study report on March 17, I realized that Mr. Trecento is expecting my review of the Venturi Agreement the same day.

Even with overtime, I doubt that I can complete both projects by March 17. Ordinarily, I'd have more help in the Research Department, but one person is on leave to get married, another is in the hospital, and the remaining staff members are already on assignment. This has compounded my scheduling problems, so I'm wondering if I may have an additional week to complete the time-work study report for you.

Please let me know what you think, Laurie. Thanks very much.

Student probation. We know that any serious problem with students in a school must be reported to parents or guardians. But this is a very touchy situation because little Tommy or Susie may be someone's pride and joy who can do no wrong. So it's important to state the facts not only clearly and objectively but also tactfully and to explain your reason for taking certain action:

Dear Mr. and Mrs. Chuckwalla:

I'm sorry to report that Dewey has been placed on probation for six months for participation in defacing the walls of the boys' locker room. He has admitted his action and has indicated that he and two other classmates considered the act a harmless prank. However, the school board views any form of vandalism as a serious offense.

Since we do not condone destructive behavior, all three boys have been advised of the seriousness of their action and the consequences. We'll closely monitor their behavior during the probationary period and hope that they'll benefit from this experience.

Please let me know if you have any questions or if I can be of help in any way.

Sincerely,

Unsatisfactory work. Did you goof? If you receive a complaint from a customer that your work is unsatisfactory, acknowledge the criticism promptly. Since the person complaining is probably irritated and not in the mood for evasive replies or weak excuses, simply admit your mistake, apologize, and emphasize your intent to correct the situation and please the customer:

Dear Mrs. Bangtail:

I agree. The quality of our paint job was below our usual standards. Not only can it be improved, but it *will* be improved in future assignments.

The painter and I have inspected the offices and have noted areas that were missed and others that are splattered with fresh paint. He believes that the need to paint after hours, with inadequate artificial lighting, caused him to miss things that he would surely have seen under different conditions.

However, we want to correct the problem *at our expense* as soon as possible. I've asked the painter to call you on Monday to arrange a suitable time to return.

We appreciate your concern and are very sorry that the work did not meet your expectations. You may be certain that we value your business and will do our utmost to provide satisfactory work at all times.

Sincerely,

Follow-ups

We've said it before: Although business letters and memos should be acknowledged promptly, some people take forever to reply or never reply at all. Because this happens so often, an office must have follow-up procedures that identify correspondence that was sent but for which no reply was received. It's a time-eating nuisance, but by a certain date the writer must write again to ask whether an original letter ever arrived and if the recipient has had time yet to consider the matter in question.

When you're preparing a follow-up, keep the message brief, mention the pertinent facts of the letter being traced, and request a prompt reply. Avoid offending the reader, however, by implying that the person is thoughtless or forgetful, even though he or she may well be both.

Not all follow-ups are necessary, however, only because someone failed to acknowledge an original message. In fact, some occasions requiring follow-up have nothing to do with someone's tardiness in replying. Various events and activities, for example, may warrant a follow-up letter of thanks, and the next letter fits that description.

Company hospitality. It's common courtesy to follow up business or social hospitality with an expression of appreciation, but such messages also serve another purpose: They help to build successful business relationships:

Dear Mr. Salmagundi:

I certainly enjoyed meeting you and your associates last week. Your assembly operations are very impressive, and I learned a lot from observing the enthusiasm and efficiency of the personnel.

Thank you for taking time to show me your facilities and to explain your well-organized and expertly managed activities. I appreciated the opportunity to get better acquainted with all of you and to learn more about our mutual interests.

Best regards,

Customer inquiry. It's not only a common procedure but also a smart one to follow up on inquiries while customers are still interested. Just ask anyone in sales. If you wait, the customers may lose interest or buy elsewhere:

Dear Ms. Dichondra:

Last week you asked about a form guide for printers, and I wanted to let you know immediately that a new shipment has arrived. Would you like to visit our store to see how they work?

A guide attaches to the rear of a printer and keeps up to four kinds of forms, such as labels and order forms, neatly organized. Moreover, it guides the output so that it isn't swept into the printer to cause jamming. Hooks on each side hold printer cards out of the way of the paper flow, and the black steel frame will interlock with printer stands if desired.

I hope that you can stop soon to see for yourself how handy these guides are. We're open from 9 to 5 o'clock every day except Sunday. In the meantime, though, if you have any questions, just call 555-9000. Any one of our clerks will be happy to help you.

Cordially,

Missing enclosure. Considering how often we forget to send what we say we're going to send, you would think that we're all brain-damaged. When someone writes to you and forgets to include something, follow up immediately. Although the writer may realize later that the enclosure was omitted and may send it then, don't count on this happening:

Dear Ms. Crookneck:

I'm so glad that you let me know about your graphics seminar. It sounds very interesting. You mentioned a program, however, that wasn't enclosed, and I wonder if you'd mind sending me a copy. Several of us in the Art Department would like to see it.

Thanks very much.

Sincerely,

Missing order. One doesn't have to be terribly clever to assume that an unfilled order, with no acknowledgment from the supplier, may mean a missing order. At least it's a possibility. If you're following up on such an order, refer to your follow-up order as a *duplicate* to ensure that it won't be treated as a new, original order or as an additional order—in case the earlier one turns up:

TO: Metacenter Office Supplies

FROM: D. G. Hemicycle
OUR PURCHASE ORDER X1772011

On January 16 I placed an order for ten boxes of self-adhesive tab labels, $3\frac{1}{2}$ by $^{15}/_{16}$ inches, for data processing (catalog no. 116-S-9292-WZ4). Since the labels have not arrived, I wonder if my original order went astray; if so, please consider this a duplicate.

We're in urgent need of replacements and would appreciate having this order sent immediately. The labels should be delivered to our letterhead address to my attention.

If the labels are out of stock or can't be sent on a rush basis, please telephone me right away at 555-3131. Thank you.

Unacknowledged gift. If you haven't received an acknowledgment of a gift after eight weeks, stop stewing and send a follow-up. It's possible that the recipient is simply a rude, thoughtless person who never sends thank yous, but it's also possible that the gift never arrived. Or the gift may be one of many that the person received, or it may have been opened by an assistant or someone else who misplaced it. Who knows? In any case, you'll need to describe it to help the intended recipient trace it. Also, explain what can be done if it never arrived. Although it's annoying to have to ask people if they received a gift, etiquette requires that you avoid suggesting the recipient is a thoughtless cretin for failing to send you a thank you note:

> Dear Ben:
>
> I've been thinking about you since your promotion and hope that the hectic first months have passed successfully. I'm sure that you're having an exciting time with your challenging new position.
>
> The news of your promotion was exciting to me, too, and I sent you a little gift to wish you well—a leather-bound desk planner for busy executives like you. I was wondering if perhaps it went astray in the midst of your transfer to another department. Could you let me know whether or not it arrived safely? If not, it was insured, and I can contact the post office to have it traced.
>
> Best of luck in your new position, Ben.
>
> Cordially,

Unanswered request. Here's an example of another type of follow-up that you may have to do: If you sent an important, *detailed* request that was never acknowledged, you might enclose a copy of the original letter and indicate that your request evidently went astray in the mail. But if you sent a brief, routine request for information that was never answered, simply restate your request in another brief letter:

Ladies and Gentlemen:

Last month we requested descriptive material and a price list for your five-drawer, eight-drawer, and ten-drawer workbenches. The information has not yet arrived, and we would like to have it sent by return mail so that we can place our order immediately.

Thank you.

Sincerely,

Unreturned call. An unreturned telephone call is just as irritating as an unanswered letter and usually must be followed up in the same way. If this happens often, you may be ready to kick a table—or the unresponsive person. As usual, though, you have to be careful not to let your irritation affect the tone of your message:

TO: Mandy Lancet

FROM: Rob Harbinger

DIPLEX PROJECT

I wonder if you received the voice-mail message that I left for you last week concerning complications we've encountered with the Diplex project. I'm afraid we're at a standstill, and I'll need to clarify a few points with you before we can continue.

If you could telephone me right away (555-6129) or stop by my office, I'll bring you up to date.

Thanks, Mandy. Hope to hear from you soon.

Goodwill

I hope that I didn't put everyone in a bad mood by talking about people who ignore our letters and calls, forcing us to write follow-up letters. This next subject—goodwill—should be more uplifting.

We know that businesses need the support of people and other organizations because the sale of products, services, and ideas in part depends on the feelings and attitudes of others toward the seller. Very simply, to build a favorable image, companies must do things that others view as kind, generous, and impressive.

Letters of goodwill are perfect for building confidence in a company and in stimulating favorable attitudes. Almost any occasion can serve as a reason for expressing concern for or interest in others. As you've no doubt observed, people are very susceptible to flattery or any other form of thoughtful personal attention. For example, you can't help but be a little pleased with someone who wishes you a happy birthday and tells you how young you look or how magnificent you are.

If you want to build goodwill among employees, prospective and current customers or clients, and the entire community, say something nice whenever the occasion rises. For example, send your good wishes when someone gets promoted, has an anniversary, celebrates a holiday, makes a helpful suggestion, or suffers misfortune—anything.

Follow a few basic rules, and you won't go wrong: Talk *only* about the other person. Although you probably have all sorts of incredibly exciting things to say about yourself, it's important not to detract from someone's moment in the spotlight by talking about yourself or your company. Also, if you send a gift or do a favor, don't ask for anything in return in that letter. I realize that in business it's not uncommon to exchange gifts, favors, and so on, but save it for later, in a separate letter. Finally, be natural and sincere, but don't gush or the reader will think that you don't mean a word you've written.

Anniversary. Business-related anniversaries or non-business events such as a wedding anniversary are all great opportunities to recognize someone and send your warm wishes. Special anniversaries, such as the twenty-fifth, should definitely be recognized, but others are occasions for goodwill too. You might, for instance, congratulate someone on the first anniversary of a new business. Don't forget long-term anniversaries either. They're always a good choice for special recognition:

Dear Mr. Parbuckle:

It's a great pleasure to send you my very best wishes, along with those of the entire Board of Directors, on your fortieth anniversary at the Jonquil Corporation. We've all benefited from your loyal service and important contributions to our organization's growth and progress.

For all of these years, you've given generously of your expertise and experience to coworkers and customers alike. You've truly earned the respect of everyone who knows you and has had the pleasure of working with you at some time during your impressive career. We share with you a well-deserved sense of accomplishment at having reached such an important milestone.

Please accept our congratulations, Mr. Parbuckle, and our very best wishes for many more rewarding years at Jonquil.

Cordially,

Guest speaker. Here's another chance to play nice: Outside speakers will gain a favorable impression of an organization when on-the-spot praise for an address is followed with a letter of congratulations from someone in the company. The speaker can't help but be pleased. Such letters should be written as a matter of courtesy in any case, but they also give you an opportunity to improve your company's image:

Dear Ms. Emu:

Let me congratulate you on your excellent speech to members of our organization Friday evening. The attendees were totally absorbed with your presentation, and afterward, I heard many of them excitedly discussing your ideas for efficiency in packaging.

Your suggestions are especially pertinent to our operation,
Ms. Emu, and I want to thank you for sharing them with
us. We hope that you'll join us soon again as our guest.

Cordially,

Holiday greetings. As you can imagine, holidays such
as Thanksgiving and New Year are among the most suitable occasions for goodwill letters. You can send the
letters in place of a card to customers and clients. You
can also send a form letter to all employees to encourage
a feeling of unity and goodwill within the firm. A letter
to employees might come from the president, and it
might be sent on behalf of the board of directors or
company management:

Dear Employee:

We're always happy when the holiday season arrives and
the New Year is upon us. It reminds us that we have a lot
to be thankful for and much to look forward to, thanks to
the loyal and dedicated efforts of employees like you.

It's gratifying to see the friendly spirit of cooperation that
exists in our company. There's always a place for individual
contributions and at the same time a need for unity and
team activity. Although we've accomplished a lot in the
past, we hope to achieve even more in the future. In
particular, we hope to be able to make your position more
satisfying and rewarding each year.

We appreciate having you as an employee of our company
and look forward to sharing another year of progress with
you. Warmest regards to you, your family, and your friends
during this holiday season, and my sincere wishes for a
peaceful and bountiful New Year.

Cordially,

New business. The list of opportunities to spread
goodwill goes on and on. Take the opening of a new

business—yet another opportunity to build goodwill, this time in the community:

Dear Jim:

I was delighted to learn that Better Business Services has already opened for business—congratulations! With your experience and enthusiasm, I know that your organization will be a huge success.

My very best to you, Jim. It's wonderful to know that all your hard work has paid off.

Best regards,

Previous customer. A business doesn't necessarily write off a customer just because the person suddenly stops buying. More likely, the business will try to entice the person to return to the fold. So it's goodwill time again. Often these letters are no more than simple thank yous for patronage:

Dear Mr. Overstory:

It was a pleasure to serve you and your guests at the dinner held in our restaurant on November 10. We hope that all of you had a wonderful time.

We're always excited when we have an opportunity to prepare a special meal for a very special occasion such as this. We hope that you found both the food and the service satisfactory, and we trust that the decorations you requested provided a special attraction for you and your guests. Since we're always eager to maintain strict standards and complete customer satisfaction, we hope that you'll feel free to offer comments or suggestions concerning the arrangements.

Many thanks for choosing the Roadside Gourmet for your dinner. We're looking forward to serving you soon again.

Sincerely,

Prospective customer. Anyone who works in sales knows that selling is a many-faceted game, and sales personnel must use a variety of techniques to stimulate interest among prospective customers. A popular device is the so-called free gift, which often accompanies some other product that the customer is expected to purchase. Customers love gifts, and often they're invited to keep them regardless of whether they buy the product being sold. Of course, if the customer feels terrible about keeping the gift and therefore buys the other product out of guilt, that's okay too. Coupons or certificates to be spent in the seller's establishment are one such type of gift that merchants and others frequently use:

Dear Mr. and Mrs. Pandowdy:

Welcome to Hillside Manor Estates! We hope that you're enjoying your new home in our beautiful community as much as we enjoy having you here. Many of your neighbors have been shopping at Toehold Grocers for years, so we feel as if we're a regular part of daily life in the neighborhood.

We realize that the first weeks in a new community can be hectic—and expensive! To help make your move a little easier, please accept this special ticket, which entitles you to one full cart of groceries *absolutely free.* Just come on over, load up, present the ticket to our cashier, and walk away with as many groceries as you can fit into our regular cart, all with our compliments. Not only will this help you fill those new cupboards, but it will also give you an opportunity to become acquainted with our store.

If we can do anything else to make your introduction to Hillside Manor Estates more enjoyable, do let us know. We're delighted to have you as a neighbor and look forward to meeting you on your next visit to our store.

With best wishes from the staff at Toehold,

Suggestion. Wouldn't you agree that a useful suggestion deserves recognition, even if you were unable to put the suggestion to work? Also, the occasion offers still another opportunity to send a goodwill letter, one that additionally will encourage future contributions and will foster warm relations in the meantime:

Dear Ellie:

Your idea to use economy diskettes for nonpermanent filing is intriguing, and the savings you project for one year are significant—nearly 30 percent. I'd like to think more about this.

Company policy at present doesn't provide for automatic elimination of any material, although a lot of our paper files are clearly intended to be temporary, as you pointed out. I'll ask for some opinions concerning company policy in this matter, and perhaps we can work out something later.

For now, I just wanted you to know how much I appreciate your suggestion. Practical ideas like yours are always welcome, Ellie. Many thanks.

Regards,

Inquiries

Sometimes it's necessary to ask questions before making a decision or taking some action. Everyone does this. In fact, a huge amount of business correspondence is accounted for by such routine inquiries. Some of the inquiries are general: Perhaps you wonder whether a mail-order supply store sells surge protectors. Others are specific: You wonder whether the store has a five-compartment noise-suppression protector.

People ordinarily don't mind composing inquiry letters because they're straightforward, specific messages. They're usually just long enough to describe adequately what you want to know. Some are combination inquiry-request letters, however, and they may be more detailed. In such cases, if you want the reader to take some action, you'll have to make that clear in addition to explaining what information you want.

If you deal with inquiries long enough, you'll discover that the reply to an inquiry frequently requires more detail than the inquiry itself—unless you're enclosing something and the reply is just a simple transmittal letter. But either way, when you reply to an inquiry, you need to provide as much information as you can to answer a writer's question and thank the person for his or her interest. If the person making the inquiry should look elsewhere, try to recommend another source.

Available product. Let's start with a common routine inquiry, such as a question about a product when you have specific features and capabilities in mind. You can probably handle this type of inquiry in one to three sentences:

Ladies and Gentlemen:

I noticed in your April 17 catalog, page 28, a description of the Wonder Computer, its operating system, and the software package. Nothing is said about the monitor, however. Would you please send me details about it, including resolution and screen size?

Thanks very much.

Sincerely,

Available service. The general inquiry—when you *don't* have specific features or capabilities in mind—is one of the simplest of all messages to compose. One to three sentences, again, should be enough to ask whether a particular service or item is available:

Ladies and Gentlemen:

Do you offer maintenance agreements for the model JT-4000 copier? If so, please send details about the type of servicing provided and the annual cost.

Thank you.

Sincerely,

Delivery requirement. I'm sure you know that deliveries are *always* the subject of numerous inquiries. But can you guess what is the most common inquiry about deliveries? If you said the date, you guessed right. When you have to meet a deadline, you'll definitely want to ask about the delivery date before placing an order to be certain that the material will arrive on time:

> Ladies and Gentlemen:
>
> We're considering placing an order for five hundred embossed binders to be distributed at our annual meeting and technical conference this fall. Would you please let us know by return mail how much time you would need to fill such an order?
>
> We're prepared to place the order at any time provided that you can guarantee delivery on or before September 1, 200X.
>
> Thank you.
>
> Sincerely,

Informational response. When you get an inquiry letter asking for *detailed* information, you can do one of two things: Put all the facts in a long letter of response or write a short note to say that you're enclosing, or sending separately, additional information such as a list, report, brochure, or catalog:

> Dear Ms. Oleander:
>
> We have two types of energy-rating guides—one for business customers and one for residential customers—and I'm enclosing both for your review. I believe these booklets will answer many of your questions, but please let us know if you need additional information.
>
> We appreciate your interest and hope that the enclosed material will be of help to you.
>
> Sincerely,

Negative response. Do you find it hard to say no without sounding awkward or even mean? After saying no hundreds of times, many people still can't get the hang of it. But when an inquiry letter asks if you'll do something and you're not interested, you obviously have to say no and, one hopes, do it with tact and consideration. After all, you wouldn't want to squash the writer's enthusiasm:

> Dear Mr. Snick:
>
> Thanks so much for telling me about your plan to rent roller skates to mall shoppers.
>
> Although it's not likely that competition will be a problem, I'm afraid that mall safety regulations and the potential for accidents would prevent any such venture from becoming a reality. Also, as much as I appreciate your thinking of me, I'm sorry that, because of other commitments, I'm not in a position at present to consider additional ventures.
>
> I'm returning your information sheet and want to wish you much success in finding the right project to pursue.
>
> Sincerely,

Positive response. Writing a *yes* letter is obviously easier or at least more fun than writing a *no* letter. If an inquiry also asks you to do something and if you *want* to do it, don't hesitate to let your enthusiasm show when you say yes:

> Dear Stan:
>
> Yes, I certainly would be interested in organizing study groups on campus this summer to deal with extracurricular reading in our theology seminars. I think it's a wonderful idea, and I'd love to be involved in such a program.
>
> I'll prepare a list of ideas for us to discuss and, as you suggested, will call you next week to arrange a meeting.
>
> Cordially,

Standard reply. Large and small companies do some things differently; in fact, they do a lot of things differently. If you work for a large firm, for example, you probably use more form letters for matters such as routine inquiries. The standard message may have blank spaces where you fill in certain information, or it may be a brief, general reply suitable for most inquiries. The customer's name may be merged with the rest of the letter by computer, or a general salutation such as *Dear Customer* may be used:

Dear Customer:

We appreciate your inquiry about our products and are enclosing a copy of our most recent catalog for you. The order form provides complete instructions on ordering as well as shipping details.

If we can answer any other questions, please feel free to call us anytime between 9 a.m. and 5 p.m. eastern standard time. Our toll-free number is 800-555-7198.

Thank you for writing to Hopscotch Traders. We're looking forward to receiving your first order.

Cordially,

Instructions

I wonder who writes the instructions that are sent with certain goods, such as how to assemble a bird feeder. Anyone who understands them ought to receive our country's highest honor.

Often such instructions are printed on sheets or in booklets enclosed with the product. Sometimes they're put in, or repeated in, a letter or memo. The memo format is suitable for most in-house instructional messages, whereas the letter format is more appropriate for outside messages. Either way, the instructions should be very clear and specific, or they'll drive exasperated readers to the brink of insanity.

Agreement. Some instructions, such as those in a cover letter sent with a document, are much simpler than others are. For example, if a document has to be signed, whether it's an informal agreement or a formal contract, all that's needed is a letter briefly explaining where to sign and what to do with the signed copies. A letter of agreement may have a line for the signature at the bottom of the letter, whereas a separate document will have the signature lines on the document itself:

Dear Mr. Skittle:

Here's the computer service agreement that we discussed by telephone on May 9, 200X.

You'll notice that the period of service is May 12, 200X, through May 11, 200X, with automatic renewal until we receive thirty days' advance notification from you canceling the agreement. Our Billing Department will send you an invoice for the amount specified in the agreement.

After you've read the entire agreement, please sign both copies at the bottom of page two and return the two copies. Upon receipt of your check covering the amount specified in the agreement, we'll countersign the copies here and return one of them to you.

We're happy to have an opportunity to provide this service for your organization and hope that you'll be pleased with the many cost-saving features of our arrangement.

Sincerely,

Caution. I hope you haven't discovered the hard way that equipment may be damaged if it isn't cared for properly. An admonition about proper care usually appears in the equipment guide, which some people may never read if it's too complex, and may also be mentioned in an accompanying letter, which some people also may never read if it's too complex:

Dear Customer:

It's a pleasure to send you the most advanced compact electronic calculator on the market today. In spite of its convenient size, it has all the best features of larger machines—full keyboard and large display.

Speed, accuracy, and dependable operation are yours with the compact model 600. Nevertheless, to ensure that you have many years of reliable service, we urge you to read the enclosed owner's manual and, especially, to observe these three cautions:

1. Do not cover the machine while it is turned on.
2. Clean the housing only with the enclosed silicon-treated cloth.
3. Do not keep the machine in hot, dusty, or damp places.

We're very pleased that you've chosen the compact model 600 and hope that you'll call us if you have any questions not covered in the owner's manual.

Cordially,

Enrollment procedure. Sometimes it seems that educational programs and organizations issue more instructions than any other type of organization. Think about it: Schools, workshops, seminars, conferences, company training sessions, and any other educational or developmental program or organization all have to provide registration details to enrollees—and that's only the beginning. You might handle such initial instructions as part of a sophisticated promotional packet, or for a small program, you could send a form letter to prospective enrollees:

Dear Manager:

We're happy to send you the enclosed outline of our Action
Seminars for Managers, available for one week in
September in a city near you. Enrollments are accepted on
a first-come, first-served basis, so we urge you to act today:

1. Telephone us at 213-555-1026 for immediate
   confirmation of your registration, or mail the enclosed
   registration card today (allow two weeks for
   confirmation by mail).
2. Make your check for the one-week seminar payable to
   Action Seminars. Refer to the registration card for
   further details.
3. Sign up six or more persons from your organization
   and receive a 10 percent group discount.
4. Remember that late cancellations—four days or less
   preceding the opening—are subject to a $50
   cancellation fee. No refunds are available after class
   has begun.
5. For help with hotel accommodations and
   transportation arrangements, call 213-555-1020.

We hope that you'll take advantage of this opportunity to
learn the management techniques that leaders in business have
tested and proven to be essential for the successful
manager. But don't delay. Registration is limited, and we
want to be able to reserve a place for you at this important
event.

Sincerely,

Operating procedure. As you know, when you buy
equipment or other devices, the operating instructions
are typically enclosed with the item. Sometimes an accompanying letter summarizes the main points, leaving
the details for the operator's manual:

Dear Customer:

We're very pleased that you've chosen the world's finest
electric pencil sharpener, the X-Cel-Matic 22. Your new

sharpener is designed to ensure trouble-free operation for many years. To use the X-Cel-Matic 22:

1. Plug the device into any 120-volt AC outlet.
2. When you insert the pencil at the front, apply only *slight* pressure. Strong pressure will damage the sharpening mechanism.
3. When a red light goes on next to the pencil opening, withdraw the pencil immediately to avoid breaking the fine point from repeated grinding.
4. Periodically, check the clear plastic cup beneath the pencil opening, and when it is full, pull it out and discard the shavings. Do not allow the shavings to become impacted since that may clog the blade area where the pencil is sharpened.

We urge you to read the enclosed operations pamphlet for additional information on maintenance and servicing. If you have any questions about your sharpener, call a nearby service center listed on the back of the pamphlet.

Thank you for trying the X-Cel-Matic. We know that you'll enjoy its reliable performance, even with heavy daily use.

Sincerely,

Product registration. When you buy a product, what do you do with the warranty material? Read it? Keep it? Send in the registration form, file it on-line, or file it in your wastebasket? Some people totally ignore warranty material and later regret doing so when a product breaks. If you've kept your material, you'll notice that often either a letter of instruction accompanies the registration card or a message is printed at the top or bottom of the registration form:

Dear Customer:

Congratulations on purchasing an ASTRO Travel Cooler! You've made an excellent choice and should enjoy many years of dependable use.

Would you please help us by completing and returning the enclosed registration card within ten days from the date of purchase? This information will formally register your product to qualify you for a free replacement should the product develop a problem within the thirty-day warranty period. It also will enable us to learn more about you and your needs. Just go down the brief list and check off your answers—no need to write out anything.

Thank you for choosing the ASTRO Travel Cooler. We're delighted to have you as a customer.

Cordially,

Replacement part. We know that things break or wear out—sometimes all too soon. Because this happens, it's necessary to instruct customers about obtaining replacement parts. This message may be a separate letter, part of the warranty form, or part of the equipment guide:

Dear Customer:

We're very pleased that you chose the Shredder Wizard for your office and hope that you'll enjoy the speed and efficiency of this remarkable machine.

To keep your equipment in perfect working condition, follow the instructions in your owner's guide. This product has been carefully engineered and manufactured to meet rigid quality standards and will give dependable service for many years. But if you should require replacement parts or maintenance, please write to the Shredder Wizard, 101 Lost Lane, Norman, OK 73069, or call us at 405-555-6262 and provide the following:

1. Model number, part number and description, color, and other details listed in your owner's guide
2. Date and store from which product was purchased
3. A description of the trouble you're having

Replacement parts are furnished at current prices plus the cost of shipping.

We wish you many happy, trouble-free hours of shredding.
If, however, you have any questions, please feel free to
write or call.

Cordially,

Request. You have my sympathy if ever you ordered
anything by telephone or some form of mail because by
now you're probably on every mailing list in the universe. If so, you no doubt get so many catalogs every
day that you now understand what's happened to the
rain forest. If you've actually looked through any of the
catalogs, you'll know that they ordinarily explain how to
order merchandise, how to return it, and so on. Other
companies, though, that don't regularly mail items may
forget to include something as simple as instructions for
returning a product. So if you receive an order without
such instructions and you need to return the material,
the rule is very simple—when you don't know, ask (by
telephone or letter):

Ladies and Gentlemen:

On February 27 we ordered a variable-speed, three-way
compact grinder/polisher *with* extension. Today we received
a single-speed grinder/polisher *without* extension.

Since our shop is in urgent need of the variable-speed
grinder/polisher, I'd like to return the other merchandise
that we received. Also, I'd appreciate it if you would
immediately send the variable-speed machine that we
ordered.

Please send me instructions right away concerning the
return of this machine. If there's any reason that you cannot
process this order on a rush basis, please telephone me at
215-555-2232 so that I can make other arrangements
without further delay.

Thank you for your help.

Sincerely,

Introductions

Letters of introduction are meant to introduce not only people but also products, services, policies—anything that you want others to become acquainted with. Although this is a common subject, you may have discovered that such letters aren't exactly a snap to write.

Often composed by specialists, the letters must entice readers to want to see and, then or later, *purchase* the product or service being introduced or to want to accept or adopt something else being introduced. In addition to being descriptive, therefore, the letters also need a strong persuasive quality.

Letters involving people can be as hard to write as letters about products or services. On the one hand, you need to portray the person in a favorable light so that the reader will respond positively to the introduction. On the other hand, if you exaggerate or make misleading comments, the reader may suspect your integrity and doubt the validity of your claims.

In general, the objective is to offer information about the person being introduced that will be useful to the reader. In other words, you needn't tell the reader what the person eats for breakfast, only what the reader wants or needs to know. You should also explain why the reader might like to meet the subject. But always—this is important—give the reader a chance to decline. People hate to be trapped into wasting time with someone they don't want to meet.

Business associate. It's not unusual for sales representatives, new employees, business associates, and others to be introduced by letter before having a personal meeting with someone. This type of letter typically gives a brief biographical sketch of the person, with the emphasis on the business or professional characteristics that will interest the reader:

Dear Ms. Mangosteen:

I'm happy to introduce Ted Lanugo to you as a possible candidate for a supervisory or administrative position with your company. He'll be contacting you soon to ask about available jobs and arrangements for an interview.

Ted is presently employed at the Trampoline Corporation as a line supervisor. We previously worked together before I moved to Chicago. During the eight years of our association, he was the perfect employee—reasonable and capable—as well as a thoroughly delightful person to know.

If you believe it might be worthwhile to consider Ted for a present or future opening, I'd appreciate any consideration you can extend to him. Thanks very much, Ms. Mangosteen.

Sincerely,

New form. Has your bank changed its statements recently? If it did, I'm not surprised. From time to time, organizations change credit card statements, checking account statements, and various other forms, sometimes because computerization and other advances make the changes necessary. When this happens, the organization has to introduce the new form to its customers, and it usually does this by way of a form letter accompanying a sample statement:

Dear Customer:

Beginning with your next statement, you'll find a more detailed description of your purchases from, and account status at, Exciting Creations. We're enclosing a sample of our new statement so that you can see for yourself all the new features we're introducing.

The first line states the department, such as Jewelry, in which the purchases were made. Next to the amount due you'll see the amount of credit still available within your credit limit. The specific date by which the payment needs to be made to minimize finance charges is shown separately at the top of the form, along with the date through which your payments and purchases are included in the statement.

To reduce our costs and to be able to pass the savings on to you, copies of the sales tickets will no longer be included with the statement. But as usual, you'll receive a copy at the time the sale is made. To achieve even greater efficiency, the statement date on all retail accounts is being moved to the end of the month, and your next statement will cover activity through June 30, 200X.

We want you to know how much we appreciate having you as a customer, and we believe these changes will help us serve you better. Please let us know if we can answer any questions about the new statement.

Cordially,

New product. It's not likely that you'll see a new product treated with a ho-hum attitude. Businesses shift into high gear when they're ready to unleash their latest creation. Usually, they introduce the birth to potential buyers; members of various media, such as trade journals; and the general public. They do this by sending a variety of messages, from formal announcements to advertisements to press releases to letters. The letter may serve all purposes by itself, or it may be only a transmittal letter that accompanies a product sample or other descriptive literature:

Dear Mr. Silverberry:

We're pleased to introduce a completely new series of aerobic exercise equipment, ready for distribution to quality outlets such as yours.

You'll be amazed at the durability of our new lightweight rowers, treadmills, and cross-country skiers. However, we believe that you and your customers will be equally surprised at the low prices that accompany the new series. Three fliers describing these remarkable values are enclosed along with a price list and order form.

If we can provide further details, please let us know. We're looking forward to hearing from you and will welcome your comments and suggestions.

Cordially,

New program. Even those who fight change to the bitter end usually have to accept it eventually or face obsolescence. So it's not unusual to learn that a school, insurance company, or some other organization has developed a new program. The details are often introduced to interested persons by means of a form letter:

Dear Friend:

We'd like to tell you about our new life insurance plan designed specifically to provide money for funeral expenses. It's common knowledge that planning ahead now can spare you and your loved ones much grief and financial stress later. A new plan is available just for this purpose, and its sound and dependable features deserve your serious consideration.

Recent surveys indicate that 85 percent of those who die in the United States leave no funds designated to pay for their funeral expenses. But if you act now, your good judgment today will ensure:

- Coverage up to $10,000 written from age 0 to 80 and good for life
- Coverage that will never be reduced
- Coverage for all children in the family up to $2,500 each
- Coverage that is good anywhere in the world

For full information, without cost or obligation, about our single-payment or whole-life plan, please mail the enclosed postage-paid card today.

Should this letter arrive at a time of misfortune in your home, we sincerely apologize.

Cordially,

New service. Let's not forget that businesses and professional people introduce new services as well as new products. Like other letters that are distributed to a large mailing list, the messages of introduction are prepared as form letters. Sometimes they use a headline rather than a person's name or a general "Dear Customer" salutation:

INTRODUCING A NEW 24-HOUR BANK SERVICE!

Now you can have instant access to your Great Global USA Bank money at more than 30,000 locations in more than 4,000 cities in the United States and Canada!

By using the enclosed 24-hour bank card, you can obtain cash, check your balance, or transfer funds anytime, day or night, weekends or holidays, wherever you see the All-Hours Bank or Anytime Bank sign. Deposits, however, can be made only at Great Global.

This card is personal and private, *and it's free!* Moreover, you may select your own personal identification number according to the combination described in the enclosed brochure.

We hope that you'll enjoy the convenience of this exciting new service. If you have any questions about it, inquire at your nearest branch of the Great Global USA Bank or telephone us at 516-555-2688. We'll be happy to help you any way we can.

Sincerely,

Refusal. Let's say that one day someone asks you to write a letter of introduction, but circumstances make it impossible or at least undesirable for you to oblige. What to do? First, say no as tactfully as possible, then briefly state your reason, and, finally, wish the person success anyway:

Dear Mr. Sinciput:

As much as I'd like to provide the letter of introduction that you requested, I'm very sorry that our company policy prohibits this practice. We do, however, reply to organizations that request a reference. If that would be helpful, and if you're able to arrange for a company to contact me, I'd be happy to respond on that basis.

Although I can't help at present, please do accept my very best wishes for much success in making your contacts.

Sincerely,

Invitations

Some things never change: Businesses have always devoted, and still do devote, a lot of time to entertaining. When you're new at it, the practice may seem like a huge, endless party that someone else pays for. But as we soon learn, the purpose of business entertaining is much more serious than that. Businesspeople set up lunches, dinners, parties, and special events (theater, exhibitions, and so on) to conduct business and build better relations with prospective, current, and previous customers or clients.

In the following models you'll see that *formal* business invitations, such as those to dinners or receptions, resemble formal social invitations in wording and format. Compare the examples here with those in **SOCIAL MODELS: Invitations.** Printers have many samples of invitations in both modern and traditional styles suitable for all sorts of businesses and professions.

If you want to avoid a last-minute hassle, plan ahead in ordering printed invitations. Keep in mind that you need to check proofs and prepare the invitations for mailing as much as four to six months ahead for out-of-town, out-of-state, and especially out-of-country dinner guests. Allow two to four weeks for cocktail parties and receptions and about five weeks for lunch and local dinners.

Before you decide on a mailing date, therefore, take time to review the guest list to determine the distance that guests must travel and the time that they need to make such arrangements. Also consider the timeliness of the event. Some confidential occasions, for example, must be announced almost at the last minute. The *type* of event may also influence the mailing date. Therefore, you would likely mail invitations to a conference banquet whenever you mailed the entire conference program packet.

You would prepare *informal* business invitations, such as those to business associates to have lunch or to guests to speak at a conference, on business letterhead. Your familiarity with the person you're inviting should help you decide on either a memo or a traditional business letter format. Always opt for the latter when you're uncertain.

But wait, we're not done yet. There's still another type of invitation to consider—the *sales*-oriented business invitation. In this case, you would *invite* customers and clients to a special sale or to stop and see (and purchase, one hopes) new merchandise. Retail stores usually prepare these invitations as form letters and mass-distribute them.

Annual meeting. If you belong to an association, such as a manufacturers' association, you probably know all about annual meetings. Some businesses, associations, and other organizations issue separate invitations to an annual meeting, particularly if a meal is offered in conjunction with the meeting. (The invitation may have to be sent apart from any formal notice required by the organization's bylaws.) When large numbers are involved, an organization may decide not to include reply cards. Instead, it may simply make arrangements for meals and other matters based on an estimate of attendance:

> *You are cordially invited to attend*
>
> *the annual meeting of the*
>
> *Centroid Architectural Society*
>
> *October 22, 200X*
>
> *at the Skyway Hotel, Denver*
>
> *Cocktails at 6 p.m.   dinner at 7 p.m.*

Dinner party. It's not likely that you would invite a hundred thousand people to dinner, so invitations to most business openings that are handled as mass mailings don't include dinner (but refreshments are common). However, some organizations do issue dinner invitations to *selected names* on the mailing list:

> *Red Spruce Development, Inc.*
>
> *cordially invites you*
>
> *to attend a dinner party in honor of the*
>
> *Grand Opening*
>
> *of our Seattle, Washington, office*
>
> *Tuesday, the sixth of August*
>
> *from five to eleven o'clock*
>
> *at the Bootjack Inn*
>
> *12 Seaside Drive*
>
> *Seattle, Washington*

Guest speaker. Need to ask someone to speak at a dinner, banquet, meeting, or other occasion? Organizations usually invite speakers by way of a business letter. (*Hint:* If you want to make it easy for yourself, also enclose a data sheet on which the speaker can provide biographical information. You'll need these facts to prepare program copy and to develop notes to use in introducing the person.) Unless you want the event to be a disaster, give the speaker plenty of factual information about it. Be very clear about matters such as time, date, and place; the type of speech desired; length of the address with or without a question-and-answer session; and so on:

Dear Dr. Cornflower:

Members of the Friends of the Caterpillar Society have long admired your study of wormlike larvae and would enjoy learning more about the results of your work. Toward that

end, we'd like to invite you to speak at our December 5
meeting.

The meeting on the fifth will be held at 8 p.m. at the
Treetop Motel, 1512 Grassland Avenue, Lexington, Kentucky.
A twenty-five-minute address followed by a ten- to fifteen-
minute question-and-answer period would be ideal.

About thirty persons are expected to attend, all of them
with backgrounds in, or a strong interest in, moths,
butterflies, and their larvae. We're particularly interested in
your findings pertaining to the effect of local insecticides on
the development of plant-eating larvae.

In the hope that you're able to be with us, I'm enclosing a
data form for you to complete. This will provide appropriate
information for us to use in publicizing your appearance.
Details about transportation and accommodations for
speakers, as well as our standard guest honorarium, are
included on the enclosed summary information sheet.

We do hope that you can join us on December 5, and I'd
appreciate having your reply by November 1 so that we can
complete our program.

Sincerely,

New merchandise. Even if you object to using the
word *invitation* for a message that's really a sales pitch,
you have to admit that it's a successful sales practice.
Prospective buyers are *invited* to see new products or to
shop on a special day—before the general public is notified. The letter is written to sound personal, but it's actually a form letter sent in a mass mailing. If the letter is
computer generated, the customer's name may be
merged in the salutation, or you may use a general greeting such as *Dear Customer:*

Dear Ms. Trinitron:

Occasionally, an opportunity so important comes along that I
want to write to you personally. Such an opportunity is here.

We've assembled more than $12 million in fine-quality leather coats, shoes, wallets, and handbags and are offering an impressive selection in each of our stores in Wisconsin, Illinois, and Ohio.

This sale, with the entire collection priced at up to 50 percent off, will be open to the public on Saturday, November 5. But I'd like to invite you to shop this sale in advance so that we can give you special attention. Your courtesy day is Friday, November 4. Extra salespeople and fashion-leather experts will be available to help you with your selections.

To let you know how impressive this sale will be, I've attached a representative listing of what you can expect to find. We're looking forward to seeing you on this exciting day.

Sincerely,

Open house. When you hear about an open house in business, do you automatically think that it's for a new office or store? Many people do. But special occasions such as expansion, remodeling, or an anniversary are also good reasons to have an open house. The invitations are usually handled as a mass mailing with no replies expected. However, you may additionally send *special* invitations to selected persons for a certain time and day:

The officers and directors

of the

Saddle Rock Loan and Trust Company

cordially invite you to attend an

Open House

in celebration of their 25th anniversary

Friday evening, February twenty-second

from five to nine o'clock

180 Saddle Rock Boulevard   Cheyenne, Wyoming

Reception and exhibition. Yes, it's okay to combine events in an invitation, for example, cocktails *and* dinner or a reception *and* an exhibition. Replies are usually not necessary for something such as an exhibition mass mailing:

The Hoatzin Gallery

cordially invites you to attend a

Champagne Reception

and

Preview Exhibition

of the latest paintings by

Hogan Puttee

May 24th, 200X

from five until eight o'clock

201 Raven Drive

Boston, Massachusetts

Reply card. If replies are desired for your event, as they often are, many people include a printed reply card with the invitation so that the recipients won't have to handwrite a formal reply:

Kindly respond on or before

May 19, 200X

M_____

Number of persons_____

Store account. I'm sure you've discovered that stores have all sorts of ingenious ways to tempt customers to shop there. Mass mailings inviting the public to shop at a particular store or open an account are one means of soliciting new business. Charge cards or courtesy cards also may be offered to lure shoppers to the store:

Dear Friend:

We'd like to invite you to stop at the Customer Service booth in the Savemore Supermarket and pick up a free courtesy card.

This card offers you easy check writing in our store without having to show your driver's license or other identification and without having to worry about carrying cash. Simply sign your name, and when you've finished shopping, show the card to our checkout clerk along with your check.

We hope that you'll pick up your courtesy card soon and start enjoying trouble-free shopping in the Savemore Supermarket, where you always save every time you shop.

Sincerely,

Orders

Processing orders in most companies involves more than ordering pizza for lunch. Although sending and receiving orders are largely routine transactions, you can usually count on errors or changes to make the work more interesting.

Your company may use standard purchase-order forms for outside orders and requisition forms for requesting supplies from an in-house purchasing department. For Internet shopping, it will follow the prompts of the on-line advertiser, and for print catalog supplies, it may use the order form provided in the catalog. When none of these options is available, there's no law that says you can't also order from the supplier by letter or memo.

However, unless you want someone to dump something you didn't order on your desk, you'll need to be very accurate in describing the material you're ordering. In general, specify all facts, including catalog or order number, price, quantity, delivery date required, and so on. If you're revising an earlier order, *clearly* explain any changes you want. Although most routine order acknowledgments, confirmations, back-order notices, and so on are processed on forms, some organizations send standard responses by letter. When you're acknowledging an order by letter—original or form letter—include a note of thanks to the customer.

Cancellation. Have you ever placed an order one day only to have to cancel it the next day? Cancellations are a big nuisance for everyone, but when you have to cancel an order, the sooner you do it, the better. As always, repeat the item number and other pertinent facts. If you paid by check, ask for a refund. If you charged the purchase, ask to have your account credited. If your company requires a written confirmation, ask for one. However, with most charges, the transaction and any subsequent cancellation are clearly recorded on one's monthly statement:

Ladies and Gentlemen:

I'd like to cancel my order of August 27 for one (1) #H-UVM-6100 microcassette recorder for $47.99. This item was charged to Ordermart account no. 7-21459. Please credit my account in full.

Thank you for your help.

Sincerely,

Change. As circumstances change, so may your need for supplies or other items change. Sounds like a proverb, doesn't it? Anyway, if your need does change, give the supplier full details about your previous order and state the precise changes that you want:

TO: Supervisor Productivity Seminars

FROM: William Setose

REGISTRATION CHANGE

We'd like to change our enrollment for your June 22, 200X, one-day seminar from two persons to three persons.

On April 24 we mailed our check for $200 along with our registration form to cover enrollment for Noel Rapport and Daniel Liege. We now want to add the name of Julian Doyen to this list, and our check for an additional $100 is enclosed to cover the fee for the third registration.

Please send your confirmation to my attention at the letterhead address. Thank you.

Charge. Nowadays most orders are charged either to a company or credit card account. Sometimes, especially with telephone, fax, or e-mail orders, that's the only way you can order. But the description of the order would be the same as it would be in any other type of order. If the delivery date is important, state that you need delivery by a certain date. However, if you only want to know when something will arrive, simply ask for the expected delivery date:

Ladies and Gentlemen:

Please send us the following item from your April 30, 200X, spring catalog of office supplies:

One (1) #JM-207143, 10" x 12" x 14", portable overhead projector with extra lamp and roll of transparent film, $299.90 plus shipping and handling

The cost should be charged to our account no. XC-10100, and it should be delivered to James Flaxen, Colt and Blixen Consultants, The Professional Building, 10 North Street, Stroudsburg, PA 18360.

I'd appreciate written acknowledgment of this order if it will not be shipped immediately, along with an estimated delivery date. Thank you.

Sincerely,

Confirmation. If you're not used to seeing order confirmations, it's probably because organizations ordinarily don't confirm routine orders. But sometimes orders will be delayed or have to be back-ordered, and a confirmation is then sent explaining the situation. Telephone orders are handled much the same way. For example, the confirmation should restate the facts—description, price and handling charges, delivery date, and so on—to avoid misunderstandings later, especially since details of telephone conversations may soon be forgotten:

Dear Ms. Chirk:

Thank you for your March 16, 200X, telephone order for five (5) #667-X410, three-shelf, 42" x 31" x 12", 60 lb., oak finish bookcases, $399.95 plus $32 shipping and handling.

The bookcases will be shipped by truck from our factory in Atlanta in four to six weeks and will be charged to your Wondercard no. 107-642-981-305, as you requested.

We appreciate your order very much and hope we can be of service again.

Sincerely,

Delivery confirmed. Delivery confirmations are more important than you might think. If you're the one filling an order, and if the individual or business doing the ordering asks for confirmation of a delivery date, repeat any important details in the order. (It's necessary to do that because the company may have placed other orders at the same time.) Your company probably uses a form letter or a standard wording, such as this:

Dear Mr. Juju:

This will confirm our delivery date of July 30, 200X (on or before), for the following order placed with us on June 29:

Two (2) #7-7723H, dual-cable transfer switches, $105.98 each plus shipping and handling

One (1) #T-32130, four-outlet Internet UPS System, $289.99 plus shipping and handling

If I can be of help in any other way, just let me know. We appreciate your order and look forward to hearing from you again.

Sincerely,

Insufficient information. I doubt that anyone will faint from reading that people don't always provide all the information you need to fill their orders. If this happens often, rather than reach for the painkillers, you could develop a form letter for this purpose. Otherwise, write an original letter to thank the customer for the order and to explain what additional information you need:

Dear Mrs. Antiquark:

Thank you for your letter requesting membership in the Crocus Society. We're looking forward to adding your name to our membership roster.

We'd appreciate it if you would complete the enclosed application and return it to us with your first year's membership fee of $25. As soon as we receive these items from you, we'll promptly process the application, and your first issue of our monthly newsletter will soon be on the way to you.

Thanks so much for your interest in the Crocus Society. I hope that you enjoy and profit from your membership.

Cordially,

On account. Purchasing is obviously easier for organizations that have an account with a supplier. They can simply place their orders by telephone, fax, e-mail, or postal mail and ask to be billed. But the order itself has to be just as clear no matter how the payment is arranged, and you need to follow the usual procedure in providing full facts:

TO: Imperial Supplies

FROM: Troy Centaur

OUR ORDER NO. 11765

Please send us the following items, to be billed to account 126498-0, Downstage Productions, 195 Farwell Street, San Francisco, CA 94107:

One (1) #FRC-XX1000, 8" x 17" x 12", punch and bind machine, $359.98

Twenty-five (25) #771-500-77, 8½" x 11", black, pocket folders, $1.12 ea., $28.00 total

Sixteen (16) #632-124-69, 6½" x 12½" x 3½", brown, wall pockets, $4.99 ea., $79.84 total

Please send these items to my attention, Room 502, at Downstage Productions. Thank you.

Proposals

Most of us think of proposals as simple suggestions, such as the suggestion to have a two-hour siesta every day at work. If you're really fearless, you could walk into your boss's office and simply state your proposal. However, the term *proposal* is used to mean anything from a long, formal submission to a funding agency to a brief memo explaining a new idea to a business associate. Really formal proposals have to be prepared according to strict specifications.

Funding agencies often provide forms on which you must prepare the proposal. At a minimum, they provide guidelines concerning topics to be covered, order of the topics, and various format specifications. I once worked with others on a proposal exceeding one hundred pages, with every page prepared according to strict specifications. If there had been the slightest deviation, the proposal would have been rejected.

But most of the daily proposals in business are suggestions prepared in a letter or memo format, often running to no more than one page. Some of the correspondence about proposals, in fact, is a forerunner to the proposal itself—sort of a proposal to do a proposal.

All proposals—even brief ones—should summarize the essential details in the beginning: the overall idea, the cost, and the major recommendations. Facts should follow in a logical order, and the conclusion should include qualifications such as the period after which the proposal will no longer be valid and costs no longer in effect.

On the other side are responses to proposals. Like any response, a response to a proposal may accept the idea or—tactfully, one hopes—reject it.

Acceptance. It's nice to be able to say yes to someone, isn't it? Depending on your organization and the formality of the proposals that you receive, you may accept on a special acceptance form, or you may simply write a brief letter of acceptance:

Dear Mrs. Fiddlehead:

We're happy to let you know that your November 6, 200X, proposal to develop a one-hundred-piece slide presentation on our laboratory procedures has been accepted. Three copies of our standard agreement are enclosed. Please sign all copies and return one to me.

We're especially eager to begin this project and are pleased to have an opportunity to work with you. Your credentials are excellent, and I know that the slide presentation will be a huge success. In the meantime, if I can be of help in any way, please don't hesitate to call.

Sincerely,

Contract-proposal combination. If you like the idea of accomplishing two things in one step, you'll love the idea of a contract proposal. When you combine a contract and a proposal in one form, the offer or proposal to do something is accepted on the same form, and presto, it then becomes a contract:

Dear Mr. Banquo:

Garibaldi Landscaping hereby proposes to provide full design services, furnish all material, and perform all labor necessary for landscaping of the lot containing your new dental offices. The materials to be provided include:

Sixteen (16) yards concrete rock, all sides of building
Two (2) rolls black plastic, all sides of building
Four (4) 16' silver maple trees
Two (2) 12' honey locust trees
Twelve (12) nandina shrubs
Twelve (12) juniper ground cover

This work is to be performed at 100 Morgan Lane, Dobbs Ferry, NY 10522, for Jason Banquo, D.D.S., owner, based on the design submitted by Roy Perfidy on March 3, 200X, for the above work.

The total cost, including tax, will be $1,989.95. Payments will be made as follows: $989.95 to be paid upon approval of this agreement and the balance of $1,000.00 to be paid upon completion of the work described here.

Any request for alteration or deviation from the above specifications will be submitted in writing to Garibaldi Landscaping. Plans to accommodate such changes and the additional cost will be submitted in writing to Jason Banquo.

All such additional agreements must be made and accepted in writing.

This agreement will be null and void if not signed within thirty (30) days. The work described here will be completed within forty-five (45) days from acceptance of this agreement.

Submitted by:

GARIBALDI LANDSCAPING

_____

Owner

Date_____

Accepted by:

_____

Jason Banquo, D.D.S.

Date_____

Delayed decision. What's the first thing you should do when you receive a proposal? Okay, other than read it? You should acknowledge it, right? If a decision on the proposal is going to be delayed, you also need to tell that to the proposer and give the person at least a general date when a decision will be forthcoming:

Dear Ms. Candy:

Thanks for giving us an opportunity to review the proposal for your firm to modify our assembly area to accommodate a new product line.

Your suggestions are impressive, and your costs appear satisfactory. However, the general manager will be out of town until the beginning of August, and I must consult him before making a commitment to retain your firm for this work. Therefore, I should be able to let you know our decision by August 10. I appreciate your effort, Ms. Candy, and do hope that this delay won't inconvenience you.

Cordially,

Letter format. How do you know when it's okay to prepare a proposal in the letter format? Generally the letter format is fine for most simple proposals. For example, you might use a traditional letter for brief comments that constitute a proposal but don't have the organizational detail requiring subheads or other characteristics of a formal proposal or even a memo-report proposal:

Dear Nora:

While in the library today looking for a videotape of last year's marketing seminar, I was told that all audiotapes and videotapes are kept in the conference-room storage cabinet. Unfortunately, there was a meeting in the conference room at that time, so I had to wait three hours to get in and find the tape I needed.

I'd like to propose that a special section be set up in the library to file all tapes. Unless some material is sensitive, it should be in a spot accessible to everyone at all times. The library seems like the obvious place, especially since many of the tapes are supplementary to reading material. It makes no sense to separate the two.

Could we make this adjustment right away? If you're in agreement, I think we should set it up and send a form letter to all department heads announcing the change and asking them to notify others in their respective departments.

Let me know what you think, Nora. Thanks very much.

Best regards,

Memo format. Same question: When should you prepare a proposal in the memo format? Generally, you might choose the memo format over the letter format if the proposal wouldn't be long or formal but nevertheless would look more proposalish than a simple letter. For example, a relatively short proposal prepared for persons in authority within a company might be sent in a memo format (a longer proposal might be prepared in a report format and sent with a cover letter). Subheadings are often used in the memo format just as they would appear in a longer, formal report:

TO: Walter Cavalier

FROM: David Fantail

PROPOSAL TO INCREASE EFFICIENCY
WITH OFFICE FORMS

Based on a three-week time study of selected routine staff operations in our office, I've identified several areas in which we can save substantial time. By using forms for communications and record keeping, for example, we can not only save time but can also increase worker efficiency.

COSTS: After computing the labor and materials costs in handling tasks conventionally and comparing this to the costs in handling tasks using printed or photocopied forms, it's clear that there will be a 12 percent reduction in office overhead if we use the forms. This will result mainly from the reduced hours required of part-time help now used to handle overflow from the regular staff. With greater efficiency, less part-time and outside service help will be required. Copies of the time-study sheets and materials-cost analysis sheets on which these conclusions are based are attached to this proposal.

FORMS: On a test run, using photocopies of forms from published books and samples from office-supply stores, I recorded a noticeable increase in efficiency with the forms. Most of them are printed checklist or fill-in styles designed for rapid entry, often by handwriting without the need for computer setup and entry. Six samples are attached to this proposal: activity-record form, documents-receipt form, long-

range schedule form, meeting-dates record form, routing
slip, and visitor-message form. A complete file of all
suggested forms is available in my office.

CONCLUSION: By making greater use of forms, we could
increase worker efficiency and reduce office costs by as
much as 12 percent. This would result in savings in staff
time that would lessen the need for part-time assistance to
handle staff overload. The forms cost would not exceed the
present cost of other paper and stationery for conventional
use. Additional study and testing would reveal which forms
could most economically be purchased, printed, or
photocopied. Some we might decide to revise, and many
could be stored in the computer for future alteration.

Let me know if you'd like to make this adjustment in office
procedures. I'll be glad to put the plan into effect
immediately. Or if you'd like to discuss the idea, I'll be
happy to meet with you at your convenience.

Thanks very much, Walter.

Rejection. It's not likely that you'll love every proposal you receive, and some you may not love a lot. But
when you have to say no, you nevertheless need to use
tact and sensitivity to avoid hurting the writer's feelings.
Always acknowledge the *effort* of the writer and, assuming that the proposal isn't completely absurd, be as complimentary as possible. If you may be able to consider
the idea later, say so. But if you know that you won't,
don't lead the writer on. Simply be honest and politely
state that you won't be able to accept the proposal:

Dear Hal:

Your proposal to expand our mail services by subcontracting more
of the list maintenance has a lot of merit. I really appreciate
the time and effort you put into this suggestion, although I'm
sorry that we can't move in that direction at present.

As you know, we're considering some further modernization
in the coming years, and our computer needs are top

priority. We haven't decided which direction to move yet, but I do know that we want to eliminate time-sharing as an option and expand our in-house capability. As a result of this expansion, we may be able to increase our list-maintenance service without subcontracting.

I expect to know more about the situation after the October board meeting, and I'll contact you then. In the meantime, Hal, I want to thank you for giving me some valuable information to consider. It always helps to have the total picture supported by detailed research and reliable facts.

Best regards,

Request. At times you may wish that all those unsolicited proposals clogging your in box would just go away. But now and then you'll *want* a particular proposal so much that you may even ask someone to prepare it for you. In fact, requesting proposals isn't at all uncommon. For example, businesses ask other businesses or individuals for proposals to provide a required service or to perform certain work. An employer might ask an employee to submit anything from a brief suggestion to a long, formal proposal:

Dear Tom:

I was really interested in the sales literature you sent about the psychology of colors in work productivity. According to the Sunflower study, the right combination of color and lighting can increase productivity by as much as 30 percent.

I'd like to have you look into this for me in relation to our offices. Using the Sunflower formula, please develop a plan that we could follow. Let me know what modifications we would have to make, what they would cost, and what results we could expect.

I know that you're busy with the Hudson account at present, but next I'd like to have you prepare a brief, five- to ten-page proposal for better color and lighting in our offices. Could you have something ready by August 5? Let

me know if you have any questions, Tom. Thanks very
much.

Regards,

Recommendations

Let's admit it: We all love to give advice. But that's
fine, because useful suggestions are valuable contributions in the business world. Aside from formal proposals,
examples of other, less formal types of recommendations
are referrals to appropriate people or sources, suggestions to meet to discuss something, and suggestions how
to handle some activity.

A recommendation may even be incidental to something else. It may be offered freely, or it may be given
in response to a direct request for suggestions or advice.
If a recommendation involves criticism, however, it
should be *constructive* criticism.

Messages with recommendations may be sent in the
letter format or, to in-house personnel and other close
associates, in the memo format.

Further evaluation. Not surprisingly, some recommendations involve doing nothing or making further studies
before doing something. There's nothing wrong with
that, and the letter should not be apologetic for that
reason:

Dear Phil:

The budget you prepared generally looks fine, and I want to
thank you for sending me an advance copy. Also, the notes
you attached were very helpful, and I'm pleased with the
overall plan.

The only recommendation that I have concerns the proposed
$2,500 for resurfacing the parking lot. You're certainly right
that most people are in favor of asphalt, but I understand

that, as an economy measure, some businesses around here are using chip and seal.

Since we're not dealing with an urgent need, I'd suggest a little further research before formalizing this activity and the amount in the budget. I realize that the budget will be voted on a week from Friday, but we should be able to get more bids and information by then. It would not be too hard to change that one figure if further evaluation suggests a revision in our thinking.

Please follow through on this, Phil, and let me know your findings. If I can help in any way, just call.

Regards,

Meeting. It would be hard to count the number of times that people want to have a meeting to discuss something. Most of us can't count that high. But when you have a recommendation or want someone else to make one, a meeting may be necessary or at least helpful. You can then use a letter or memo to introduce the idea or to confirm an earlier decision about it. The message can usually be brief, because the details will supposedly be discussed during the meeting. However, if it would help the other person arrive at the meeting better prepared to make a recommendation, you should include more details or attach pertinent material:

Dear Ronda:

Would it be possible to meet with you for about an hour next week to discuss our September data-processing seminar? I wasn't very happy with the high number of dropouts after the first night during last month's seminar, and I was hoping you might have a recommendation or that together we could plot some strategy to prevent excessive dropouts in September.

I'd appreciate a call from you (extension 6611) so that we can set a time to get together. Thanks, Ronda.

Best wishes,

Notification. Have you ever felt that there's no end to anything? Or, as the cliche says, that one thing simply leads to another? Therefore, even when an action has already been taken or a decision has already been made, you still may have another recommendation. For example, the question of notifying others may arise, and you may want to recommend sending notices—to whom, when, and how:

TO: Ed Torchwood

FROM: Gene Wallaby

TIME RECORDERS

Ed, I believe that we should let the supervisors know about our plans to modernize our time-recorder system. We also could invite their comments. After all, they're close to the action and may have some valuable recommendations. I'd rather hear from them before we commit ourselves to a new system, and I'm sure that you would too.

If you agree, I'll prepare a memo explaining our plan. Could you let me know what you think by next Monday? You can telephone me at extension 7922 or send me a note with your decision. Thanks very much, Ed.

Other person. As you know, we recommend not only things but also people. For example, we're often asked to do things we haven't the time to do or don't want to do. Sometimes called *passing the buck,* a common response is: "No, I can't, but I know just the person for that":

Dear Ms. Birchbark:

Thanks so much for asking me to be the company's representative this year in the Hillside Business Association. As much as I'd love to accept the assignment, I'm sorry that I'm unable to do so.

I know that the association is very useful, and one can make some valuable contacts there. Unfortunately, I took on another extracurricular job last week—helping set up our new company day-care center. However, it occurs to me that Terry Stillwater was a member of a similar business organization in Buffalo, so he might be interested in being our representative. He's certainly qualified.

Let me know if you can't arrange for Terry to handle the assignment. Perhaps we could then find someone else who would be suitable.

Thanks for thinking of me, Ms. Birchbark, and good luck in filling the position.

Cordially,

Other source. Just as you may refer someone to another person, you may refer someone to another source of information. In this case you would say: "No, I don't have what you want, but you might try here or there." In any such situation, it's important to thank the person for writing and to be as helpful as possible in guiding the individual elsewhere:

Dear Mr. Beltway:

I'm sorry that we don't have the information you need on the destructiveness of cankerworms in our forests. However, I called our local Conservation Office and understand that the director may have exactly what you need.

You can write to the Conservation Office and request a free copy of their booklet *Controlling Harmful Larvae,* which discusses the species of moths you're studying. The address is 11215 Third Street, Flagstaff, AZ 86002.

Good luck with your research, and thanks for thinking of us.

Sincerely,

Preventive medicine. What do you do when you go to the doctor and sit in the waiting room? Stare at the other patients and try to decide if they're contagious?

Then, to get your mind off that, read the magazines and other available literature? If you do that, you'll know that doctors, dentists, and veterinarians have brochures and flyers in their waiting rooms to alert people to matters such as necessary vaccinations and other preventive measures. Of course, people don't always take the necessary steps. Neglect of animals in particular is not uncommon, and when serious outbreaks occur, the medical facility may notify the people on its mailing list by form letter:

Dear Pet Owner:

In the past month we've been asked to treat an unusually large number of cats infected with the feline leukemia virus. Although diagnosis in the early stages is difficult, we urge you to watch your pet for signs such as depression, fever, appetite loss, and swollen glands in the neck or abdomen.

If your cat shows any of these signs, there's a single blood test that we can use to help us in a diagnosis. If your cat shows no signs, you may be able to protect your pet against this disease by preventing exposure to other cats, some of which may be carrying the virus. Vaccination, however, is the only safe protection for cats nine weeks of age and older that do not already have the virus.

Stop by our office if you would like a free brochure with life-saving information. If you want to arrange for a vaccination, we urge you to bring in your cat now.

Faithfully,

Program benefits. Businesses have all sorts of programs for employees, some of which are mandatory, some optional. Employees aren't always thrilled about the ones that are mandatory and may feel less pressured by the ones that are voluntary. A company may therefore recommend some of the programs without actually requiring participation:

Dear Employee:

We're happy to let you know that Bridgehead Industries has expanded its on-the-job training program to include retraining for employees who have been with the company one year or more. This program will complement the training program that we've always provided for new employees.

The enclosed brochure describes the total program and details the three-week night sessions and the optional twelve-week day sessions—all *free*. The night sessions are available Monday through Thursday evenings from 7:30 until 9:00 p.m. The day sessions are available every weekday from 8:00 until 9:00 a.m. or from 12:30 until 1:30 p.m. To make arrangements to leave your workstation for any of the sessions, contact your immediate supervisor.

The retraining programs are offered by rotation of subject matter. Starting in October, for instance, the program will cover sales, administration, word processing, and electronics. The next session will have a different selection to be announced about three weeks in advance.

I urge each of you to enroll in one or more programs to increase your knowledge in the area in which you now work or to broaden your capabilities by becoming knowledgeable in other areas. Again, the program is *free,* and it offers an excellent means to increase your opportunities for career advancement and flexibility as well as to enhance your qualifications for promotion. If you have any questions, feel free to call Lauren Azeotrope at extension 6161 or Bill Brightman at extension 6109.

I hope you'll enjoy and profit from this new program. Here's wishing you a rewarding future at Bridgehead Industries.

Warmest regards,

References

Remember the last time you applied for a job? For a mortgage? For college admission? You had to supply one or more references, right? Like introductions of people, references involve comments about someone's personal and professional characteristics. So tact, honesty, and sensitivity are necessary in any letter that involves someone's welfare or perhaps that of both parties.

A well-written reference letter will offer useful information pertinent to the recipient's interests and needs. Also, any comments you make should be objective and honest. If the situation is reversed and you've asked someone to provide a reference for you, remember to send the person a letter of thanks.

Business. Although these letters can be tricky to write, at least you can treat a letter about a business the same as one about an individual. The only difference is that you'll be discussing *business* characteristics instead of *personal* traits and abilities. So if you become skilled in composing one type, you'll also be skilled in preparing the other. In each case you'll want to provide *selected* information of use to the person requesting the reference, and you'll want to be honest, accurate, and diplomatic in doing it:

Dear Mr. Geophyte:

DOVE TEMPORARY HELP AGENCY

We've used the Dove Agency for occasional temporary and part-time clerical help since 1985. During this period we've been generally satisfied with both performance and rates, and we expect to continue to draw on Dove's personnel pool.

The agency has both experienced and beginning workers available, all of whom we found to be honest, hardworking, and reliable. The experienced personnel—Linda Baluster and Sean Carpus, in particular—provide far more satisfactory assistance than the beginners in more demanding areas such as word processing as opposed to less demanding areas such as mailing-list cleanup. My only suggestion is that you request one of the experienced individuals for more difficult assignments.

If you would like additional information, please let me know.

Sincerely,

Individual. What if you're asked to supply a *character* reference for someone or a reference for someone who has never before held a job? Obviously, you'll have to focus on the person's character or perhaps on both character and educational background, depending on the circumstances. Such references are needed in special situations, such as for a security check or for a situation in which the person has no suitable employment experience to report:

Dear Ms. Fructose:

Sylvia Perfume attended Sloop College from 200X to 200X and received a baccalaureate in chemistry. During that time she was a student in two of my chemistry classes and maintained a high grade average in each case.

I believe that Ms. Perfume would be well suited for the laboratory position you have available. She's intelligent, diligent, and cooperative. I was impressed with her thoughtful and positive outlook on life, and it was always a pleasure to have her in my classes.

Let me know if you would like any further information.

Sincerely,

Open letter. You've no doubt seen this type of letter or have written one. Often it begins with a general salutation such as "Dear Sir or Madam," "Ladies and

Gentlemen," "Dear Reader," or "To Whom It May Concern" (some people dislike the last example). An open letter of reference is really a general recommendation that's often given to the subject to use as he or she wishes. For example, a student may make copies of such a letter and give them to prospective colleges that are requesting references, or a job applicant may give copies to prospective employers. Since you may not know who will eventually see the letter, you can't tailor it to one type of school or business:

> Dear Reader:
>
> It's a pleasure for me to comment on the excellent work that Tony Sluice did for us at Octopod Discount Stores. As assistant manager for nearly ten years, he was responsible for numerous aspects of our operations from personnel management to purchasing to store display and advertising to customer relations.
>
> Tony successfully applied his natural managerial ability and broad experience to every task. He's an exceptionally capable and personable individual, and I have great respect for his high-quality work and his responsible and trustworthy character.
>
> If I can provide additional information, please don't hesitate to call.
>
> Sincerely,

Refusal. It's not likely that students who were expelled or employees who were dismissed will ask to use you as a reference. But what if they do? If someone whose record was unsatisfactory does want a reference, you'll probably have to refuse to provide it. Unless the person did something criminal or otherwise outrageous, however, be certain to end your refusal with a polite good-luck comment. Using a tempered tone in such letters may be important for other reasons, too, considering that sometimes it doesn't take much to motivate a disgruntled former student or employee to commit a violent act:

Dear Mr. Grimly:

As much as I would like to be of help, Mr. Grimly, I'm very sorry to let you know that I won't be able to provide the general letter of reference you requested.

Upon reviewing your file I noticed that your employment with us was not entirely satisfactory. In such cases, it has always been company policy not to furnish a letter unless a prospective employer contacts us and requests one. We would, of course, be happy to respond to any such request that we might receive.

Although I can't be of help to you in this respect, I personally wish you the best of luck in finding more satisfying and successful employment elsewhere.

Sincerely,

Request. What if you're on the other side? That is, you're the one checking someone else's background and requesting information from the sources listed by the subject. If this is the case, let the person to whom you're writing know what type of information you need. Be specific—"Tell me *something* about Mr. X" isn't sufficient:

Dear Mrs. Redstart:

Charles S. Lantern, one of your former employees, has applied for an operator position in our Word Processing Department and has given your name as a reference.

I'd appreciate it if you could tell us about his experience and ability as a word processing operator. We would be especially interested in knowing about his word processing speed, accuracy, and overall skill; his ability to work under pressure and meet deadlines; his cooperative spirit; and his punctuality and respect for company policies and requirements. Please be assured that your comments will be held in the strictest confidence.

Thanks very much for your help.

Cordially,

Thank you—job accepted. If a reference helps you snag a job, always send your thanks to the person who provided the reference. Although such a thank you is usually very brief, it should mention any results obtained from the person's letter and obviously should show sincere appreciation:

Dear Mr. Barcarole:

Thanks very much for your generous remarks to Mr. Owl of J. Baron & Sons. Your letter of reference was extremely helpful, and I have been offered the position of investment analyst. It's an excellent opportunity, and I've already accepted the offer.

I certainly appreciate your help in finding this exciting position.

Sincerely,

Thank you—job declined. When you're job hunting, if you're a real catch or at least are very lucky, you'll probably have many offers, some of which you'll then have to decline. Even when you decline a position, however, your thank you to the person who sent a reference should still have a positive tone and express sincere appreciation:

Dear Mr. Dahlia:

I certainly appreciated your recent letter to the Virtual Arts Corporation. In fact, they offered me a position, although it wasn't quite what I was looking for. Therefore, I've decided to continue my search for something more suitable.

I hope I may continue to use your name as a reference, Mr. Dahlia. Clearly, your remarks were beneficial, and I very much appreciated your help.

Sincerely,

Reminders

If ever you've forgotten anything—I know: Who hasn't?—you should be able to appreciate how important a reminder can be. A *reminder* is a special type of follow-up message that's meant to jog someone's memory about something the person is supposed to do.

The typical reminder restates key facts, such as the date, time, and place of an appointment. If the facts are lengthy, the reminder letter or memo needn't repeat everything. In that case, it might be simpler to enclose a copy of the original message. Most of the time, however, you'll briefly describe the original message or reconfirm something arranged earlier.

Appointment. Lunch, dinner, conference, and other appointments may be forgotten if they're made far in advance. Of course, that's why we have something called *calendars*. But if you think that someone doesn't have sense enough to record an appointment on a calendar or might forget to look at the calendar anyway, a brief reminder would be helpful:

Dear Lisa:

This is just a note to say that I'm really looking forward to meeting you for lunch at noon on October 21 at the Cotillion.

I reserved a table for us in my name, and I'll see you there, Lisa.

Best regards,

Demonstration. It's hard to imagine that a salesperson would miss any expression of interest from a customer, but stranger things have happened. If you believe that a salesperson has forgotten your interest in something or didn't take it seriously, send a brief letter reminding the person that you're still expecting a call or other response:

Dear Mr. Lector:

In November last year I expressed an interest in the Panchax 2100 copier for our office. You mentioned that a new, improved version would be in shortly and that you would call me to arrange a demonstration.

Although I haven't heard from you, I was wondering if you now have the new 2100 on the floor. If so, I'd still like to see it in operation.

Please send me a note or telephone me at 555-1001 as soon as you can set up a private demonstration.

Thanks very much.

Sincerely,

Inquiry. Although inquiries should always be acknowledged, things happen in a busy office (a slightly worn-out excuse that we keep hearing), and your letter may be misplaced. You'll then have to send a reminder. If you think the recipient is the type of person who again may forget to reply, you may want to include a deadline in your reminder message, especially if time is important:

TO: Rolf Radar

FROM: Andy Thorn

INSURANCE BROCHURE

You may recall that in July I sent you a memo to ask whether you wanted me to continue distributing the brochures listing our insurance benefits even though part of the coverage listed is no longer available.

I indicated then that I would wait for authorization from you before printing new brochures but that I thought we should have new ones at our annual meeting in December. The printer tells me that we have to place our order within two weeks to meet that deadline, so I wanted to remind you that I still have it all on hold pending a green light from you.

To meet the printer's deadline, I'd appreciate a call (555-0400) or note from you by Friday, November 14. Thanks very much, Rolf.

Invitation. Isn't it annoying when you invite someone to go somewhere or do something and never get an answer? An unanswered invitation—formal or informal—obviously warrants a reminder. Even if the delay is intentional because the person simply doesn't know whether he or she will be available, a reminder is in order anyway. Guest speakers, for example, are often busy traveling, so a letter of invitation to a prospective speaker might remain unanswered a long time. Of course, there's always the possibility that the person is a great orator but a terrible administrator or manager. He or she then may simply have forgotten about your invitation. This is an instance in which you may want to enclose a copy of your original letter with the more extensive details:

Dear Mr. Sidereal:

Have you had an opportunity to consider our invitation to you to address the November meeting of the Tiglon Institute on Wednesday, November 7, at 7:30 p.m.? I wanted to remind you that our deadline for the program is next Friday, October 23.

Because we haven't heard from you, I'm wondering if my invitation went astray in the mail. In case that happened, please refer to the enclosed copy of my original letter. It

has full details about the meeting, dinner, and other
arrangements.

We all hope that you'll be able to participate. Your
experience in Kenya would add a great deal to the success
of our meeting. Could you let me know this week so that
we can finish our program?

Thanks very much.

Cordially,

Meeting. As you know, meeting dates are sometimes
scheduled far in advance, sometimes even a year or
more ahead. So it's conceivable that someone may forget
or that complications may arise for people who originally
planned to attend. A reminder notice is essential if you
need to determine attendance before the meeting:

Dear Joe:

I hope that you're still planning to be at the April 9
meeting of the Cygnet Club. We'll open the meeting at
10:30 a.m. in the Blue Room of the Jupiter Motel on Route
9 in Wexford.

Since I'm trying to estimate attendance, I'd appreciate it if
you would telephone me at 555-6709 or send me a note
to confirm that you're planning to attend.

Thanks very much, Joe. Hope to see you then.

Cordially,

Payment. Not everyone is a financial deadbeat.
Some late payments are truly the oversights of very
busy people, and full-fledged collection efforts are unnecessary. You may have talked to the person and may
have received a promise to pay. In any case, a reminder note is usually sufficient in situations involving
simple oversight:

Dear Ms. Scoutcraft:

I know how busy you are, so I thought that I'd send you this brief note to remind you that your membership in the Blimp Rejuvenation Association has expired.

You were planning to put a check in the mail after I saw you at the convention, but we haven't received it yet. To keep your name on the mailing list so that you won't miss any issues of our magazine, we'll need your check by Friday, August 13. So I'm sure you'll want to take a moment to put it in the mail right away.

We hope to hear from you soon, Ms. Scoutcraft.

Best wishes,

Request. How many times have you asked someone to do something and, each time, felt as though you may as well have been talking to a fence post? If this happens to you, briefly summarize your original request in another letter or, if the request was too detailed, refer to it in your reminder message and enclose a copy of the original letter. Either way, if the person's failure to respond is causing a problem, politely point this out. With luck, your reminder may be enough to prod the individual to pay better attention:

Dear Mr. Thrip:

Four months ago we sent you a change of address for all future payments on your account. However, our bookkeeper recently let me know that your checks are still arriving at our old address—now an abandoned building—although she has sent several reminders of our new address to your office.

Although we can imagine how very busy you must be, we're concerned that some of your payments may go astray if they continue to be sent to the abandoned building. Since they involve substantial sums of money, I'm sure you wouldn't want that to happen. Perhaps you'd like to alert the appropriate person in your office to change the address immediately—before mailing any more payments.

Thanks very much, Mr. Thrip. It's always nice to hear from you, and we want to be certain that nothing interferes with your mail.

Cordially,

Reports

Each time that I talk to friends in business, they're busy working on a report. I wonder when they have time to do anything else. However, they're not always working on a huge, thousand-page document. Some of their reports are brief, simple letter or memo reports.

Short, informal reports are commonly sent as letters or memos and sometimes as fill-in forms. Some letters or memos, of course, are meant only to accompany and explain a lengthy report that's prepared in a special format on other paper. Such explanatory messages are really cover or transmittal letters.

A formal report may be as complex as a book and may have many parts. Even shorter versions usually contain a summary, an introduction, a presentation of data, the conclusions and recommendations, and an appendix. Letter and memo reports, however, may be considerably more abbreviated. When fuller details are needed, it's best not to use a correspondence format but rather to prepare the report as a separate document.

Credit. We all know that when you apply for credit, the provider usually checks your credit background. So credit checks are fairly routine matters. However, those who do the checking may handle this in various ways. For example, if you needed to collect facts about someone's credit history, you might use a regular letter to ask for the information. If you wanted to make it easy for the recipient, however, you'd also enclose a fill-in credit report for the reader to complete. Depending on the amount of information you needed, you might even be able to add a short, fill-in form at the bottom of your letter:

Dear Mr. Bibelot:

To help us process a credit application by Mensch Interiors, 200 Old Stage Road, Skokie, IL 60076, we would appreciate your providing the information listed below and detaching and returning the form to us. Your response will be considered strictly confidential.

Thank you very much for your help.

Sincerely,

Robert Benson
Credit Manager

- -

Account: _____

Date credit granted: From_____to_____

Credit limit: _____Terms: _____

Highest current/recent credit: $_____

Current balance due: $_____

Amount past due: $_____

Average monthly balance: $_____

Payment practice: ( ) prompt   ( ) due date   ( ) late

Comments: _____

_____

Signed: _____Title: _____

Company: _____

Address: _____

Daily-call form. Is it fair to say that if you're busy, you tend to like anything that saves time? The pressure of time is one reason that forms are so popular. The other obvious reason is that, in business, anything that saves time probably saves money too. Businesses therefore provide standard forms to use in transmitting comments and other information. Sales call reports, expense reports, and shipping reports are common examples. But forms can be devised for almost any purpose. For example, you might have a form to use in reviewing different software, to comment on job applicants, to prepare job descriptions, or to report the progress or status of a project. Use the following example of a sales representative's calls on customers and prospects to trigger your imagination:

DAILY CALL REPORT

Date _____ Zone _____
Customer/Prospect _____
Contact _____
Title _____ Department _____
Address _____
City, State, Zip Code _____
Telephone _____ Fax _____ E-mail _____
Product/Service Presented/Sold _____
Remarks _____
_____
Representative _____

Information request. What would you rather do: *write* a report or *research* it? In most cases, you may have to do at least a little of both. So if you're researching a report, part of your search for information may involve contacting others. Although a research request letter can be relatively brief, you still need to define your topic well enough for the reader to know what type of information you want:

Dear Mr. Minstrel:

I'm preparing a report on the economics of desktop publishing. Since your firm has one of the most popular software programs in this area, I was wondering if you have any available studies or statistics on the cost of desktop publishing versus the conventional means of publishing various types of material: newsletters, magazines, catalogs, and so on.

I'd very much appreciate receiving any information that you have about this or a price list if there's a charge for any of the information. Should you not have anything available, perhaps you could recommend another source.

Thanks very much for your help.

Sincerely,

Letter format. A *letter report* is written in the format of—let's all say it together now—a *letter*. Of course, it's a special kind of letter. For example, it may follow the outline of a separate, short report—summary, introduction, data presentation, and conclusions and recommendations—with attached supplementary material. It also may include subheads similar to those used in a formal report or in some memo reports. But usually, it doesn't. In fact, the letter may be used only as a preliminary *report summary* sent in advance of a larger, more detailed study:

Dear Ms. Goldeneye:

On April 6, 200X, Derrick Basilisk, director of communication, authorized our firm to make a study for your organization to determine the advantages in using electronic- and voice-mail systems. A detailed report of our findings will be sent on May 14. However, I can summarize the pertinent results now.

The main advantages of these systems are the speed in conveying information, the elimination of time-zone and delivery delays common in other types of messaging, the ability of both sender and receiver to transmit at convenient times, and substantial cost savings over conventional fast mail delivery, such as Express Mail.

The forthcoming detailed report will describe the time and cost applicable to messaging by conventional telephone, conventional mail, private delivery services, electronic mail, fax, and voice mail. As will be clear in the report, electronic

mail, fax, and voice mail compare favorably with one
another and surpass conventional mail in many respects.

Our final report will suggest system costs for various
configurations you might choose. However, our
recommendation will be that, when possible, you rent or
lease first so that you can study actual costs before
committing yourself to a large investment. Moreover, we
suggest that you conduct an in-house telephone traffic study
to determine delays in calling and reaching a number and
the extent to which the delays affect employee efficiency
and productivity.

Please let me know if you'd like further information now.
Otherwise, you may expect our detailed report very soon.

Sincerely,

Memo format. The other principal correspondence
form, besides the letter, used for reporting is the memo.
The memo report is simply a short, informative memo
that fills the needs of both a report and a transmittal
letter in one document. Like the letter report, it may
follow the requirements of a separate short report—summary, introduction, data presentation, and conclusions
and recommendations—with attached supplementary
material. Or it may focus on reporting information without formal evaluation and conclusions. Subheadings,
lists, or any other organizational pattern that helps make
the information clearer is not only appropriate but also
is common in the memo format:

TO: Jeremy Singspiel

FROM: Loni Mooneye

BEHAVIORAL HEALTH CENTER STAFF

We've been very successful in securing commitments from
most of the psychiatrists and psychologists that we asked to
join our Behavioral Health Center following the opening of
another branch in Concord.

ON-CALL DOCTORS: The following highly qualified doctors (listed with their areas of expertise) will participate on a part-time, on-call, rotating basis. The cost will be within our annual operating budget of $1,800,000.

> Dr. Forrest Hardtop, geriatrics and psychiatric consultation
> Dr. Dixie Nasturtium, therapy and forensic psychiatry
> Dr. Bruce Speedwell, general adult psychiatry and clinical psychiatry
> Dr. Jeanette Bascule, addictive diseases and psychopharmacology

With the addition of these impressive individuals to the psychiatric staff, we're fully confident that our expanded facilities can provide outstanding support and treatment programs for the community.

BIOGRAPHICAL DATA: A biographical summary of each person is attached along with the hours for which they've registered for service.

Let me know, Jeremy, if I can send you any additional information.

Progress. This is another subject that doesn't require a lot of brainpower: A *progress report* obviously reports *progress.* Not everyone has occasion to prepare this kind of report, although people handling projects for their organizations often have to submit periodic status or progress reports to an immediate supervisor, a board of directors, or a head office. The report gives a summary of what's been done and what's left to do, with any other significant comments. Progress reports are often prepared in the memo format:

TO: Bella Bullwinkle

FROM: Arnold S. Graffito

DEPARTMENTAL REORGANIZATION PLAN—STATUS REPORT

September 1 is the deadline we set to complete departmental reorganization and the establishment of our new Word Processing Department. Today we're eight weeks from that goal and on schedule. All employees were given preliminary notice on June 1 and are cooperating fully.

JULY 1: Managers from the Business Office, Purchasing Department, Sales Department, Advertising Department, Research Department, and Personnel Office have submitted a list of routine and special word processing activities and the time and personnel requirements, based on their experience for each one. George Sippet is getting this information classified for computer input, and we expect to have a combined time-work report by July 5.

JULY 15: Based on the computer analysis of time-work requirements to transfer all significant word processing from each department or office to the new Word Processing Department, we'll start to generate a computer list of personnel requirements.

AUGUST 1: We'll begin computer matching of personnel data with the personnel requirements and will generate a list of recommended personnel transfers to the new department.

AUGUST 15: Department heads will submit their individual proposals for internal staffing after the transfer of selected personnel to Word Processing and will prepare for internal reorganization effective September 1. We'll then send a memo to all employees confirming the transfer date.

SEPTEMBER 1: The transfer of personnel, equipment, and supplies will occur. Within one week before the actual move, we'll send details of the transfer to all employees.

Although we expect some confusion as a result of such a
massive reorganization of offices, the departments are so
strongly in favor of the plan that cooperation and support
are at an all-time high. Therefore, we expect to handle any
associated difficulties with a minimum of disruption.
Throughout the period, key personnel will be working to
ensure that the company continues to serve its customers
without distraction or interruption.

The next progress report will be mailed July 15. In the
meantime, please call if you have any questions.

Transmittal letter. Until now we've been talking about
reports that are also letters or memos—a two-in-one sort
of document. But many reports are too large to be formatted like a letter or memo, and they're set up as a
separate, formal document. Such documents need a
cover letter to explain the purpose of the report, to mention important features and persons who helped prepare
it, and to refer to the authorization or other circumstances that prompted the report. Note that a cover, or
transmittal, letter is *not* mailed separately. Rather, it's
inserted in the report itself, after the title page and before the table of contents. The tone of this letter should
be consistent with that of contemporary correspondence
(personal, conversational, and so on) rather than be objective and impersonal like the tone in the report body:

Dear Ms. Hackney:

I'm pleased to send you this copy of "Implementing a
Productivity Program," the study you authorized in your
March 23, 200X, letter to me.

An evaluation of five leading productivity programs in
organizations the size of ours indicates that several steps
must be taken to ensure the success of such programs. The
first step is to set a goal of high ethical or social value.
Thereafter one can set important guidelines, select the
participants, set performance-improvement deadlines, review
progress, and provide appropriate rewards.

Since the program can be implemented by senior executives and routinely monitored by junior executives throughout the organization, the additional time requirements can be controlled. Therefore, no outside labor or materials costs are anticipated, other than those normally associated with work assignments that would be undertaken with or without the existence of a productivity program. The positive results evident in the five programs evaluated suggest that we can expect an increase in efficiency and morale as a result of establishing this program.

I enjoyed preparing this report and hope that the study will prove beneficial. Please let me know if I can offer any additional information.

Sincerely,

Requests

This subject—requests—is a lot like an earlier category—inquiries. Remember it? Letters and memos that inquire about or ask for something are among the most frequently sent messages in the business community. People ask for information, products, services, advice, favors, money, credit—everything imaginable.

Whereas most straight inquiries are brief, the amount of detail in a request message can vary greatly. For example, if you're asking for a contribution to something, you'll have to explain the nature of the cause or the group and present a persuasive argument. But if you want something such as a copy of a brochure, you can make your request in one or two sentences.

Generally, to make a request, state in your letter or memo what you want; what the reader has to do, such as take some action or make a decision; and where and when the reader should do something or send what you want. Always close with an expression of appreciation, especially when you're requesting a favor or special effort from the reader. For some requests, such as for certain types of information, you might enclose a form that the recipient can use in replying, along with a stamped, self-addressed envelope.

Business introduction. Somewhere there's probably someone you know who also knows a person you want to meet. When you request a letter of introduction, explain why you want or need it, show appreciation, and leave the door open for the person to decline if he or she can't or doesn't want to write the letter for you:

Dear Rich:

I was recently mulling over alternative ways to approach the National Bighorn Association as a prospective customer for our mailing services when I remembered that you know the director, Boyd Finback.

Would you be willing to write a brief letter of introduction for me? I'll be in Denver on May 1 and will be calling to request an appointment with Mr. Finback. But it would be ideal if a letter of introduction reached him first.

If you can find time in your busy schedule to do this—and wouldn't feel you were imposing on him—I'd certainly appreciate it. Many thanks, Rich.

Best regards,

Fund-raising. I don't know what the situation is nationally, but of the thousands of samples I have in my files, fund-raising letters are second only to sales letters in number. A day seldom passes that I don't receive at least one (let's not even talk about the telemarketers). The variety is staggering, but all of them make a strong, persuasive appeal for support. Have you noticed that many of them also include an incentive such as a "free" gift? I now have enough complimentary address labels to last until the year 2100:

Dear Alum:

After I accepted the job of directing Chalet University's annual fund drive, it occurred to me that you and I have something in common. As students at Chalet, we helped shape this important institution with our participation. I don't know about you, but that gives me a deep sense of satisfaction. Suddenly, I can understand the enthusiasm that the students and faculty feel. Most important, though, I realize why they depend on us for support.

Every great university has supportive alumni, and Chalet is no different. You and I are supportive, and I know that *we make a difference*. This university is on a course of great achievement, and we—the alumni—are the keys to its success. Therefore, I'm asking you to give as generously as possible to this year's annual drive—to *increase or match your last contribution*. Believe me, your gift *does* make a difference.

Most of us give because Chalet will always be important to us. We don't really expect anything directly in return. But this year, I have a surprise for you: Your contribution will be recognized by Chalet through the *dedication of a book in your name* to be placed on the shelves of the university library! How about that? The librarian will keep a list of all such books dedicated to alumni so that you can locate yours when you visit the campus.

Give today, and your name will be among the great books in the library. Let's make this the best annual fund in the university's history!

Sincerely,

Information. How much time do you spend thinking about information requests? Probably none. Information requests are so common that most people make them without thinking about the task of composition. After all, how much effort could be involved in writing "Please send me a free brochure"? But other types of information requests need an explanation not only of *what* you need but *why* you need it:

Dear Ms. Coffee:

We're compiling our annual directory of independent research services and would appreciate your taking a few minutes to complete and return the attached questionnaire in the enclosed, self-addressed, postage-paid envelope.

Whether or not you or your organization has been listed previously, we'd like to update our records with any new information about your services. More than 30,000 readers depend on the listings in our directory as a guide to available research services in the United States.

Should you want to reserve a copy of the directory, an order form is enclosed.

Thank you very much.

Sincerely,

Past-due payment. The earlier models about collection—remember them?—illustrated that efforts to collect unpaid accounts are endless. This next letter requesting payment has another twist: requesting payment *and* also refusing to fill future orders on credit until payment is received:

Dear Mr. Intaglio:

To confirm our recent telephone conversation, the current balance due on your account is $7,980, of which $2,600 is now more than sixty days past due. As much as we'd like to fill your October 8 order, our credit policy requires that all accounts be current for us to make additional shipments on credit.

As soon as we receive the past-due payment of $2,600, we'll promptly review your account and discuss future arrangements with you. Won't you, therefore, send us your check today?

If you have any questions about your account, please feel free to contact me at any time.

Sincerely,

Reason for action. If you're dying to know why someone did something, why not simply write and ask? In many cases, though, you won't get a reply or at least may have to wait quite a while for one. However, if you devise a check-off form that makes it easy to reply, the odds are better that the recipient will soon answer your request:

Dear Ms. Whaleback:

It's hard to give up something valuable, and we're concerned about your recent decision to discontinue your insurance coverage.

From past experience we know that the needs of our policyholders change, and we'd certainly like to help you make the necessary changes to keep your coverage in force. Therefore, we'd appreciate it if you would take a few minutes to answer the following question and return this letter in the enclosed postage-paid envelope.

I discontinued this coverage because of the following reasons:

Cost ( ) Other insurance ( ) Other ( )_____
_____

Let us hear from you, Ms. Whaleback. I'm sure that we can help you resolve any problem that may exist.

Thank you very much.

Sincerely,

References. Although I hope not, you may have already learned the hard way that it's risky to hire someone without first checking his or her references. Individuals and firms that bid on jobs may not routinely provide a list of others who have used their services. So if you want to check references before retaining outside help (always a good idea), you may have to request names and addresses of people or organizations that you can contact:

Dear Ms. Cupronickel:

To help us relate your service to our accounting requirements, we'd appreciate having a list of individuals and firms for whom you previously provided or currently are providing a similar service. Please include the firm name, address, telephone number, and person to contact.

Thanks very much. I hope that we'll soon be able to move forward with our arrangements.

Sincerely,

Refusal. Earlier, I mentioned the fact that it can be hard to say no. But I didn't add that in some situations it's harder than in others. In some cases, you simply have to decide how candid you want to be. Usually, when you can't agree to someone's request and you want to be frank about the reason, you should briefly state why, thank the person for asking, and wish the person good luck (if appropriate):

Dear Mack:

Thanks for reminding me that contributions to the Flicker campaign are now being accepted. However, I won't be able to make a donation this year since Bud Flicker's stand on the school bond issue is generally in opposition to my own views. In addition, I recently agreed to lend my support to another candidate.

I hope your campaign work won't keep you so busy that we can't have lunch sometime. I'll look forward to hearing more from you later, Mack.

Regards,

Reservations

Have you ever been turned away from a nice restaurant on a Saturday night because you didn't have a reservation? If so, you know that you need to make reservations for anything that has limited availability or capacity or anything that requires advance preparation for use—transportation, rooms, meals, and so on.

If you don't know the details, such as rates or hours, you should ask for information before making a reservation. Of course, after you've made it, you may still have to cancel or change it for another reason. That's life. With reservations, a lot of up-to-the-minute information is needed, and a lot of back-and-forth contact may be required. To complicate matters, time is often short. In general, it's important to state full details of what you want, the time, the date, the method of payment, and other important facts.

Although most reservations are made by telephone, some for major events or activities, such as a banquet, should be stated or at least confirmed in writing. The same is true for changes, such as a cancellation. Even if it's initially handled by telephone, sending a letter of confirmation is a good idea.

Cancellation. It never fails: Just when you've got your reservations set up and confirmed, something comes up to derail your plans. But most of us have had to change reservations often enough that the procedure for canceling them is no longer a huge mystery. When you cancel something by letter, repeat the main facts of the original reservation and ask for a refund if you paid by check or a credit to your account if you charged the reservation:

Ladies and Gentlemen:

Please cancel our reservation for four tickets to the Cranberry Society's annual banquet, March 17, 200X.

The reservation was made on January 22 and was paid by our company check number 3077 for $240. Please confirm this cancellation and send a refund to my attention at the letterhead address.

Thank you.

Sincerely,

Conference room. Common sense suggests that you need to know something about a proposed meeting before you decide where to hold it. For example, businesspeople usually don't go to an outside facility to hold a relatively small, routine employee meeting. Even when some clients or customers are invited, the meeting may be held in-house. Your company may therefore have one or more rooms set aside for business meetings, sales presentations, and other activities. Or for larger gatherings, perhaps you have a favorite motel or conference facility that you regularly use. In either case, contact the person in charge of assigning space and state the desired time and date, number of attendees expected, equipment and supplies needed, and any other special requirements:

TO: Todd Glockenspiel

FROM: Marla Neoprene

CONFERENCE ROOM RESERVATION

I'd like to reserve the Sales Room for Tuesday, January 30, from 1 p.m. until 4 p.m. for a training session.

About fourteen persons will be present and will need seating at rectangular group tables. Two rows of tables, theater style, with chairs facing the front of the room, would be ideal. Each table should have a water pitcher, and each person will need a water glass, notepad, and pencil. I'll also need one overhead projector, a tape recorder, a dry-erase marker board, and two presentation easels.

I'd appreciate a telephone call (extension 4232) from you, Todd, as soon as you can to confirm that the room is available. Thanks very much.

Confirmation. Let's reverse roles for a moment. Assume now that you're on the receiving end of a reservation request: You've been asked to confirm someone else's reservation. Or perhaps it's your company's policy to confirm everything in writing anyway, whenever there's time to do so. In that case, repeat the essential facts of the reservation, offer to provide anything else the customer might need, and include an expression of appreciation:

Dear Mrs. Netsuke:

Thank you for your dinner reservation for eight for Friday, February 21, at 7 p.m., in our Jungle Room.

We'll be happy to provide a choice of cocktails, house wine, and our $15.95 lemon chicken menu, including asparagus soup, the main course, salad, chocolate mousse, and regular or decaf coffee. As you requested, the charges for the evening, including gratuity, will be charged to your company account number 7214-J.

If we can do anything else to make your evening more enjoyable for you and your guests, please let us know.

Sincerely,

Theater tickets. Do you like to see plays? If so, you'll know that tickets for the theater are sometimes requested far in advance. Therefore, if you want to have a written record, you must have time to send a traditional letter to make the arrangements. If you need tickets at the last minute, though, you'll probably telephone the box office or a ticket agency and take whatever is available. When you send a written request, specify your preferred seating location and the performance date, give your credit card number or indicate if a check is enclosed, and state that a stamped, self-addressed envelope is enclosed for the box office or ticket agency's reply:

Ladies and Gentlemen:

Please reserve four center mezzanine seats for the August 1 performance of *Cats* and send the tickets to my attention at the letterhead address.

Our company check for $160 is enclosed, along with a stamped, self-addressed envelope for your reply.

Thank you.

Sincerely,

Sales

Salespeople will tell you that selling is an art. It's also big business, because organizations spend huge amounts of money to promote and sell their products, services, ideas, and goodwill to customers, prospects, and the general public.

Sales letters are meant to stimulate an immediate sale, and promotional sales messages are meant to stimulate interest, with the hope that this will eventually lead to a sale. Both are crucial aspects of a good sales program. Specialists often write these letters because they're so vital to a company's success. Very simply, an effective letter can produce profits, and an ineffective letter can create losses. With so much at stake, a letter must be appropriate for the audience, and it should arouse interest and stimulate action.

Often a sales message begins with some remark that catches the reader's attention, and then it follows with adequate information to interest the reader, emphasizing key features. It also appeals to something the reader wants, such as security or prestige. In closing, it tells the reader what to do, encouraging immediate action. Easy-to-complete paper or on-line forms, postage-paid reply envelopes, and other conveniences and incentives are used to make it easy and desirable for a reader to reply.

The language in a sales letter tends to be more exaggerated than that in a regular business letter. Since the letter writers aren't at all shy about stating or overstating the features of their products or services, you'll see plenty of dramatic or descriptive words, such as *acclaimed, amazing, beautiful, colorful, enchanting, exciting, leading, prestigious,* and *valuable.*

For a mass mailing, the letters are usually standard form letters. But with computer merge features, the customer's name and other information can be merged with the standard message on each letter.

Advertising. If you get mountains of books, magazines, and other publications or material that carries advertising, you'll know that the sender often uses cover letters to accompany the rate cards and other advertising information. When the enclosures contain rates, specifications, and a sales message, the cover letter can be brief (compared to other sales letters):

Dear Printing Professional:

A completely updated edition of the *Printers in America Directory* will be published in February 200X, and it's time to plan your advertisement for the next edition.

PAD is the *only* annual source of detailed, up-to-date information about the printing industry. For this reason, *PAD* is consulted daily by decision makers and represents the *best medium for your advertising dollars.* Space in *PAD* will give your printing operations *daily exposure for a full year,* putting your name right before the countless buyers of printing and related services.

Use the enclosed media kit to help you select your space in *PAD* 200X. To confirm your reservation immediately, call

800-555-7708. If you have any questions in the meantime, just let me know.

I hope to hear from you soon.

Cordially,

First order. Understandably, businesses take advantage of anything suitable to build customer relations and stimulate sales. A new customer's first order offers a good opportunity to send a letter. Sometimes the salutation is omitted, and a welcome line is used instead:

Thank you—and welcome!

We were delighted to receive your first order and hope that it marks the beginning of a long and satisfying association with Busby Business Supply.

The enclosed catalog will introduce you to Busby's entire line of office supplies and accessories. There you'll find the best values in quality supplies and accessories at low, low prices. And we *guarantee* these prices for the full life of the catalog!

Every *item is offered at a discount.* In fact, you'll be amazed to discover that our discount prices on manufacturers' national brand products are usually *15 to 40% below list prices*—sometimes more! Especially, watch for our "Busby Bargain" items that represent the greatest value of all.

We believe that you won't find better quality for your money anywhere else. And we ship within one to two days of receiving your order! At Busby we guarantee what we sell too. If you're not completely satisfied, return your purchase for full credit or a refund. *You'll receive prompt, courteous service.*

We're certainly glad that you came to Busby. We all sincerely appreciate your business and look forward to serving you on a regular basis.

Sincerely,

Follow-up. Not everyone is a spontaneous buyer, so you may have to send one or more follow-up letters to make a sale. One common tactic is to threaten that if the reader doesn't order something, you'll take the person off the mailing list. I know—that would suit you just fine. But it worries a lot of people who are afraid they'll miss out on something later:

FINAL NOTICE!

I thought you should know that this is the *LAST* packet of bargains that I'll be able to send you.

Recently, we noticed that you haven't ordered anything from Blarney for a long time. We've sent you hundreds of exciting offers in our regular mailings and notices of many truly special values. But since you haven't placed an order, I must assume that you're no longer interested in hearing from us.

You see, the cost of printing and mailing has gone up sharply, and the truth is that it's too expensive for us to send these packets to folks who aren't interested. One way that we keep our direct-to-you prices so low is by keeping our expenses as low as possible.

However, before I finally remove your name, I wanted to send you this one *LAST chance* to shop with Blarney. An order for *anything at all* will again restore you to our active customer list, and you'll continue to receive our bargain notices on a regular basis.

To give you time to place your order, I'll hold our file open for two more weeks. Won't you take a few moments right now to look through the enclosed special offers? Notice the marvelous household helpers and the unique gifts that you won't find anywhere outside of Blarney. And check those *low, low prices!* In these days of tight budgets, wouldn't it be nice to know where you can get the things you want and need at sensible prices?

Why not order today, while we still have your name on the active customer list?

Sincerely,

Gift. As we've said before, consumers love so-called free gifts, and sellers know it. That's why almost every other letter you receive nowadays promises to give you something—*if* you subscribe to a publication, join some club, or do just about anything short of selling your soul (maybe next year):

Dear Ms. Sternpost:

Why shouldn't *you* have a powerful vocabulary like other successful people?

A lot of people are discovering that word power and earning power go hand in hand. And we have just the thing to help you build a dynamic vocabulary virtually overnight—a self-study course from the publishers of the best-selling handbook *Vocabulary Unlimited.* We'd like to give you this amazing book absolutely free. All you have to do is initial the enclosed postage-paid card and drop it in the nearest mailbox.

Along with your free book, I'd like to give you a 15-day trial examination of our vocabulary-building self-study course developed especially for people like you.

Each month for a year, you'll receive a self-study lesson to complete in the convenience of your own house. It starts with basic fundamentals and, with each lesson, shows you a simple way to increase the size of your vocabulary almost overnight.

There's no obligation to continue if you're not completely satisfied with the first lesson of our self-study course. At the end of 15 days, you may return the lesson and not owe a cent. Or you may continue at the low rate of only $3.50 a month plus a small charge for postage and handling. The book *Vocabulary Unlimited* is yours to keep—free—in any case.

If you want to develop your word power, mail the enclosed card today. I guarantee that you'll be glad you did.

Cordially,

Services. As you know, both products and services are routinely promoted and sold by conventional mail or over the Internet to customers or clients and prospects. The service described in this next letter happens to be free—with no catch:

Dear F. T. Butcher:

We'd like to do something for you, and it won't cost you a thing!

Banyon National Bank has an *optional,* free service—now used by more than 85 percent of our customers—whereby we store your canceled checks for you. It's called MicroCheck.

With MicroCheck we're able to offer you complete safety and security because your canceled checks are stored on microfilm in our vaults for seven years. Should you ever need one of your checks, we can mail you a photocopy of both sides of the check within two working days. (Photocopies of canceled checks are accepted as legal proof of payment in every court and by the IRS.) Up to five copies a year are free, and there's only a small charge of $2 a copy thereafter.

MicroCheck makes balancing your checkbook easier and faster. You don't have to wade through all those canceled checks, which greatly cuts down on the time you spend each month doing paperwork. And it saves you storage space as well.

If you'd like to join our many other banking customers and add MicroCheck to your Banyon checking account, just let us know by detaching and mailing the attached reply card in the enclosed postage-paid envelope.

We hope you'll agree that our MicroCheck service is just another way of making your banking with us even more convenient.

Sincerely,

Subscription. Whoever said that you can always count on death and taxes should have said death, taxes, and magazine subscriptions. To talk you into subscribing, magazines offer an endless variety of incentives from free cameras to free issues. The assumption is that once you're accustomed to receiving the magazine, you'll continue to subscribe:

Dear Mary Daylily:

I'd like to add your name to our *Professional Educator* subscription list—*at no cost to you*—for four months! That's right, *four free issues* without any obligation on your part. In fact, since we're enclosing a free sample with this letter, you'll actually be receiving five free issues.

I can't think of a better way to introduce you to the range of ideas in the *Professional Educator* and to convince you that it belongs regularly on your library shelves.

I hope, of course, that you'll make the copies available to teachers, administrators, and school officials—in fact, to *anyone working in the world of education.* But we won't force it on you. If you'd rather not receive the next four issues *free of charge,* just check the *no* box on the attached reply card and return it in the enclosed postage-paid envelope. However, do keep the enclosed free copy—or pass it on.

I hope that you'll join the millions of others who rarely spend a day without an issue of the *Professional Educator* nearby.

Cordially,

Sympathy

This will probably be your least favorite subject in the book, but because death, accident, illness, natural disaster, and other misfortune can't be ignored in real life, we can't ignore them here. When these things happen in business, the resulting sympathy messages are treated almost the same as such messages in the social world, as you'll see from similar sympathy models in **SOCIAL COR-RESPONDENCE**.

You may not know the victim or the family of the victim as well as you know your personal friends and relatives, but if you know the customer, client, coworker, employer, or other person at all, it's appropriate—and important—to send a message of sympathy. These messages should be brief, but they must have a caring, sincere (though not effusive) tone. The better you know the reader, the more personal your remarks can be, including an offer to help.

The choice of stationery depends on how well you know the person. Perhaps you're friends as well as business associates, or perhaps the person experiencing the misfortune is your boss. A handwritten note on personal, or Monarch, stationery is appropriate when you're friends or have a very close working relationship. Foldover cards are ideal for handwritten messages. See **BUSINESS COR-RESPONDENCE: Letterhead stationery** and **SOCIAL CORRESPONDENCE: Foldover cards**.

However, if you don't know the person very well, you might prepare the letter by computer on business letterhead. Or you might print out the message on personal stationery or plain bond paper if it's going to an employee within your company.

For instance, a sympathy letter to the general manager of an outside firm that lost its president would be sent on business letterhead. A letter acknowledging the death of the spouse of an executive whom you don't know very well in another firm, perhaps a customer, would also be prepared on business letterhead. A message to a coworker whom you see occasionally might be prepared on plain bond paper or personal stationery. It's always proper, however, to use handwriting for business acquaintances in your own company, and it's essential to handwrite notes for friends, relatives, and close working associates.

Acknowledgment. If you're the one *receiving* expressions of sympathy from coworkers and outsiders, send a brief thank you. In selecting the stationery, follow the example of the sender. If you receive a handwritten message on personal stationery, send a handwritten reply on personal stationery. If you receive a computer-printed message on business letterhead from someone outside the firm, print out your reply on business letterhead:

Dear Ms. Scrip:

I sincerely appreciated your kind expression of sympathy on the death of our board chairman. Thank you very much for remembering us.

Sincerely,

Death—coworker's mother. When a member of a coworker's family dies, immediately send a personal note—handwritten on personal stationery if you know the person well:

Dear Mr. Primrose:

I was saddened to learn from our supervisor today about your mother's sudden death. You and your family have my heartfelt sympathy.

If I can help in any way, Mr. Primrose, do let me know.

Sincerely,

Death—customer's spouse. You may learn that the spouse of an executive in a customer's firm has died. If you don't know the person well, send a very brief computer-prepared message on business letterhead:

Dear Mrs. Granadilla:

I and my staff were saddened to learn of your great loss, and we want to extend our sympathy to you during this very difficult time.

Sincerely,

Death—outside official. When an official in another firm dies, send a computer-prepared message on business letterhead to the president or other head of the company:

Dear Mr. Borneol:

My associates and I were shocked to learn about the death of Mr. Cloche. We know that he will be greatly missed not only in your firm but also in the entire business community. We want to extend our condolences to you and to the family.

Sincerely,

Illness—in-house. If you've ever been sick for quite a while or hospitalized following an injury, you may know from experience that employees sometimes worry about being replaced at work or about losing their jobs. Although it's important to tell the absent person how sorry you are, it's also necessary to have an upbeat tone. Suggest that the person's job will be handled (if that's true) until he or she can return:

Dear Neil:

I was so sorry to learn about your accident this morning, and I hope that you'll soon be up and about. Although we'll miss you at the office, don't worry about your work— we're all going to pitch in to keep things moving until you return.

Take care of yourself, and please get well soon.

Best wishes,

Misfortune—outside business. Some types of misfortune, such as the loss of a job, require a slightly different message. Although you'll want to be sympathetic and not treat the situation lightly, say something encouraging to give the person a lift:

Dear Wayne:

I just heard that Portly Fashions is closing its doors after twenty years. No doubt this was a blow to you, but considering your talent and energy, I'm sure that the setback will be only temporary. In fact, it wouldn't surprise me if this opens up even better opportunities for you.

If you're not already totally immersed in plans for the future, let's get together for lunch and toss around ideas. I'll call you early next week, Wayne, and am looking forward to seeing you soon.

Best regards,

Staff response. When an employer is away and a death occurs, someone else in the office has to decide whether to contact the employer or send an interim message. If the person was a close friend of the employer, someone should let the employer know right away. If the employer didn't know the person very well, someone in the office can send an interim message:

Dear Mr. Tasse:

Although Ms. Wilder is traveling at present, I wanted you to know that she will undoubtedly be shocked to learn about the death of your wife. I'm certain that she'll send a personal message as soon as she returns.

Sincerely,

Thank Yous

Everyone can relax now. We're moving on to a much lighter subject—thank yous. Those two words, *thank you,* are seldom used too often, unless you get into one of those annoying "Thank you—No, thank YOU—NO, thank YOU" exchanges.

It would obviously sound phony, or at least excessive, if you kept repeating *thank you* in every paragraph of a letter. But it would also seem rude if you didn't say it at all in response to assistance, a favor, a gift, hospitality, or any other thoughtful occasion or gesture.

We know that people in business do nice things for each other every day, whether out of kindness or for purely selfish motives. Regardless, every opportunity to thank someone is also an opportunity to build good working relations or to spread goodwill on behalf of a company.

Don't worry: Thank yous can be brief. The important thing is to sound genuinely pleased, without becoming gushy. If you were passing out inexpensive company souvenir letter openers to customers, you would expect the people to say thank you when you handed them the souvenir. But imagine opening a letter the next day that said:

> The beautiful letter opener that you gave me for my desk is absolutely exquisite. Never have I seen such marvelous craft work. This is the nicest thing anyone has ever given me. I was so excited yesterday that I didn't sleep a wink all night. How can I ever thank you enough? The truth is that I can't because words will never be sufficient to express my endless joy at such a wonderful gift.

Even with an expensive gift, wild exaggeration sounds downright silly. The proper approach is to offer thanks, make a sincere comment about the gift, and end with a pleasant remark—something more original than the trite "thanks again."

Assistance. Everyone needs help at some time, right? For example, busy employees sometimes have scheduling problems, an overload of work, and other difficulties. When someone does something exceptional to help you in a time of need, it's important to write a thank you letter as well as to give thanks in person. The following example would be computer-printed on business letterhead:

Dear Sid:

It was very thoughtful of you to take over my duties on the trade-show committee. With the sales seminar this week and customers coming for a meeting and tour next week, all on top of my usual hefty workload, I was in over my head.

I really appreciate your help, Sid, and hope that I can reciprocate one day. Many thanks.

Best regards,

Bonus. If you're lucky enough to get a bonus to write about, address your letter (printed out on business letterhead or personal stationery) to the person in the company giving the bonus to you, probably your immediate supervisor or boss:

Dear Mr. Scuttle:

Thank you so much for the Christmas bonus. With the holidays already here and the tax season around the corner, you may be certain that the check will be especially helpful in selecting presents for the children, taking care of taxes, and even saving something for a rainy day. Christmas will definitely be a happy time at our house this year!

We sincerely appreciate the bonus, Mr. Scuttle, and want to wish you and your family a very happy and peaceful holiday season.

Sincerely,

Customer referral. In our ad-happy society, it's almost surprising that not all business comes from advertising. But it doesn't. Some of it comes from the referrals of friends, associates, and other customers or clients. Therefore, when someone sends an important new customer to you, promptly send a letter of thanks. A brief message on business letterhead is sufficient (unless you know the reader well enough to say more):

Dear Mr. Racemose:

We were happy to meet Virginia Nutria from the Community College and equally delighted to accept her as a new client. Thank you so much for referring her to us.

Your kind remarks about our graphics service were certainly helpful, and we want you to know how much we appreciate your interest and confidence in our work.

Sincerely,

Gift accepted. If you receive a nice gift from a business associate, and company policy doesn't prevent you from accepting it, immediately send a thank you message. If it's clearly a *business* gift, you can send a computer-prepared message on business letterhead:

Dear Mr. Krummhorn:

I'm completely intrigued with the compass you sent. You must have known that as a field representative, calling on customers by car most of the time, I could really use this.

It's a handsome unit, too, with a very impressive case. My boss saw it today and commented that I now have no excuse for getting lost—as I've done on more than one occasion!

Many thanks, Mr. Krummhorn, for such a useful and enjoyable gift.

Cordially,

Gift refused. A strange sort of thank you is one in which you're actually saying thanks but no thanks. Although it would be unthinkable to hurt the feelings of someone giving you a gift, some companies don't allow employees to accept gifts from outsiders for various reasons. For example, the company may want to prevent an employee from being bribed to do something not in the company's best interests. In any case, to handle this type of situation properly, you need to use extraordinary tact as you explain your reason for returning the gift:

Dear Mr. Hutment:

How very thoughtful of you to recognize my promotion at Obelisk Engineering.

As much as I deeply appreciate the generous gift you sent, company policy won't permit me to keep it. Regretfully, I must return it, but I sincerely thank you for your kind thought.

It was wonderful to hear from you, and I look forward to seeing you soon.

Cordially,

Invitation. We're all used to sending and receiving *informal* invitations in business, such as those to have lunch with someone or to be a guest speaker. This type of invitation is usually prepared on business letterhead, and the thank you is returned in the same format. If the thank you also acknowledges an *event*, repeat the facts (day, time, and so on) for confirmation:

Dear Ms. Cudgel:

Thanks for inviting me to give a thirty-minute presentation at your Friday, July 16, meeting of the National Mole Society at 7:30 p.m.

It will be a pleasure to discuss the star-nosed mole in North American habitats. Since some of my slides are excellent close-ups of the pink, fleshy projections surrounding the nostrils, I'll plan on interspersing the discussion with a slide presentation.

I appreciate this opportunity to meet others who study this fascinating creature and look forward to meeting you and your associates Friday evening.

Cordially,

Party. Have you ever arranged a dinner, cocktail party, or other type of party for customers or clients, members of the community, or employees (on important occasions)? You probably have at least attended such a function. You may even have been the guest of honor or a special attendee. Anyone who's honored in that way should promptly send thanks to the host. The message may be either computer printed or handwritten on personal stationery:

Dear Ms. Clerihew:

What a wonderful time I had at the retirement party you held for me. Thank you ever so much. It made me realize, though, how hard it will be to leave my work and good friends in this company.

The party was a very special occasion for me, and I'll long remember this generous and joyful conclusion to my twenty years with Eschar Petroleum. I sincerely appreciated all the thoughtful sentiments that were expressed, and I'm grateful to everyone who made the evening possible.

I'll always be glad I chose Eschar and that Eschar chose me. But it's clear that I'm the one who came out ahead!

Cordially,

Transmittals

I'm sure that you're superprofessional and always handle things properly. So when you send something to someone, you presumably always enclose a note or letter identifying whatever you're sending and explaining why you're sending it. Even with a merchandise order being sent to a customer, your company may have a policy of always enclosing a form letter saying here it is—thanks for ordering from us.

If you had nothing to explain and no sales pitch to make, all you would need is one or two sentences. But if more information were involved, you would probably send a longer letter or memo—unless you could enclose something such as a report or brochure that would sufficiently explain everything.

Missing material. Let's start by assuming that you're *receiving* a transmittal letter. One of the first things you'll do is check to be certain that the material described in the letter is actually there. If it isn't, your follow-up notice to the sender should clearly describe what you were expecting but didn't get:

Dear Julie:

I was happy to get your letter stating that the blueprints were finished and ready for my examination. However, they weren't enclosed with your letter. Are they being sent separately? If not, I'd appreciate it if you would send them by return mail.

Thanks very much, Julie. I'm really eager to see them.

Best wishes,

Order. If you're ordering supplies or goods on an order form and also want to say something, you may be able to put your comments directly on the form. If that won't work, though, you'll have to enclose a separate letter or memo. If you do that, you may want to write "See enclosed letter" on the form:

TO: Artemis Software Press

FROM: Ozzie Brabble

INSTRUCTION DISKS

Enclosed is our check for $175.85 along with a completed order form.

We're in need of these training disks for an upcoming training session and have marked the order form for *rush service.* Therefore, if any of the titles are currently unavailable, we'd appreciate having an immediate refund rather than having the disks back-ordered.

Thank you.

Payment. If you're someone who is *never* late, you can skip this model. For everyone else, if you're sending a payment well past the due date, and you want to maintain good relations with the creditor, include a letter of explanation or apology:

Dear Mr. Trephine:

Please forgive me for sending the enclosed check to you nearly sixty days late.

I mistakenly thought it had been paid before I left on vacation, but your invoice had been misplaced. Fortunately, our bookkeeper discovered it yesterday stuck to the back of another piece of correspondence.

I hope this delay hasn't caused you any problems. To be certain that this doesn't happen again, we've all agreed to be much more careful hereafter.

Sincerely,

Printed material. Not many people would send an important document, such as a contract, without a letter of explanation. Other documents, though, such as printed material, need only a short, straightforward message:

Dear Mrs. Plenum:

Here are the proceedings of the November 19 UFO fair. I hope this material will be useful to you.

We appreciate your interest and want to thank you for writing.

Sincerely,

Product. Sometimes it seems that businesspeople spend 99 percent of their time explaining to customers what they should do if so and so is necessary. For example, businesses that ship products requiring some action on the part of the customer often enclose a form letter telling the person what to do and how to do it:

Dear Customer:

Here's your BP 3107 backup power unit. Although it was inspected before shipping and packed with care in our warehouse, we urge you to examine the unit immediately upon receipt.

Defective merchandise will be repaired or replaced, and return shipping charges will be reimbursed. Please follow these instructions if you must return your unit:

1. Return the product in its original carton.
2. Address the package to Customer Service, 1149 South Street, Redondo Beach, CA 90277.
3. Enclose a letter describing the problem.

We sincerely hope that you'll enjoy the safeguard of having the BP 3107 to rely on when your utility power fails. If you have any questions about your new unit, please let us know.

Cordially,

Recommendation. Transmittal letters aren't always simple cover letters announcing what is being sent. Some transmittal letters also serve another purpose. You might, for example, send someone some literature and attach a cover letter that also (briefly) makes a recommendation:

TO: Warren Gimcrack

FROM: Alice Bryony

ABSENTEEISM

Following our last board meeting, I did some further research into the increasing problem of absenteeism in our plant.

Although this is a widespread problem, I found two interesting case studies, one a Ph.D. dissertation from the University of Alabama and the other a report published by an independent consultant. The studies reported some improvements in this area through job counseling and special incentives, or rewards, for good records.

Copies of both studies are enclosed for your review. Their solutions could be incorporated into our policy, and I'd be interested in your impression of them. Perhaps we could have lunch before the next board meeting to discuss this further.

I'll look forward to hearing from you after you've had a chance to examine the reports.

Shipment. You would probably send a packing slip or a standard transmittal form letter with routine shipments from a large company. But if you were sending an important package from your own office, you would likely want to create your own transmittal message especially for that package:

Dear Mark:

Here, in one carton, is the full collection of clippings dating from 1981 to the present from the Sharp Clipping Service. As I mentioned by telephone, I believe these files would be more useful to you at headquarters. They're simply too remote in our branch office.

I hope it all arrives safely. You'll notice that the sixty-one files are arranged by subject rather than by year. Within each subject file, however, the clippings are in chronological order. But let me know, Mark, if you have any questions about any of it.

Thanks very much for taking care of them.

Best regards,

Social Correspondence

Someone who was reading the first edition of this book said that he was looking forward to the topic *social correspondence* because he really wasn't sure what that meant. When, he wondered, does *business* correspondence become *social,* and what's the difference between *social* and *personal* correspondence? Those are fair questions, because people tend to be vague about the terms, and even authorities differ.

Look at it this way: An invitation to a dinner party may be either business, social, or personal correspondence, depending on the issuer. If a company or a representative acting on behalf of the company issues the invitation, it's a *business* (or *social-business*) *invitation.* If someone issues the invitation on behalf of or to others in a social group—but without company affiliation or sponsorship—it's a *social invitation.* If a family member issues the invitation to other family members or if a friend sends it to other friends, it's a *personal invitation.* Get the idea?

At least that's the way we're looking at it in this book. However, the distinction between personal and social correspondence isn't as clear as that between social and business correspondence. Since either personal or social correspondence may involve messages written by and for oneself, one's family, or a social group—rather than on behalf of a company—personal and social matters are combined in this book, whereas business correspondence is considered by itself.

But whether someone wants to call correspondence business, personal-business, social-business, social, or personal correspondence, one thing applies in each case: You have to follow the same rules for writing thoughtful and effective messages described in **MESSAGE COM-POSITION**. This means that the language and tone you use, your attitude, and the appearance of your letters all paint a picture of you to the readers. So put your best foot forward if you want to make a good impression.

Format

Basic formats. Remember this discussion in **BUSI-NESS CORRESPONDENCE**? As I mentioned there, three of the basic formats—block, traditional, and sim-plified—illustrated in the **REFERENCE SECTION** are primarily business formats. But they're also suitable for many of the letters that you write to companies about household problems, such as repairs, or letters that you write to a member of the community about personal or social activities, such as community fund-raising. The personal format, also illustrated in the **REFERENCE SECTION**, is different from the other formats, as you'll see in the forthcoming discussion.

For strictly *formal* social matters, such as invitations to a dinner party, you would use still a different format, and the next chapter, **SOCIAL MODELS**, has examples of formal social invitations. At the other extreme, for very *informal*, personal letters, such as a note to a family member, you would probably use whatever format you like, without worrying about specific rules or guidelines.

Let's think of some examples: Assume that you've in-stalled a new ceiling fan in the dining room, and it sud-denly sucks up the dinner napkins and a fresh bowl of lettuce. If this happens, you may be inclined to shoot a letter of complaint to the manufacturer. In fact, if it hap-pens in the middle of an important dinner party, you may be inclined simply to shoot the manufacturer. But I assume that you'll use a letter to register your displea-sure and will either handwrite it or, more likely, use a typewriter or computer to prepare it in a business-letter format.

On the other hand, if your cousin Nellie sends you a

pet alligator for your birthday and you're writing to thank her, you'll probably use whatever personal format you like. You may even pen a few sentences on a commercial thank you card, expressing your total ecstasy at becoming the proud new parent of a cuddly reptile.

Handwriting versus machine preparation. Some things should always be handwritten. For example, you should handwrite personal or social thank you notes (unless they're part of a larger typed letter), sympathy messages, formal invitations that aren't printed, and replies to formal invitations when no reply card is provided. Invitations to a large social event would always be printed, of course, simply because there would be too many to handwrite all of them.

For most other types of social and personal correspondence, such as a newsy letter to a friend, do as you please. Therefore, if you prefer to use a typewriter or computer, go ahead. But remember that anything personal or social that you send by e-mail will be subject to the same concerns that you would have with business e-mail. Especially, keep in mind that someone other than the intended recipient may see what you transmit electronically. So be careful if you want to say mean things to your cousin Bob about his brother Joe, because Joe may be using their computer when your message comes in and therefore may be the first one to see your nasty barbs.

Incidentally, except for e-mail messages, memos usually aren't appropriate for social or personal correspondence. Although you might send a memo to a company about some household product that you ordered, this format would look too businesslike and impersonal for messages to your family, your minister, or one of your neighbors.

For more about e-mail, see **MESSAGE COMPOSITION: Electronic Mail, How to prepare e-mail, When it's okay to use smileys,** and **Other e-mail shorthand.**

Personal format. Just a few comments about the *personal* format, which some people describe as "anything you want it to be": Whereas the *social* format often is essentially the same thing as the *business* format (discussed in **BUSINESS CORRESPONDENCE**), the personal format is much less strict about things such as the parts of a letter—where they're positioned or even if they're included at all.

For example—this is important—the personal format omits the inside address, typed signature line, and special notations, such as *Enc.* (See the model in the **REFERENCE SECTION**.) It usually begins with the date, unless you don't have your return address printed on your stationery. Then it would be helpful to the recipient if you would put your address at the top of the page.

The date should follow the address, with one or two spaces between the two:

. 1416 South Street
Prescott, AZ 86303

June 7, 200X

In a business, social-business, strictly social, or personal-business letter, a colon follows the salutation (see the many examples in **BUSINESS MODELS**). But in a personal letter, a comma follows the salutation:

Dear Aunt Matilda,

For the proper style of writing addresses on envelopes for personal or general social correspondence, follow the suggestions here and those in **Mailing Guidelines**. For an example of an envelope used with social-business or personal-business correspondence, refer to the envelope formats in the **REFERENCE SECTION**.

The complimentary close you use depends on your relationship with the recipient. *Love, Affectionately,* and *Faithfully* are common closes to family members and close friends. If that's too gooey for you, use a less intimate close such as *Always* or *As ever.* Some persons also write something such as *Your niece* for letters to relatives.

The most familiar placement for the complimentary close in a handwritten personal letter is slightly to the right of the center of the page, with a space between the last line of the letter and the close. If the letter is typed in a block style, the close would be flush left. For more ideas, look at the examples of the block, traditional, and personal formats in the **REFERENCE SECTION**.

You should omit the typed signature line and sign only your first name in a personal letter or in a social letter to someone you know well. However, in a social letter to someone you don't know very well, you should include a typed signature line, such as those illustrated in the **REFERENCE SECTION** formats, and also should sign your full name.

Again, if you're writing to a company about some household matter, use a business letter or memo format. The business-letter format has an inside address, a complimentary close, and a signature block, and you would sign the letter with your full name.

Social and Personal Stationery

Writing paper. If you already think this discussion is a little boring, I have to warn you that it's going to get worse before it gets better. But if you skip it, you may miss something crucial and therefore may make a terrible blunder one day. This unspeakable catastrophe may force you to leave society forever and spend the rest of your life in a cave, forced to relive through all eternity your decision to skip this discussion. Convinced?

Okay, to begin: Personal and social writing paper is usually smaller than standard business letterhead, which is 8½ by 11 inches. If you're writing a letter to a company about a household matter, however, you might use the standard business-size paper, such as regular typing paper.

Personal stationery is usually about 7 or 7¼ by 10 or 10½ inches (Monarch size) for men, folded in thirds to fit into a matching Monarch envelope. In business, women also use the Monarch size for social-business letters. Otherwise, for personal and social situations, they use smaller size paper, about 5½ by 6½ inches, folded in half to fit into a matching small envelope. (For computer-printed social or personal messages, you'll have to pick a size paper that your printer can handle.) However, don't bet your life on stationery measurements because sizes may vary depending on the manufacturer.

Paper used strictly for social purposes should be white, off-white, or a conservative pastel color. However, informal personal writing paper, such as that used to write to family members or close friends, may be any color or design that appeals to you.

A man may have his name (but no title), full address, and telephone, fax, and e-mail numbers (optional) printed at the top of the page. Plain, matching sheets are used for additional pages. A man also may have a family crest positioned in the top center or upper left corner of the paper. If it's placed in the left corner, the address, telephone number, and any other numbers may be placed in the upper right corner.

Although engraved stationery is elegant, it's also very expensive. Therefore, in most cases, plain printing or raised printing (by a process called *thermography*) is used instead.

Traditionally, a married or widowed woman has the title *Mrs.* and her husband's full name printed on formal social paper, such as on the front of foldover cards (see the description in the next section):

Mrs. John Winter

On social paper meant for informal use, though, she would probably omit the title *Mrs.* and use her own first name. An unmarried woman would also omit the title *Ms.*:

Diane Winter

For more about the proper use of names and titles for women, see **Forms of Address** in the **REFERENCE SECTION.**

Foldover cards. Foldover cards or paper (also called *informals*), folded once to a size of 3½ by 5 inches (or more), with matching envelopes, is very useful and popular for brief thank you notes, replies to invitations, and other short messages. See the examples in **SOCIAL MODELS: Invitations.** Some people have their initials, their name alone, or (less likely) their name, address, and telephone number printed on the outside front panel (visit a printer to see samples):

Eva Marie Wall
Mrs. Dennis Wall
EMW

If the name, initials, or other information is centered on the front panel, you'll have to open the note and start writing at the top of the inside two panels for a long note or at the bottom for a short note.

Envelopes. You may have your return address printed on the upper left front or the back flap of the envelope. For formal social correspondence, it looks nice to have it on the back. For personal-business letters, though, it's preferable to have it on the front (also preferred by the U.S. Postal Service).

Put the recipient's address on the front of the envelope in the same style that you would use for a business letter. However, in formal social correspondence and in personal notes, use the traditional style, not the all-capital-letter style sometimes used in business for fast machine reading in the post office. Again, see the envelope formats in the **REFERENCE SECTION** and **Mailing Guidelines** in this chapter.

Social cards. You don't see many social cards (also called *visiting, calling,* or *gift-enclosure cards*) anymore. Nowadays, these cards, when used at all, are primarily used in graduation announcements or to accompany gifts and flowers. (Florists and gift stores also have small commercial cards that you can use.) For gifts and flowers, however, the foldover cards described earlier are more popular when you want to write a brief message.

Social cards for men are about 3 by 1¼ inches. For women, they're about 3 by 2¼ inches. Usually, they consist of shiny- or matte-finish card stock in white or an off-white color, with matching small, plain envelopes. The cards are printed or engraved with small, black letters. Either script or nonscript letters are acceptable.

Use only the person's name on a social card, not an address or telephone number such as you would use on a business card. If the name isn't too long, spell out each part in full, adding *Mr., Miss* (optional), *Mrs.,* or any other title, such as *The Reverend.* When space permits, spell out *Doctor* and other professional titles preceding the name. (On a business card, you would omit the personal titles and professional titles such as *Dr.* preceding the name but would include initials such as *M.D.* after the name.)

Spell out the designations *junior* and *senior* after the name and write each with a small initial *j* or *s.* (On a business card, you would abbreviate and capitalize *Jr.* and *Sr.*) In both social and business usage, you may set off *junior/Jr.* and *senior/Sr.* with commas or omit them, as the person prefers:

Doctor Wilfred Bluestone III
Mr. Wilfred Bluestone III
Judge Wilfred Bluestone junior

Married and widowed women use the title *Mrs.* with their husband's full name in the same form that he uses:

Wilfred Bluestone III, Mrs. Wilfred Bluestone III
Wilfred Bluestone junior, Mrs. Wilfred Bluestone junior

A divorced woman may put *Mrs.* in front of her own first name and her married or maiden last name. In contemporary usage, however, some divorced women adopt the style of an adult single woman (no title):

Mrs. Jeanne Bluestone (*former married last name*)

Mrs. Jeanne Pyle (*maiden name*)

Jeanne Pyle (*maiden name*)

Single women also write out their names in full (no initial) but usually drop the title *Miss* (*Ms.* is not common on social cards):

Frieda Anne Bluestone

If a professional woman uses a title, she should include that title on her social cards as well as on her business cards:

The Reverend Jeanne Bluestone

Unlike other social cards, on joint husband-and-wife cards, which are about 3½ by 2½ inches, you might have the address printed in the lower left corner. Also, you might have to abbreviate personal and professional titles because of space limitations:

Mr. and Mrs. Wilfred Bluestone junior
Dr. and Mrs. Wilfred Bluestone III
Dr. Jeanne and Mr. Wilfred Bluestone junior
Drs. Wilfred and Jeanne Bluestone III

For more information about professional or business cards, refer to the discussion in **BUSINESS CORRE-SPONDENCE: Business cards.**

Mailing Guidelines

Method of transmission. Okay, we made it through the format and style tedium. Let's see how fast we can zip through the mailing guidelines. First, how are social or personal letters sent? Invitations and most social letters are sent by first-class mail, with postage stamps applied to the envelope (rather than a postal-meter tape or imprint). Personal letters are another matter. You can mail them, fax them, e-mail them, send them by carrier pigeon, or put them in a bottle and throw them in the ocean. You decide.

Envelope address. The envelope should be sealed, although hand-delivered letters are usually left unsealed. For formal social correspondence, such as a formal invitation to a dinner, the address should be handwritten. However, for informal social letters, such as a letter of congratulations to an award winner, and for personal letters, such as a letter to your nephew, the address may be typed.

Use a title (*Dr., Mr., Ms., Mrs.,* and so on) with the name on the envelope:

Ms. Rita Pennywort
19 Elm Street
Princeton, NJ 08540

A traditional envelope format (the most common format in personal and social correspondence) and an optical-character-reader format are illustrated in the **REFERENCE SECTION**.

Folding and inserting letters. You may not think it matters how you put a letter in an envelope, but there's a right way and a wrong way. Follow the example in **BUSINESS CORRESPONDENCE: Mailing Guidelines** for folding a standard-size paper (8½ by 11 inches), which you might use to write about a household or other personal-business matter.

Generally, fold this type of letter in thirds to fit into a No. 9 or a No. 10 envelope, leaving a small (up to ¼ inch) edge protruding at the top. Then insert the letter so that this small edge is at the top of the envelope. But if you must fit the letter into a smaller envelope, first fold the sheet in half to 8½ by 5½ inches. Then fold it again in thirds, but with the last fold, leave a small edge protruding and insert the letter so that this edge is to the top in the envelope.

Usually, you would fold smaller stationery only once (in half) to fit into a small envelope. Foldover notes, for instance, are commonly packaged already folded in half to a size of 3½ by 5 inches or more. Personal or social writing paper commonly is sold with matching envelopes and should be folded in half or thirds as needed to fit the envelopes. In most cases, you should insert the paper so that the reader can pull it out, open it, and start reading without twisting or turning it. But for an exception, read the tips about using paper clips with correspondence in **BUSINESS CORRESPONDENCE: Conventional mail**.

Mailing dates. The date that you mail a social or personal letter or invitation is very important. After all, invitations must be sent in time for the recipient to make plans to attend the event. Follow the suggested dates in **SOCIAL MODELS: Invitations**.

However, other social and personal letters must be sent on time also. For example, a gift—no matter how small—should always be acknowledged promptly. I've received acknowledgments as much as several months after sending the gift, sometimes only in response to my inquiry whether the gift ever arrived. People should *never* have to ask whether you received their gift simply because you think you're too busy to let them know.

For some gifts I've sent, I never did receive an acknowledgment. I happen to know that the people received the gifts, or I would have asked to be certain that the items weren't lost in the mail. It's probably an understatement to say that I'm not very impressed with their manners. Invitations, too, must be acknowledged promptly, and other messages, such as sympathy notes, must obviously be sent without delay. So timing is just as important in the social world as in the business world.

Commercial Cards

Cards for special occasions. One thing I'm certain we can all agree on is that people enjoy receiving cards—holiday cards, birthday cards, anniversary cards, graduation cards, get-well cards, all sorts of cards for every imaginable occasion. No wonder. Sending a card on a special occasion is a nice gesture. If your computer has the right software, you can even make your own cards and print your own greeting inside.

However, whether it's a commercial card or your own computer creation, the recipient will enjoy it even more if you handwrite a message inside in addition to any printed message. I have to confess that I never read the printed message, especially the long, syrupy ones. But I always look carefully to see if anything is handwritten inside or on the back of the card. People who are ill have told me that even a very brief, handwritten message means the world to them.

Let's clear up one mystery right now: It's fine for Jews and Christians to exchange general-message holiday cards during the winter season. Instead of sending a card that says "Happy Hanukkah" or "Merry Christmas," simply choose a message such as "Peace" or "Season's Greetings," and be certain that it depicts a general scene without a religious tone. Also, be certain that the message and scene in a holiday card to someone in mourning is not offensively festive.

A belated greeting card may be better than no card, but most people have only a feeble excuse for failing to send a card on time. Everyone should keep a list of birthdays and anniversaries of friends and relatives in a prominent location or record them on a calendar at the start of each new year.

When you sign cards sent to family members and close friends, use only your first name but include your last name in other cases. Although it may seem redundant, sign your name and pen a few words even on cards that you had printed with your name and a selected message. It will add a personal touch. If a card is being sent from a couple, the person signing it usually puts his or her name last. If a lot of children are included, it's sufficient to add "and family" rather than write all the names.

Personal newsletters. This is a controversial subject that authorities haven't yet straightened out. As you know, some people like to enclose a detailed form letter, or newsletter, with their holiday cards telling recipients everything they, their children, and their pet turtle did during the past year. Since authorities differ on the wisdom of this practice, there's no firm social rule preventing it. In fact, some people believe it's a wonderful way to bring friends and relatives up to date. Also, parents and grandparents tend to relish the extensive news about their children and grandchildren.

However, unless you add a personal, handwritten message to this type of letter, it may seem cold and impersonal to some people. After all, a *form* letter for *personal* correspondence is a contradiction in terms. Also, keep in mind that it's probably all about *you* and *your family* and doesn't ask about the other person or discuss his or her life to any extent and possibly not at all. Since truly gracious people say a minimum about themselves and focus mostly on the other person, the newsletter may come across as conceited and self-centered.

Many people have told me that they never read Christmas or other form letters. They say that it's too boring and time-consuming to read one or two single-spaced pages of trivia (to them). They simply don't want a step-by-step account of little Lily's dental work and don't care how many cars son Jamie counted at the campground last summer, who came from where for Thanksgiving dinner, or which former neighbors Ed met for dinner last October in Idaho.

But if you can't face life without sending your annual memoirs, what can you do to make people more receptive? First, try to resist the urge to tell everyone *everything* you and your family thought, said, saw, visited, or did during the past year. If the urge to tell all totally overpowers you, though, at least try to edit out some of the microscopic details about travel and children that others might find excruciatingly tedious. Finally, if you're convinced that some people, such as your parents, will be heartbroken if you don't tell them everything—including what color bathroom tissue you're using this year—by all means send a copy of the newsletter to them. Just *don't* send it to the other people on your list, such as the more remote family members or various friends and acquaintances who are probably more interested in their own lives, loves, travels, and bathroom tissue.

Thank you cards. You'll be happy to know that most people are at least receptive to other messages, such as thank you messages. Although some authorities recommend a thank you letter, a commercial card is acceptable if you add a handwritten message. As I've said before, thank you messages *must* be sent promptly for any gift received, except a gift that's given in person for which you express your thanks at the time. Even then, following up with a written message is always proper and very thoughtful.

If you receive a thank you *gift,* you should acknowledge it the same as you would acknowledge any other gift. But don't send a thank you in return for a thank you *letter* that you receive. You could get dizzy trying to thank everyone for thanking you.

Sympathy cards. Both foldover cards and commercial sympathy cards are widely used for sympathy messages, although proper etiquette requires that you add a brief, *personal* message on any commercial card sent to a close friend or relative. You may also send commercial *acknowledgments* to those who sent you commercial sympathy cards. But you should send handwritten acknowledgments to those who sent you handwritten letters. In other words, follow the example of the sender when you reply.

The Cassette Letter

Both audiotapes and videocassettes can be used in place of a handwritten or typed letter if you know that the recipient has the right equipment to play them. Men and women in the military services, especially those who are in foreign countries, in combat areas, or at sea, are sometimes separated from loved ones for long periods. They have good reason to send a recorded message— especially if telephones are not available or are too expensive—and they also enjoy receiving a recording.

Children and grandchildren can brighten the day of an elderly person who lives far away by sending an audio or video recording—perhaps a family message in which everyone takes a turn saying something. Students also enjoy sending voice letters, particularly if they don't like to *write* letters. If you goof while you're making the recording, it's easy to record over your words. Take care, however, not to erase or record over someone else's recording to you until you've jotted down the contents or sent a reply.

Social Models

Remember when you learned to write? You've probably forgotten, but at least you'll recall that we all learned to write personal and social letters before we learned to write business letters, which for most of us worked out just fine. That first letter to Santa Claus and all the letters that followed were good training for the coming challenges of business writing. Of course, if we didn't handle our personal and social correspondence correctly, we probably carried over all our bad habits to our business writing.

You can probably guess what I'm leading up to: Yes, like business writing, social writing has rules too. Sorry. We can't seem to get away from those evil rules. Although people who are tactless or messy in their social letters won't risk losing a customer, as they might in business, they may lose a friend or the respect of someone important to them. Anyone with a healthy sense of pride should want to avoid that.

Social correspondence is also important in other ways. In particular, personal and social letters help people to bond and maintain lasting connections in a highly mobile society. E-mail, though considered less personal by some people, nevertheless makes a contribution, too, because it connects people rapidly—as quickly as a telephone call—over long distances. In the future, it will be used even more to foster twenty-first-century relationships.

The social models in this chapter are examples of the messages people write not on behalf of their employers but at home or in a social group. In addition to the models given here, the collection of business models earlier in the book includes examples that you can tailor to personal-business and social situations.

For example, you may need a sample of a *follow-up* letter if your order for a new breadmaker is ignored. Perhaps you want to send out a lot of *inquiries* about available homeowner's insurance. Or you may be ready to make a *reservation* for a night at the theater. Turn to the business models for such examples. But instead of writing the letters on company letterhead, prepare them on personal stationery or plain bond paper.

You'll notice that some salutations in the following models end with a comma and some with a colon. How do you know when to use which? Easy. Use a comma if your letter is a personal message to a family member or a close friend. Use a colon if your letter is a personal-business letter, such a letter to your telephone company about your resident phone bill. Also use a colon if your letter is written to someone you know, or know of, socially and is about a social matter, such as holding a benefit to raise money for charity. For more about salutations, see **SOCIAL CORRESPONDENCE: Personal format** and **REFERENCE SECTION: Letter Salutations**.

Announcements

Let's start the models on familiar territory with an especially common social activity: making birth, engagement, wedding, and other announcements. If you haven't sent such announcements, I'll bet you've at least received them. As with business announcements, many of the social announcements we make are formal or at least semiformal, although some are informal.

For example, you might use a formal card to announce a birth or a wedding, but you might prefer an informal letter to announce a divorce or a new address. Printers have numerous samples of modern and traditional announcements, and stationery stores have commercial cards that you can purchase for events such as a birth.

Adoption. As you know, nowadays single men and women as well as married couples adopt children. In either case, those who adopt the child often send an announcement to family and friends. You may use fill-in commercial cards to make the announcement, or if you insert the word *adopted* or *adoption* in an appropriate place, you may have standard announcements printed. The wording in the next example is suitable for a basic card that you would order from a printer:

Ms. Holly Knight

is proud and happy to announce

the adoption of

Michael

age, twelve months

Birth. Excited parents are usually eager to tell the world about the latest addition to their family. You would usually send such announcements to friends and relatives very soon after the event. (Although no gift is required with a birth or other announcement, recipients should send a note of congratulations.) The fill-in commercial cards from stationery stores are less expensive than those prepared by a printer. However, many of these cards have designs that may be too gaudy or cute to suit you. In that case, a more conservative card ordered from a printer may seem more tasteful. You could also design and print your own announcements by computer. If you want to send something simple, follow this example:

Mr. and Mrs. Jonathan Q. Piper

take pleasure in announcing

the birth of a daughter

Natalie

on Monday, March second, 200X

Death. Sometimes it just isn't practical to call or write to everyone who should know about a death. Fortunately, you can put a notice in the newspaper. Since the announcement has to be made immediately, you can fax or e-mail it, deliver it, or read it over the telephone. In the following example, you could use or omit words such as *beloved* and *devoted,* as preferred:

CATALASE—Samantha Catalase, on October 6, 200X. Beloved wife of Martin, loving mother of Dennis and Lauren. Services Tuesday, October 10, 2 p.m., at Resthaven Funeral Home, 62 Grove Avenue, Culver City. In lieu of flowers, please send contributions to the Cancer Society.

Divorce. Although you probably wouldn't send cards *celebrating* your divorce—even if you were breaking out the bubbly at home—you would likely notify friends and relatives who should know. If nothing else, you might have to send them a change of address and, in the case of women, explain a name change. If you're not in the mood to write newsy letters discussing the matter, simply send printed change-of-address cards and add a brief, handwritten comment referring to the divorce. For cards to persons who might not recognize your maiden name, add your former married name in parentheses:

Sheila Strobe

(formerly Mrs. Delbert Brighton)

has changed her address to

45 Ryan Boulevard

Roslyn Heights, NY 11577

At the bottom of the card, you might handwrite: "I just wanted to let you know, Aunt Agnes, that Del and I were recently divorced, and I have a new address in a lovely neighborhood. Do write sometime."

Engagement. This is a happier event than the previous two examples. You may personally and informally announce an engagement by letter to friends and family and, if desired, by newspaper notice. For the newspaper announcement, you may fax or e-mail it, deliver it, or read it over the telephone. However, the woman's parents usually make the formal announcement. When only one parent is living, add a sentence such as "Miss Louisa Raintree is the daughter also of the late Mr. Bertram Raintree." If the parents are divorced, add something such as "Miss Louisa Raintree is the daughter also of

Mr. Bertram Raintree of Baltimore." If both parents are living and not divorced, follow this example:

> Mr. and Mrs. Bertram Raintree of Blue Ridge Summit, Pennsylvania, announce the engagement of their daughter, Louisa Raintree, to Mr. Clifford Zebra, son of Mr. and Mrs. Elton Zebra of Trenton, New Jersey. A June wedding is planned. Miss Raintree is a graduate of Swallow College. Mr. Zebra is a management consultant at Crain and Forest, Inc., in Philadelphia.

Leaving school. Most of us learn how to cope with problems at an early age. Sometimes, though, the hard part is not handling the problem but telling our parents about it. So what do we usually do? Put it off as long as possible, which often makes it worse. In many ways, the sooner we level with everyone, the better. Lying about something or hiding it will just make our parents angry as well as disappointed:

Dear Mom and Dad,

I have some important news for you and hope that you'll support my decision. First, I'm not on drugs, I'm not getting married, and I'm not in jail! So please don't panic. My big news is that I'm working.

Yep, I'm gainfully employed full time as assistant manager in the video section of the Hale and Hearty Discount Store. This means that I've *temporarily* left school, but I want to emphasize that word *temporarily*. I have every intention of returning in a year or in two years at the most.

The reason I decided to leave school and work is that I couldn't handle both my courses and my part-time job. I could see my grades sinking and knew I had to do something. I also knew that you were already sending me as much money as you could, which I really appreciated. But college is so expensive that none of it—your money, my part-time job—seemed to be enough. So I think I've made the best choice under the circumstances. I'll work a while and save like crazy. Then, as soon as I have enough stashed away, I'll enroll again.

Hope I can count on you to back me up with this. I'll still be young when I return to classes, and in the meantime, my new job will be a fantastic experience.

I'll call you soon—I'm off Sundays and Mondays. Till then, DON'T WORRY! It's all working out great, and the job is really cool.

Love,

Wedding. I'm sure you don't expect *everyone* you know to attend your wedding or send a present. So you should send wedding *announcements,* not invitations, to those people. The bride's parents usually send the announcements, but if the groom's parents want to share in or even take over this activity, that's fine. In fact, many people think that it's nice to include both parents. Usually, you would change the wording for a second or later marriage. For a widow, the announcement might read: "Mrs. Laurence Shock and Mr. Jacob Azide announce their marriage." For a divorced woman, it might read: "Mrs. Lucille Avocet and Mr. Benjamin Resile announce their marriage." In the next example of a first marriage, both parents announce the wedding:

Mr. and Mrs. Fabian Carver

and

Mr. and Mrs. Raymond O. Gear, Sr.

announce the marriage of

Martha Anne Carver

and

Raymond O. Gear, Jr.

Saturday, the fifth of June

First Baptist Church

Jackson, Mississippi

Apologies

When I was researching this book, I asked people how many times in the past week they had apologized or received an apology for something. One woman said that she had to apologize seven times and had received three apologies. I don't know about that. I think I'd have to work at it to offend that many people in the short span of a week. I just hope that the number is above average.

However, in the social world, as in the business world, people make mistakes. The best thing to do if that happens is to apologize immediately and offer to make amends. Although you wouldn't write a letter of apology for brushing against someone in a crowded store, you should put an apology in writing—or follow up a spoken apology with a written letter—if something serious happens.

Belated thanks. Saying thank you late is better than not saying it at all. But as a rule, you should always promptly acknowledge gifts, condolences, favors, and other special considerations. Although you may have a legitimate reason for being late, not many excuses are valid. If you were in a coma in a Mozambique hospital, one might assume that you had a good excuse. But when you don't have a valid reason for being late, it's best not to shift the blame or invent something—"I was captured by a UFO" won't work. Just state that you have no excuse and that you're very sorry:

Dear Meg,

I hope that you'll accept my belated thanks for letting Bill and me use your cabin for a weekend. We haven't had that much fun in years!

When I returned, though, my boss called and sent me packing the next morning to our branch office. Instead of writing to you from my hotel room, as I intended to do, I'm ashamed to say that I collapsed in exhaustion each night and put aside everything but sleep. Please forgive me for taking so long to write. I promise to do better next time!

Your cabin, by the way, is wonderful, Meg. I do hope that the four of us can meet there in August, as you suggested. Bill says hello and to tell you how much he appreciated a weekend of peace and quiet—and no telephones.

Hope to see you soon.

Love,

Carport damage. Even if you're not a klutz, one day you may unintentionally damage something that belongs to someone else. Perhaps you'll accidentally crack someone's crystal goblet when you send it flying across the room while gesturing wildly about a recent case of road rage. The only sensible response is to apologize immediately, offer to pay for the damage (if it's strictly your fault), and, when the damage is significant, follow up with a letter repeating your spoken apology:

Dear Steve,

I still can't believe I didn't notice that my battery was boiling over when I parked in your carport Saturday. Although you very kindly insisted that the stain was minor, it was obvious to me, and I certainly do apologize.

Won't you let me send out someone from a local garage to work on it? It didn't occur to me at the time, but perhaps someone could use a solvent to remove the stain. I'll call around and let you know what I discover.

In the meantime, Steve, please excuse my inattention. I guess I was enjoying our visit so much that I just didn't pay proper attention to my car.

Yours,

Dog attack. Pets are as plentiful as weeds where I live, and it often seems that no one obeys the leash laws. Sometimes—leash or not—a dog simply breaks free and goes on a rampage. So if ever your dog gets away from you and tries to eat your neighbor's pet frog or shreds his trousers (your neighbor's, not the frog's), you may have to pay damages as well as apologize. If you don't have a pet under control and it actually attacks someone or if some other serious problem occurs, you should apologize on the spot, offer medical or other assistance, and follow up with a letter of apology. However, from a legal standpoint, if the matter is truly serious, consult your attorney before committing yourself in writing:

Dear Mrs. Derby,

Joe and I still feel terrible about our Pooky biting your beautiful cat, Frosty, in the tail. We're just so relieved that Dr. Algol thinks Frosty will be as good as new in a few days.

We've instructed the animal hospital to send us the current bill for Frosty's office call and the next bill for the one follow-up call that he recommended. In addition, we're having a carton of Frosty's favorite nibbles delivered to your house next week. I realize that this won't make up for Frosty's moment of fright, but I hope you know that we're very sorry it happened and will make certain that Pooky is securely restrained from now on.

With all good wishes to you and Frosty,

Forgotten anniversary. Do you tend to forget special dates? If so, possibly you need to jot them on your calendar each year—for the whole year—right after New Year. When you forget someone's special day, tell the person that you're sorry, but don't hide behind a weak excuse:

Dear Uncle Jon and Aunt June,

My vacation must have brought out the worst in me. I didn't look at my calendar once until today, and then I saw

the big, bold letters I had written by the date July 2:
UNCLE J AND AUNT J'S ANNIVERSARY. I hate myself for
missing such an important day and sincerely do apologize.

This is three weeks late, but—from my heart—
congratulations and all my good wishes for many more
years of happiness!

Always,

Plans canceled. I'm sure that life is hectic for you, as
it is for most people. But even so, we all have to deal
with conflicts and emergencies. For example, it's
thoughtless and rude to cancel plans you made with one
person when a better offer comes along afterward. But
when unexpected legitimate problems arise—perhaps
you break a tooth and have to rush to the dentist—you
may have to cancel your plans. If so, call, apologize, and
follow up with a letter if it means a big disappointment
to the other person:

Dear Alexia,

I'm so sorry that I had to call you yesterday to bow out
of our theater date at the end of the month. As I explained
last night, I just found out that I have to fly to the Coast
that week and can't see any way out of it, much to my
regret. Believe me, I'd rather be going to the theater with
you.

Let me know if your friend Doug can use my ticket. If
not, I'll ask around here and see if anyone I know might
like to meet you there. I'm sure we can turn up someone.
It's a great play.

Have a wonderful time, Alexia. I'll be thinking about you
while I'm knee-deep in boring meetings.

All the best,

Student probation. Even if you're not a parent, you've
probably discovered that children can make life very in-

teresting, occasionally a little too interesting. If your child is the subject of disciplinary action, it's entirely proper for you to investigate to see whether the charges are warranted. If they are, don't defend bad behavior. Send a letter to the school principal or superintendent apologizing for any problems the child has caused. You can prepare this letter in a business format (see **REFERENCE SECTION**) on personal stationery or plain bond paper:

Dear Mr. Coffin:

We were distressed to learn that Harvey has been placed on probation, although we understand the reason for your action.

Like you, we don't condone outright malicious destruction and realize that counseling may be needed. We're prepared to cooperate in any way possible to ensure Harvey's return to responsible behavior, and we've already discussed this entire matter with our son.

Please accept our apologies for the problem you and the other teachers have experienced. We hope that there will be a big improvement in the coming weeks.

Sincerely,

Complaints

Although no one likes a chronic complainer or troublemaker, it's okay to point out something that's wrong. Often, it's a mistake not to register a complaint. *How* you go about registering the complaint is the real issue.

If you're really angry about something—and perhaps you should be—and you vent your rage on the responsible person or company, you may ruin your chances of getting a satisfactory resolution. So that's not a good idea. If your letter sounds levelheaded and objective, the reader will probably respond much more favorably. Prepare your letter on personal stationery or plain bond paper.

Billing. You may have seen the notices enclosed with some statements describing your rights and what to do in case of an error. When you write about an error, however, present proof if you can. Once my first electric bill in a new house was 80 percent more than that for succeeding months, and I was certain that the utility company was billing me for some of the previous resident's usage or that there was another problem. But I forgot to read the meter when I moved in and therefore couldn't prove it, so the utility company refused to make an adjustment. With some matters, such as a credit card error, there should be no problem if you kept the original sales slip:

Ladies and Gentlemen:

SUPERSAVER CARD NO. 616-232-437-010

My December credit card statement contains an error in one of the charges.

The jewelry department item is charged at $93.89 for a watch purchased on November 6, 200X. However, the watch was on sale at $39.89, and this amount was correctly recorded on my sales slip at the time of purchase (copy attached). I therefore have deducted $54 from the total bill, the amount of the overcharge, and am enclosing my check for the corrected total of $189.73.

Please credit my account for the amount of the overcharge. Thank you.

Sincerely,

Damage. As you know, you should always notify the responsible parties immediately when someone causes damage to your property. When you can prove who did it and how it happened, your chances of being compensated are much better. At times, though, numerous persons or companies, through some repeated action, eventually cause some things to deteriorate. You can't then assign blame to any one source. Therefore, it's not likely that a specific party will reimburse you for the damage, but you have nothing to lose by contacting all the parties you can identify and asking for cooperation in resolving the problem:

Ladies and Gentlemen:

We've experienced a serious problem caused by trucks, including your garbage trucks, cutting across the northwest corner of our driveway when turning from Peach Street onto Ponderosa Drive. As a result of this, the entire northwest corner of our paved drive has split off, and the edge is beginning to crumble with repeated abuse.

The streets are very narrow in our development, and drivers of large trucks find it easier to cut across our drive to turn the corner. It isn't necessary, though, since even large moving vans have managed to avoid our driveway while turning. We suspect that the truck drivers are in a hurry and simply don't take time to maneuver carefully.

Unfortunately, the repair cost to us is too great to allow this to continue. We must therefore insist that your drivers be instructed to avoid crossing our property, and if those instructions aren't followed, hereafter we'll expect reimbursement for repairs.

With your cooperation, we hope to solve this problem before any further costly damage occurs. Thank you for your help.

Sincerely,

Defective product. It's always smart to report immediately any problems with a product that you purchase. If you buy the item locally, you may be able to report the problem or return the product in person. Otherwise, you'll have to handle the matter by telephone or letter. If the item is new and the seller is reliable, you'll probably get a replacement or a refund or credit. However, you usually can't return sale merchandise, although you can send a letter of complaint and hope for the best. If you weren't given instructions with the purchase, address your letter to the manager of customer service:

Dear Customer Service Manager:

Less than four months ago we purchased a Mr. Robot self-propelled lawnmower from your company. The machine has operated erratically since we received it, either stalling continually or running too fast. During the ninety-day warranty period we took it to the nearest authorized service center, but the problem was never corrected.

Last week Mr. Robot lived up to its name. As if it had a mind of its own, it lurched from my husband's grip, sped across our lawn (with all of my family in pursuit), shaved our neighbor's beloved bed of iris to the ground, and nearly demolished two lawn chairs while the occupants fled for their lives. Although the mower was on sale under your no-refund policy, I'm sure you'll agree that this Mr. Robot is clearly defective, and we believe we're entitled to a replacement or a refund.

If you'd like to have the machine returned to your company for inspection, we'd be delighted to remove it from the premises immediately upon receipt of forwarding instructions from you.

Thank you.

Sincerely,

Delivery. It's one thing when occasional orders aren't filled on time, but it's something else when daily or weekly deliveries are unreliable. If this problem involves something you don't need or can easily get somewhere else, you can simply cancel your order. But if you want to continue, a letter of complaint may nudge someone to straighten out the problem:

Dear Circulation Manager:

We ordered daily home delivery of the *Cavalier News* one month ago today. Although service began promptly the day after we placed our order, we've received the paper only about three days in each week. Even though we call each day that the paper is not delivered to report it, delivery service hasn't improved.

We notice a large turnover in the delivery boys and girls on this route. It may be difficult for newcomers to learn all of the addresses so quickly. However, this doesn't solve our problem. It's too expensive to subscribe to a paper that we receive only 40 percent of the time, not to mention the aggravation of waiting continually for a paper that never comes.

Please telephone us at 555-0179 or let us know by return mail whether you can correct this problem immediately. If you can't provide what we've paid to receive, we'll have no alternative but to cancel home delivery. We enjoy the *News*, however, and would certainly prefer a satisfactory resolution to the problem.

Thanks very much for your help.

Sincerely,

School. Everyone knows that parents of school-age children deal with many concerns and frustrations. It may be more common for the school to alert the parents about problems, but it could be the other way around. If you notice a problem concerning your child, and the school hasn't contacted you, it's proper—and possibly very important—to contact the school. Write to the principal or superintendent about most matters:

Dear Ms. Limn:

Recently, our son Rusty confided in us that he and other students have a great deal of trouble working and concentrating in study hall.

According to Rusty, the study hall tables are usually overcrowded during the afternoon period, and the students who arrive last are forced to sit in tight rows of chairs along the walls. The level of noise and disruption is apparently higher because of the overcrowding.

Although we realize that the school has strict budget limitations, it isn't clear to us why this problem hasn't been corrected or even recognized. The inability to study is a serious handicap to those students who have a genuine desire to learn. We're certain that Rusty is only one of many in this category.

We believe that this issue should be addressed at the next meeting of the school board. If parents should become involved financially or in some other way, we'd like to have you report this to us. In any case, we hope to see a solution to the problem very soon.

In the meantime, please let us know if we can do anything to help. We appreciate your efforts on behalf of the students.

Sincerely,

Unsatisfactory service. Poor service is hardly uncommon nowadays, and complaints aren't always effective. But if you don't speak up, no one will know, and the situation may not improve by itself. Overworked personnel, carelessness, and lack of pride in performance all contribute to poor service. However, an organization that wants to provide good service will probably welcome any constructive notice of problems:

Dear Postmaster:

My neighbors and I have been experiencing a mail-delivery problem in Rose Valley that we'd like to bring to your attention.

Some of us have repeatedly had our mail delivered to a neighbor's address. Since this has become a regular problem, we're obviously alarmed, especially because many of us have checks, interest statements, and other important items sent to us by mail. Several times a week I get someone else's mail in my box, and neighbors give me pieces of my mail that were left in their boxes.

The problem is probably due to having various substitutes working on an unfamiliar route. No doubt it's difficult for them. But even so, there must be some way for the mail to be handled more responsibly. The ongoing and excessive carelessness is very disturbing to us, and we believe it's fair to ask for greater care in the handling and delivery of our mail.

We appreciate your help and hope that some improvements will be forthcoming. Thanks very much.

Sincerely,

Congratulations

When something special happens to a neighbor, friend, relative, or someone else you know in the community, write an enthusiastic congratulatory message right away. Notice the word *special*, because I don't mean that you should congratulate someone for knowing enough to come in out of the rain. For the message to mean anything, the occasion should be something rare, important, or meaningful.

You'll want to be certain that the tone of your message is genuine and sincere. But the message can be brief and, in fact, shouldn't discuss anything else, unless it's part of a very informal letter to a family member. Generally, though, you should focus on the person's special situation and never detract from that by discussing other news.

You may use personal stationery, foldover cards or paper, or commercial congratulations cards (if you add a handwritten message). If you were congratulating a member of the community who won an election, for example, you might prepare the letter on personal stationery or plain bond paper. Such a letter could be set up in one of the business formats illustrated in the **REFERENCE SECTION**. But if you were congratulating your cousin on the birth of a son, you should handwrite the note on personal stationery, a foldover card or paper, or a commercial card.

Anniversary. It's thoughtful to remember friends and relatives on their anniversary—any anniversary, not just the obvious ones (silver or golden). Older people especially like to be remembered. In fact, if you forget, you may find that the celebrants are a little miffed at you. If you purchase a commercial anniversary card, remember to personalize it by adding your own handwritten message:

Dear Marlene,

How wonderful that you're celebrating your tenth wedding anniversary Friday! Whatever your plans are, I hope that you have a perfect day together.

Congratulations to both of you, and may you have many more years of happiness.

Affectionately,

Article. When people accomplish something extraordinary—win an award, write a best-seller, fly around the world in a balloon—it's nice to send a warm message of congratulations. Just put yourself in their place: You'd probably be thrilled, too, and it would add to your enjoyment if others shared in your moment of glory. If you don't know the person very well, you can use plain bond paper or personal stationery and prepare the letter in a business format:

Dear Ms. Arbor:

I just read your article "The Homeless: America's Secret Shame" and can't emphasize enough how impressed I am. Finally, someone has zeroed in on the fact that problems aren't solved by sweeping them under the rug. Until we accept that, the problem will only fester and grow.

Your outstanding article is an important contribution to contemporary social thought, and I think it's superb. Heartiest congratulations!

Cordially,

Birth. I'm sure you'll agree that the birth of a child is a big event. Okay, for some of you it can't compare to the birth of your Snoopy or Tiger, so let's just agree that, in general, being born is a big deal. Therefore, when you receive a birth announcement, send an immediate handwritten message or, if you prefer, a handwritten note on a commercial card:

Dear Linda,

Your exciting news really made my day! You must be so thrilled and happy. Just imagine, a daughter—and what a beautiful name: Myra. I love the sound of it.

Congratulations to you and Fred, and I wish you both much joy and a lifetime of happiness with your daughter.

Fondly,

Election. As you've no doubt witnessed, many campaigns for election to an office are grueling affairs, and whoever wins deserves recognition for the achievement.

That goes for someone elected to a school board or a church council as well as to the U.S. Senate. If you don't know the person well, you can prepare a message on personal stationery or plain bond paper in a business format. If it's a close friend, handwrite or type a warm message on personal stationery:

> Dear Dan,
>
> I knew you could do it! I'm so glad that the citizens of our community had the good sense to elect you to our City Council. Congratulations on winning a tough contest! You're the right person for the job, and everyone I know is applauding your victory.
>
> If ever you need additional support, Dan, you can always count on me. Best wishes for a successful and rewarding term.
>
> Regards,

Engagement. Let's say that someone you like has become engaged, but you despise the other person. Nevertheless, a rule of etiquette is that you should enthusiastically and unconditionally express your very best wishes. If you're truly convinced beyond a shadow of doubt that the other person is wanted in a dozen states for murder and armed robbery, you can and probably should voice your concern (to the police, not only your friend), but otherwise, as the saying goes, forever hold your peace. When you write to the woman to wish her happiness, ask her to pass along your congratulations to the man, too, or simply wish them both happiness:

> Dear Jenny,
>
> Dave and I were so happy for you when you called last night to tell us about your engagement to Harry. He's a very lucky man, as I'm sure he knows. I'll bet that you're both on top of the world.

It was wonderful to hear your news, and we want to wish you both much happiness.

Lots of love,

Promotion. Like a new venture, new contract, or new assignment, a promotion means a lot to the person who gets it. So relatives, friends, and neighbors should contribute to the happy occasion with a sincere word of congratulations. You may handwrite your letter on personal stationery or type it on plain bond paper:

Dear Ray,

I had a feeling that one day I'd be living next door to the general manager of the Antler Packaging Company. Congratulations!

That title fits you perfectly, because no one is better qualified to take on such an important post or is more deserving of it. Antler is very lucky, indeed, to have you in charge.

Nell and I are excited for you, Ray, and we want to send you our good wishes for much success in your new position.

Regards,

Holiday Wishes

Have you noticed that Americans are in love with holidays? Of course, people in other countries are too. But where I live, our few national holidays apparently aren't enough for some people, because I get all sorts of social greetings, from "Happy Summer" to "Happy Groundhog Day" to "Happy Monday" (Tuesday, Wednesday, and so on). Many people use commercial cards for the main national holidays. But some prefer to send a separate letter along with or instead of the card. Sometimes it's hard to find a card for the occasion, such as Chinese New Year, so a letter may be the only choice.

A letter to a close friend, family member, or other relative might be long, newsy, and very personal. But a letter to a neighbor or a member of the community, such as a minister, would probably be a brief one- or two-paragraph message.

It's fine to send religious cards as long as they're appropriate for the person receiving them. Otherwise, use a *general* seasonal card that doesn't mention a religious holiday. In all cases, it's important to personalize a commercial card by adding a handwritten message.

The following holiday messages may be handwritten on personal stationery or added to a commercial card.

Christmas. Although many Christians celebrate the *religious* aspect of Christmas, I know plenty who emphasize the *commercial* aspect—the partying, gift giving, and general holiday merriment. Messages to Christians, therefore, may or may not emphasize the religious meaning, as appropriate. The following message—suitable for a separate letter or a handwritten note added to a commercial card—takes a general approach:

Dear Sharon and Lloyd,

I'm so glad it's almost Christmas because I know that I'll be seeing both of you at Charlie's party.

Until then, I just wanted to say that I hope both of you and the children have a very Merry Christmas and a Happy New Year!

As ever,

Easter. As you know, Christians commemorate the Resurrection of Jesus on Easter Sunday, and some exchange Easter cards or separate letters. The tone and message for this day are primarily religious and not commercial, although I for one am always *very* concerned about the Easter bunny's plans:

Dear Donna,

Keith and I want to send you our very best wishes for Easter and all of the days that follow. We hope that the love and beauty of the Easter season will be with you throughout the rest of the year.

Always,

General. When you don't think a religious message is quite right for a certain holiday, or if you simply don't know a person's religion, you can send a commercial card with a general holiday or seasonal message. The nice thing about a general message, such as "Holiday Greetings" or "Peace" is that Christians, Jews, and others can send them to one another:

Dear Mel,

Happy holidays! This is such a great time of the year that I feel like sharing my good wishes with everyone.

I certainly hope that you have a wonderful holiday season, Mel. Let's hope for peace, joy, good health, and prosperity—for all.

Yours,

New Year. New Year's Day is a legal holiday in all states, so you may use the occasion to send greetings to virtually anyone. Because Christmas and Hanukkah precede New Year's Day, most people send general holiday wishes rather than separate greetings for both the religious holiday and New Year's Day. However, if you prefer, there's nothing wrong with sending separate New Year's greetings, such as the following message to neighbors or other acquaintances. The tone in this example is more reserved than would be the case with a personal note to family and close friends:

Dear Dr. and Mrs. Boule,

Now that 200X is almost here, we want to wish you both a very Happy New Year.

We hope that you have a wonderful celebration on the first, followed by a year of peace, good health, and happiness.

Cordially,

Pesach. The Feast of the Passover (Pesach) commemorates the escape of the Jews from Egypt. Some people send messages only for Hanukkah (Festival of Lights), which commemorates the purification of the Temple of Jerusalem. But the holy day of Pesach and other Jewish religious days are also occasions for thoughtful messages. The following one is appropriate for a family that observes the occasion with devotion:

Dear Anita,

Mike and I want to wish you and your family a joyous Pesach celebration. We truly hope that God's grace will make this day and others to follow especially happy for all of you.

Affectionately,

Thanksgiving. Although this is supposed to be a day to recognize how fortunate we are and to give thanks for our many blessings, for many it's mostly a time to get together with family and friends and pig out—or turkey or tofu out, as the case may be. But some people send commercial cards, and others use the occasion to send a separate goodwill letter. Those who can't be present at family reunions, church dinners, and other gatherings may write a sorry-I-can't-be-there message:

Dear Aunt Ruth,

Since I can't be there to say it in person, I'm writing to wish you Happy Thanksgiving! I know that you'll have a

house full of children and grandchildren for the big feast.
Wish I could be there with you.

Have a wonderful day, Aunt Ruth, and give my best to
everyone.

Love,

Introductions

If you read the examples in **BUSINESS MODELS:
Introductions**, you'll see that social introductions are
very similar to business introductions. In both cases you
put in touch two parties who might enjoy or benefit from
meeting each other. Your letter should focus primarily
on those things of interest to the reader and shouldn't
go off on a tangent about trivial matters. In other words,
you needn't supply a complete history or biography of
each person. Above all, strictly avoid making one person
feel obligated to meet the other person.

You would usually prepare introductions to a club or
other organization on personal stationery or plain bond
paper, using one of the business formats illustrated in
the **REFERENCE SECTION**. But you might introduce
one friend to another with a handwritten note on personal stationery.

Club membership. If you're a member of an organization—is there anyone who isn't?—you may want to introduce someone to the club's officers as a prospective
guest speaker or member or simply as a friend. Include
useful background information—"He's a great guy" isn't
enough—pertinent to the club you're addressing:

Dear Chan:

I'd like to introduce Lester Mew as a candidate for
membership in the Forest Hills Sports Association. I've given

him an application to complete and submit, and I hope that you'll be able to consider it at the next board meeting.

Les, a former college friend, moved to Forest Grove last year, and we did a lot of cross-country skiing this past winter. He's a real sports enthusiast with an interesting background in downhill and cross-country skiing as well as mountain climbing.

Les would fit in well with our group, and I'd like to bring him with me to our next meeting. It will give you and the rest of the executive committee an opportunity to meet him before voting on his membership.

I'm looking forward to seeing you in a couple of weeks.

Best regards,

Idea. People introductions are the most familiar kind of social introduction, but who says you can't introduce an idea? To do this, simply write to the appropriate person, explain what you have in mind, and give a good reason why the idea should be considered or adopted:

Dear Suzanne,

I just had a thought for cleaning up the vacant lot that Mr. Gumby agreed to let us use for a playground in our development. Instead of going door-to-door for donations to hire a yard service, why don't we have a neighborhood cleanup party?

At bridge last Tuesday, we were talking about a block party. Instead of that, how about expanding it to include the entire development for an evening of work and play? We could all pitch in for an hour or two to rake and mow and then conclude with an outdoor barbecue for everyone who helps.

We'll have to ask for donations later to get the playground equipment, so it would be nice to avoid it for the cleanup. We could send a form letter to everyone asking for volunteers to bring some cleaning tools and hamburgers, wieners, or a prepared dish to contribute to the meal. It could be a lot of fun.

Let me know what you think, Suzanne. Perhaps you could sound out people on your block, and if it looks promising, we could form a volunteer committee to set it up.

Best wishes,

New neighbor. In our mobile society, I assume that most of us at one time were newcomers in a neighborhood. Or have you always lived where you now live? Anyone else who moves to a new area often depends on the nearest neighbors for introductions to other persons, clubs, churches, and so on. It's always thoughtful to help a newcomer by making introductions in person or by letter to various people in the community. If the people you contact aren't close friends, you may set up this type of letter the same as a business letter:

Dear Mrs. Sleigh:

I'm happy to introduce to you my new neighbors, Helen and Morris Rider.

The Riders are a delightful couple who operated the Rider Bookstore and Newsstand in Montpelier before retiring here. Helen is an avid reader, and Morris is a serious golfer. Both have many other interests, however, such as nature study and hiking. They also support many charities and have already inquired about local volunteer needs.

As reference librarian at the Public Library, you'll no doubt soon meet Helen when she visits the library. I'm sure that she'll be a daily caller, in fact. Considering her love of books, the two of you will have a lot in common. I hope that you'll join me in making the Riders welcome and that you'll enjoy meeting them as much as I did.

Cordially,

Personal friend. If you want to do a favor for a friend who is traveling to another city, send a letter of introduction to someone you know there. The letter shouldn't make the resident feel obligated to meet your traveling friend, however. But there's nothing wrong with creating the opportunity for the two to get together and then let them decide what to do. Give the reader more specific information about the person than "she's a lot of fun." After all, the reader will already be assuming that she isn't deadly dull and depressing, or you wouldn't be introducing her:

Dear Judy,

My good friend Dee Woodbine will be in Fort Lauderdale April 9–11. She's such a delightful, interesting person that you might like to meet her while she's there.

Dee writes all those hilarious messages that you read on the Uncle Chuckles line of Meteor Greeting Cards. You may have noticed that I always send you one of their gems on your birthday! Dee is just as funny in person as she is on the cards, and she knows a lot of equally fascinating people. She also has an insatiable curiosity about everyone and everything, so she would probably soak up everything you could tell her about life in sunny Florida.

If your schedule isn't full at that time, Judy, you can call Dee (or leave a message) at the Leisure Star Report, 555-6799. I know that she'd really enjoy your company.

All good wishes.

Fondly,

Service. We probably all complain too much about bad service and don't say enough about good service. It's the old story about taking good things for granted. So this example about good service may be less common than a letter of complaint about bad service. In any case, if you want to introduce a service to family, friends, and others in the community, give an accurate, honest description with information of interest to the reader:

Dear Mr. Court:

At the last PTA meeting you mentioned the problem the school experienced last year in having its large school banners professionally cleaned. Since then, I have arranged to have a banner cleaned for my son's fraternity and was pleased with the results.

I used a dry cleaner on the west side of town. The disadvantage is that it's a little farther to drive, but I've concluded that it's well worth the extra time. Top-Notch Cleaning Professionals at 23 West End Drive did an outstanding job for me. Its prices are competitive with other dry-cleaning establishments, and it offers the same one- to two-day service on routine jobs.

Following my first pleasant experience with Top-Notch, I returned on several occasions and was fully satisfied each time. Perhaps this is the answer for the school if you're still having problems.

If you'd like to know more about Top-Notch, I'll be happy to answer any questions you have. You can reach me days at 555-6108 and evenings at 555-2951.

Best wishes,

Volunteer work. I don't know how you feel about volunteer work, but certain organizations are always in need of volunteers. Even if you don't have time to be a volunteer, you can help by introducing people who are looking for volunteer work. The following letter may be prepared on personal stationery or plain bond paper in a business format:

Dear Ms. Fleck:

It's a pleasure to introduce Sam Port to you as a possible volunteer counselor at the Community Building. He'll be calling you next week to inquire about your needs.

Sam was a social worker in New York before moving here and is now a part-time counselor at the Drug Rehabilitation Center. When the need arises, he hopes to increase his hours to full time at the center, but until then, he'd be happy to offer his services at the Community Building.

Although I'm not completely familiar with Sam's professional credentials, I do know that he's a thoughtful, intelligent, and reliable individual who has always impressed me as someone you would like to be around—personally and professionally.

If you'd like to know more, feel free to call anytime at 555-0738.

Cordially,

Invitations

Purely social invitations look a lot like social-business invitations, so if you want to see more examples, glance at **BUSINESS MODELS: Invitations**. There and here, you'll see that formal and informal invitations are very different.

Informal social invitations, which are phrased in the first person (*I'd like to invite you . . .*), are often hand-written in a letter format, usually on white, off-white, or conservative pastel personal stationery or on foldover cards or paper. Envelopes should be at least 3½ by 5 inches to meet minimum-size postal requirements.

A casual letter to family members or close friends might be typed, if you prefer, or you might use commercial fill-in cards (where you pen in the person's name and other information), available in stationery stores. Commercial cards are often used for informal events such as a cocktail party, barbecue, or luncheon.

Formal social invitations, which are phrased in the third person (*Mr. and Mrs. Horace Rivers cordially invite you . . .*), are often printed or engraved, but they also may be handwritten in a formal invitation format on plain (no address) personal stationery or a foldover card. Since engraving is rarely used anymore, the printed versions sometime have raised letters that resemble engraving. Although the address is not printed on paper or cards used for formal invitations, a coat of arms may be embossed on the invitations (if no color is used for it).

All lines may be printed on a formal invitation, or only certain lines may be printed, with the others left blank. When some lines are left blank, you would later pen in the guest's name and other information. In either case, though, you should indicate in the lower right corner if formal dress (black or white tie) is required. Also, you should spell out in full the names, states, and time (*half past,* or *after, seven o'clock,* not *7:30 p.m.*) and always include personal or professional titles, such as *Mr., Mrs., Miss, Ms.,* or *Dr.* (Although the traditional form *Miss* is correct, most single women prefer the use of *Ms.*)

If you want a reply, put *R.s.v.p.* (please reply) in the lower left corner of the invitation. However, nowadays senders often enclose small reply cards with formal invitations, such as wedding invitations, so that the recipients don't have to write out formal replies.

The proper time for mailing invitations is as follows: four to six months ahead for a dinner or other important event with out-of-town or out-of-country guests, three to five weeks for lunch or dinner with local guests, and two to four weeks for events such as a cocktail party or reception with local guests.

The following models illustrate a few of the main types of invitations and replies. For detailed information about this subject, however, consult a current etiquette book. The larger handbooks have numerous examples of invitations and replies, as well as extensive information about the do's and don't's of entertaining.

Benefit. Do you like to dance? Let's assume that you and others in your community want to hold a public ball to raise money for a charity. You would send *formal* printed invitations for such an event. If you expect the attendees to buy tickets, state the price on the invitation and give the address where the checks should be sent.

Often people are asked simply to enclose their checks with the reply cards:

> *The Directors of the Unified Aid Society*
>
> *request the pleasure of your company*
>
> *at a Ball*
>
> *to be held at the Community Center*
>
> *on Saturday, the sixth of August*
>
> *at eight o'clock*
>
> *for the benefit of*
>
> *The Community Shelter*

> *Single ticket $25.00*   *Black tie*
> *Couple $50.00*

Dinner. Most private dinners are informal events, but formal affairs are common in the political and diplomatic worlds and in certain business and social situations. You would obviously send formal invitations to a formal official event, but you might also send formal invitations for certain private occasions, such as a wedding anniversary. A formal invitation to a private dinner may be fully printed or partially printed, with the blank lines filled in later. But if you don't like the idea of writing in certain information later, you might use a fully printed invitation that would simply say "requests the pleasure of *your* company," eliminating the need to pen in a guest's name:

> *Mr. and Mrs. Foster Guyot*
>
> *request the pleasure of your company*
>
> *at dinner*
>
> *on the Twentieth Anniversary of their marriage*
>
> *Friday, the twelfth of November*
>
> *at half past seven o'clock*
>
> *307 East Wilshire Avenue*
>
> *Raleigh, North Carolina*

R.s.v.p.

Fill-in card. You may use both formal and informal fill-in cards for a variety of events. People who entertain a lot sometimes prefer partially printed formal cards where later they can quickly pen in miscellaneous information, such as the guest's name, type of event, date, and time. The same principle applies with the informal fill-in cards sold in stationery stores. Although the styles vary, the general fill-in lines resemble those illustrated here. This type of card can be used for a variety of informal occasions, such as cocktails, dinner, lunch, or even a dance:

You Are Cordially Invited

 by   [sender's name]

 for   [event]

 on   [month, day, year]   *at* _ [time]

 at   [street address]

R.s.v.p.
[telephone no., if desired]

Foldover card. Some people use foldover cards or paper (also called *informals*) to send an informal invitation. The invitation is then folded in half to fit envelopes of at least 3½ by 5 inches. You would write the information on the front outside panel, like a brief one-paragraph letter, and sign your name. If the front panel already has your name printed on it, you would simply add the basic data above and below the printed name:

Lunch

Mr. and Mrs. Homer Bovine

Sunday, April 9
12:30 o'clock
162 Prince Street

Regrets only
555-7900

Houseguest. If you want to invite someone to come for a visit and stay overnight or longer, telephone or handwrite a letter on personal stationery in your usual personal letter style:

Dear Jennifer,

Troy and I were wondering if you, Dan, and the children could spend the weekend of September 7 with us. The fall foliage should at least be underway if not at its peak, so we could take a beautiful drive through the country Saturday or Sunday.

It would be nice if you could drive over Friday after work, but if you can't manage that, Saturday morning is fine too. I do hope that you can come. We'd love to see you.

Love from all of us,

Recall. We all know how fast things change in life. So if you've already sent invitations when a complication arises, such as illness, you'll have to cancel plans by telephone or, if you're able and have enough time, by a handwritten or printed recall. If an engagement is broken, for example, you might use this wording, set up in the same style as the original printed invitation: "Mr. and Mrs. Rosamer Portulaca III announce that the marriage of their daughter Angela Portulaca to Mr. Nelson Auklet will not take place." This formal example illustrates one way to *recall* invitations (cancel plans) for a dinner party:

> *Owing to the illness of Mr. Portulaca*
>
> *Mr. and Mrs. Rosamer Portulaca III*
>
> *are obliged to recall their invitations*
>
> *for Saturday, the twentieth of May*

Replies to Invitations

The rules for replying to an invitation are easy. Answer in exactly the same style as that used on the invitation you receive. Therefore, if you get a formal, third-person invitation to a reception, printed or handwritten, you should also reply in the third person—in handwriting on either plain (no address) personal stationery or a plain foldover card or paper.

If someone handwrites a brief letter-style, first-person note, you should send a handwritten, letter-style, first-person reply on personal stationery (either printed with your return address or having no address).

If an invitation lists a telephone number, call with your reply and do not send anything by mail. If no telephone number is given, no *R.s.v.p.* designation is listed, and no reply card is enclosed, you may assume that you're not required to reply (although a telephone call or a note of reply is thoughtful when it involves someone you know at a small gathering).

Many formal invitations include a small, fill-in reply card, such as the model illustrated in **BUSINESS MODELS: Invitations**.˙

With both fill-in reply cards and handwritten formal replies, the main concern of the host is whether people will reply at all or whether they'll do it promptly. Although that may seem a bit childish, the categories of correspondence called *reminders* and *follow-ups* were created out of precisely such a need to pursue unanswered letters, invitations, and other messages.

Some people intend to reply but wait until the last minute in case their plans change. Think how difficult it would be to plan menus, seating, and so on if everyone did that. It's better to reply promptly and, if your plans change, to telephone the sender or quickly write a note of apology.

Accept. A formal, handwritten acceptance follows essentially the same pattern whether it's for a dance, a dinner, or another formal event. The reply should use one of two expressions: "the kind invitation of Mr. and Mrs. Arthur M. Clime, Jr." or "Mr. and Mrs. Clime's kind invitation for":

Captain and Mrs. Howard East

accept with pleasure

the kind invitation of

Mr. and Mrs. Arthur M. Clime, Jr.

for Thursday, the second of September

Combination reply. For some formal events, such as a wedding, where many people will be present, it's okay for one person in a couple to accept and the other to decline an invitation:

Mr. Sherman Hurly
accepts with pleasure
Mr. and Mrs. Estuary's
kind invitation for
Saturday, the sixteenth of June
at one o'clock
but regrets that
Mrs. Hurly
will be unable to attend

Foldover card. To reply to an informal invitation sent on a foldover card or paper, pen your response on your own foldover card or paper. If your name is already printed on the card or paper, you can briefly write at the top "accepts with pleasure" and underneath that line write the day and time (*Saturday at 8*). Or you can write "sincere regrets" below the printed name and underneath write the date but not the time (*Saturday, April 17*). If your name isn't printed on the card or paper, sign it immediately after your regret or accept lines and the date:

Accept with pleasure
Saturday at 8

Helen and Homer Bovine

Modern style. In replying to a *modern* formal invitation, do the same thing that you would do with a *traditional* formal invitation: Imitate the wording of the sender's invitation. For instance, if a wedding invitation refers to "sharing joy," reply with words such as "share your joy." But if the wording is complex or excessive, simply pick out key words such as *celebrate* and use them in the reply: "celebrate with you." If the invitation is issued in the name of the engaged couple rather than the parents, refer to "*your* marriage" rather than "*the* marriage," as illustrated in this example:

> *I will be happy*
>
> *to share in the joy*
>
> *of your marriage*
>
> *on Tuesday, the tenth of June*
>
> *Amy Daub*

Regret. A formal regret should essentially follow the same pattern as that used for an acceptance, except for the "regret" line. Again, you would use the wording "the kind invitation of Mr. and Mrs. William F. Banter" or "Mr. and Mrs. Banter's kind invitation":

> *Drs. Bryce and Shana Hoick*
>
> *regret that they are unable to accept*
>
> *Mr. and Mrs. Banter's*
>
> *kind invitation for dinner*
>
> *on Friday, the thirtieth of October*

Several hosts. If more than one host is named on a formal invitation, repeat all of the names in your handwritten reply. But mail the reply only to the person listed under the *R.s.v.p.* line. If no one is listed there, mail your reply to the first person named on the invitation:

Ms. Elizabeth Numbers

accepts with pleasure

the kind invitation of

Mrs. Moss and

Mrs. Lapboard and

Ms. Sprat

for Wednesday, the eleventh of December

at half past twelve o'clock

Sympathy

This is a sober subject, so it's probably a good thing that the best sympathy messages are brief. If people had to write a lot, they might become too morbid or too philosophical. Those who are grieving shouldn't be led deeper into their sorrow. It's best therefore to indicate only that you were shocked or saddened to learn about the loss or that the family and friends are in your thoughts, with a concluding offer to be of help (if you know the reader well).

Your words should obviously be completely sincere, without even a hint of a flowery or macabre tone. The exact message you use, however, will depend on how well you knew the person who died or how well you know the survivors. For example, the language in a note to someone in the community who isn't a friend or relative would be more reserved.

Write your personal message on personal stationery, foldover cards (ideal for a one- to three-sentence message), or commercial sympathy cards (choose a dignified, quiet design). Socially, sympathy messages are always handwritten, unlike notes to business organizations, which may be prepared by computer and sent from the office, as illustrated in **BUSINESS MODELS: Sympathy**. Messages of sympathy are most often sent when a death has occurred, but you can—and should—send comforting notes at other times of misfortune. For example, if someone's house is destroyed by fire, and you know the person well, you should offer comfort and help in person, perhaps following up with a sympathy note. You might also send a similar encouraging message to someone you didn't know very well. In all matters that are personal, no firm rule exists except that it never hurts to be thoughtful and let other people know that you care.

Death—adult. When someone you know dies, perhaps a neighbor or another member of the community, immediately send a *handwritten* personal message to the family. If you're writing to a relative or close friend, your message would be very personal. Otherwise, you might write something such as this:

Dear Mrs. Wall,

George and I want to send you our deepest sympathy on the death of your husband. I know that he will be greatly missed by many, and we join everyone in sharing your grief during this difficult time.

With sincere sympathy,

Death—child. It's hard to compose a message for someone who just experienced the tragic loss of a child. Whether it's a relative, a close friend, or an acquaintance, you may be certain that the grieving parents will appreciate any message that says you're sharing their pain and sorrow:

Dear Pam,

I'm still stunned by the tragic news, and my heart is filled with sorrow for you and Glen. We all loved Carol and will miss her so very much.

Please call me, Pam, if there's anything I can do to help.

With love and deepest sympathy,

Death—relative. You may write a newsy letter *later* to help the surviving spouse of a relative who died. But your immediate sympathy message should be just that—condolences—and nothing more:

Dear Uncle Carl,

Mother just called to tell me about Aunt Kerri's death, and I know what a terrible blow this is for you.

As much as we all loved Aunt Kerri, I realize that she's finally free from her long suffering, and I hope you'll find some comfort in that thought.

Please let me know if I can do anything to help, Uncle Carl. Although I won't be able to attend the funeral because of my work, I can arrange some time off later and would like to see you.

With love and sympathy,

Misfortune—accident. People who've experienced any misfortune need cheering up, and a note of concern and good wishes to an accident victim means a lot to the person. Unlike condolences following a death, sympathy messages following an accident should be upbeat, focusing on the recovery. You may send your message along with flowers, or you may mail it separately. However, you probably won't send a commercial *sympathy* card for an accident, because most such cards are geared toward bereavement. So if you want to write a brief message on a commercial card, it will have to be a thinking-of-you type of card or, if appropriate, a get-well card:

Dear Louise,

I was shocked to hear from Bill about your accident, but we're all relieved to know that you'll fully recover in time. I'm so sorry, though, that you had to have such a terrible experience.

Bill said that you will be allowed visitors in a few days, so I'll be there to see you soon. In the meantime, I'll be thinking about you, and we'll both be looking forward to your quick and complete recovery.

Love and good wishes,

Misfortune—illness. You may be feeling low, but when someone is ill, the aim of your message should be to lift the person's spirits. The length of your message will depend on how well you know the person. If someone is terminally ill, you obviously wouldn't talk about recovery or dwell on the illness. But you might mention daily pleasures still to come—visits with friends and relatives, television programs, good books, and so on. Even if you call on someone, you should still send a written note. It's always thoughtful, in fact, to send a written message whether or not you know the person well or see the person often. The following model is upbeat but doesn't mention recovery because the patient has a terminal illness:

Dear Catherine,

I was so sorry to hear about your illness, but I'm happy to know that you're getting good care and are resting comfortably now.

Lee tells me there are a surprising number of things you can do that the doctors believe are just fine. That's great! Since you've always been fascinated with stories about the African jungles, I decided to enclose something with this note that might give you a bit of a challenge in that area—a jigsaw puzzle about animals in a famous Kenyan wildlife preserve. All of those tiny pieces to put together just confuse me, but I understand that you've become an expert on puzzles, so good luck!

I plan to stop for a visit sometime next week, Catherine, and will look forward to seeing you then. In the meantime, get lots of rest—and happy puzzling!

Best wishes,

Misfortune—property. It's amazing how many things can go wrong with houses, cars, boats, and other property. In addition, Nature has a way of rendering tremendous losses through tornadoes, earthquakes, hurricanes, fires, floods, and other disasters. When someone loses a lot, a message of sympathy and concern along with an offer to help is especially important to those who suffered the loss:

Dear Mr. and Mrs. Neptune,

We can't begin to tell you how sorry we were to learn that the flood caused almost total damage to your home. I can imagine what a terrible loss it must be.

We all love our homes and our possessions, and the prospect of losing them and starting over would be almost overwhelming. That's why Richard and I want to offer our help in any way we can. We have an extra bedroom, clothes, and miscellaneous furnishings that you're welcome to use as long as necessary. Since we don't know where to telephone you, please feel free to call us immediately at 555-2100.

As your friends and neighbors join forces to offer their help and support, I'm sure that everything will seem a little brighter with each day. In the meantime, please do call if we can help.

With all good wishes,

Sympathy Replies

It's difficult to decide which is harder to compose—sympathy messages or replies to them. Neither one is easy, but both are necessary.

You should acknowledge all *personal* expressions of sympathy, assistance (such as serving as pallbearer), flowers, mass cards, contributions, and any other expression or act of kindness. But you don't have to acknowledge a printed commercial card that has no handwritten, personal message. So the rule is that you should always send a personal, handwritten reply to any personal, handwritten message (or for personal assistance and so on).

You may use commercial reply cards—with no added handwritten message—for the numerous strangers who responded to the death of a prominent person. But if you use those same cards for relatives and close friends, add a brief, handwritten thank you on the card. Incidentally, it's okay to have someone else help you when there are numerous replies to send, and the message should then clarify this: "Mother has asked me to thank you for . . ."

Death—assistance. Family, friends, and neighbors always take time to offer help and emotional support to families who've lost a loved one. Therefore, the least that you can do is to acknowledge such consideration and kindness with a warm, personal thank you:

Dear Peter and Jane,

It's hard for me to imagine how I could have gone through the past week without both of you. Ellen and I always agreed that we couldn't find two nicer friends anywhere.

From the bottom of my heart—thank you for the food you prepared, for helping me meet callers, and for generously lending so much comfort and support.

Affectionately,

Death—flowers. If you've made funeral arrangements for a family member or friend, you'll know that the cards accompanying flowers sent to a funeral home are collected and given to the family after the funeral. This group of cards, in addition to those with flowers sent to the home, provides a partial list of people who should receive acknowledgments. Send a very brief, personal, handwritten thank you on foldover cards, on cards provided by the funeral home, or on commercial acknowledgment cards:

Dear Julia,

    Thank you so much for the beautiful flowers. I did so appreciate your kindness and concern.

Fondly,

Death—message. You should always acknowledge personal, handwritten messages whether they're added to a commercial card or are sent by letter. Put your reply on foldover cards, on cards provided by the funeral home, or on commercial cards:

Dear Mr. and Mrs. Buckle,

    Thank you very much for your kind thoughts. I appreciated all of the nice things that you said about Bill and found it very comforting to know that he had so many thoughtful friends at work.

Sincerely,

Death—printed card. You may use printed acknowledgment cards, such as those supplied by funeral homes, to answer *printed* messages from persons you don't know very well. But if you want to use the same cards for everyone, pen a brief, personal message on the ones going to those who sent you a handwritten note. As illustrated in the following examples, the printed portion of the message may mention the deceased or may just name the persons giving thanks:

The family of J. Nelson Ladder

gratefully acknowledge

your kind expression of sympathy

Mrs. J. Nelson Ladder and family

wish to express their appreciation

for your kind expression of sympathy

Illness—friend. When people visit, you should always acknowledge in person any thoughtful expressions that you receive while recovering from illness or an accident. In addition, follow up in writing when you're able to do so. If you're not able to write, family members should do it for you. An illness or accident will have a strong bearing on how this is handled. Someone in a coma obviously isn't in a position to take care of social obligations. However, if you're able to write your own letters, send a short message of appreciation to those who have sent you gifts or have written thoughtful messages:

Dear Abby and Dick,

What a beautiful bouquet of spring flowers! It arrived today with your cheerful note, which I really enjoyed.

Thank you so much for thinking of me. I believe I'm feeling better already!

Always,

Misfortune—neighbor. Have you noticed that accidents, layoffs, property losses, financial difficulties, and other misfortunes often bring out the best in people? It's not uncommon for relatives, friends, acquaintances, and strangers all to pull together to help. In some cases the names of the people who give time, money, and gifts to help those in need aren't even known. But when you do know their names, send a reply of appreciation for their expressions of sympathy and their kindness. If you're not in a position to do this immediately, say thanks in person when you see them and later, when you're able, follow up with a personal note:

Dear Len,

I want to thank you very sincerely for all the help you gave me when I was out of work after the accident.

Taking care of my family, the house, and the car always seemed relatively easy before I was confined to a wheelchair. Suddenly, nothing was easy! But with your generous help in cleaning out gutters, carrying heavy boxes out of the garage, and doing numerous other chores for me, the recovery period didn't seem as long as I thought it would be.

I really appreciate your thoughtfulness, Len, and hope I can do something in return for you one day.

Regards,

Thank Yous

Everyone take a deep breath. We're moving on from pain to pleasure: responding to gifts and other nice things. From an early age we learn that it's common courtesy to thank someone who gives you something or does something for you. The size of the gift has nothing to do with it. If one relative gives you ten dollars for your birthday and another gives one hundred dollars, you should send both givers a warm, sincere expression of thanks (with money, tell the person what you're going to do with it).

The question often asked is: If you're given something in person and thank the giver at the time, is it still necessary to write a thank you note? Some etiquette authorities believe you *always* must send written thanks whether or not you thank someone in person. Others, however, believe that a *written* note is required (in addition to any in-person thanks) only in response to the following:

Any gift for which you didn't give thanks in person
Get-well gifts (when you're able), except for those from close friends and relatives whom you thank in person
Overnight hospitality, if you don't see the person frequently

Parties given in your honor
Personal condolence messages
Personal congratulatory messages
Very special favors
Wedding gifts

According to some etiquette authorities, a written note is *not* needed in these cases if you thank the giver in person:

Birthday gift
Dinner party
Get-well gifts from close friends and relatives
Holiday gift
Overnight hospitality, when you see the people frequently
Parties at which you're not the guest of honor
Shower gift
Virtually any other gift, except a wedding gift, which always requires a written thank you

All authorities agree, however, that even though you may thank someone in person in these situations, a personal, handwritten thank you note in addition is always in good taste and will no doubt be very much appreciated.

Handwrite your thank you messages on personal stationery, foldover cards, or commercial thank you cards. Send thank you messages promptly (within two to three days) unless illness, injury, or some other complication makes this impossible.

Address your envelope to the person(s) who gave you something or did something for you. With a family, write to the principal parties or the parents and ask them to thank any other family members. When you're given a gift by both husband and wife, address the letter only to the wife, but mention the husband in your thank you line: "I want to thank you and Joe for . . ."

Focus on the gift, favor, or other kindness in your letter. Save news about yourself, your job, or your own family for another letter.

Anniversary wishes. You may be lucky enough to receive gifts on your anniversary, but at least I'm sure you'll get a number of cards and letters. Or perhaps you'll get both. You would obviously thank people for any gifts that you receive, but you should also acknowledge the written messages. When you receive a personal, handwritten message of congratulations and good wishes, write a brief, personal thank you (for longtime friends whom you haven't seen for a while you may want to write more):

Dear Elaine,

What a joy it was to get your thoughtful message. Dennis and I think of you often and have many fond memories of our early years together.

We both send our love and thanks for remembering our anniversary with your kind thoughts.

Affectionately,

Congratulatory message. When you do something truly noteworthy, like discover the secrets of time travel, and people send you letters of congratulations, promptly send them your own personal letter of thanks:

Dear Mason,

Thanks so much for all of those kind words of praise. You're much too generous, but I certainly did appreciate your note of congratulations on my winning the state photographic contest.

Cordially,

Favor. All favors deserve an *oral,* or *in-person,* thank you, right? But a follow-up written message is appropriate and thoughtful too. Very special favors definitely require a written note of thanks:

Dear Marti,

I can never thank you enough for letting the children stay with you and for taking such good care of them while I was in the hospital. With Henry working, it would have been impossible for me to have had the surgery with any peace of mind.

Andy and Sally both loved every minute of their "vacation" at your house, so much so in fact that I'm not sure they really wanted to come home! They probably wore you out, so for all of our sakes, I'm glad that the three weeks in the hospital are over.

Jed and I really appreciate your helping us out, Marti, and we hope that we can do something nice for you one day.

Always,

Newspaper notice. Handwriting is always appropriate and sometimes necessary for *personal* messages. But what should you do when very large numbers are involved? It would be overwhelming to try to respond to everyone with a personal, handwritten message in that case. So on those occasions you might want to purchase space in a newspaper for a general thank you message and send handwritten notes only to close friends and relatives. Newspapers will publish your card of thanks following a funeral, a natural disaster, an anniversary, a political campaign, or any other event that prompts widespread acts and expressions of kindness:

CARD OF THANKS

Mr. and Mrs. Douglas Komondor

wish to express their sincere thanks

to all who offered their kindness

and came to their aid

with gifts and assistance

following the loss of their home by fire

Overnight hospitality. Do you frequently stay overnight with a friend? Then you wouldn't write a thank you note every time you visited. Saying thank you in person would be sufficient. But you should acknowledge infrequent overnight stays in writing in addition to thanking your friend in person:

Dear Mary,

Last weekend was wonderful, Mary. Thank you so much.

It was such fun seeing you and Herb again, and Al and I thought your apartment was absolutely beautiful. Those delicious meals were a real treat for us too. In fact, the entire weekend was perfect, and we do so appreciate your inviting us.

Until we see you both again . . .

Love,

Wedding gift. There's one occasion when you'll definitely get lots of gifts: your wedding. It's always necessary to acknowledge a wedding gift in writing—and do it promptly. Although the excitement of the wedding, leaving for a honeymoon trip, and setting up housekeeping would be captivating to anyone, people should not have to wait weeks and certainly not months to learn whether their gifts arrived safely. If you receive money for a gift, indicate what you plan to purchase with it:

Dear Aunt Dena,

When your very generous gift of five hundred dollars arrived, Tom and I were so pleased! It's really true that most couples starting out in life have many things they need to get all at once. So it's wonderful to be able to go out and select something useful.

Tom and I sat down right after receiving your check and looked at our list of things we need. We both knew immediately what we wanted—a chair for the study. I had been so worried that we wouldn't be able to afford one for a long time, so you can imagine how excited we were with your gift.

Thank you so much, Aunt Dena. We really appreciate your thoughtfulness, and as soon as we've found the right chair, we want you to come for dinner and view our selection firsthand.

With much love from both of us,

Reference Section

This final part of the book has all those lovely technical details that you need to know about letter writing, such as how to write and where to place something called a filename notation in a letter or how to address married women socially. If it seems like too much to remember, look at the various illustrations throughout the chapter, such as the models of letter and memo formats. You may be able to pick up many things just by looking. Most of the other information in this chapter is arranged so that you can check what you need to find out immediately and skip the rest until later.

Letter Formats

Let's start with the three main letter formats used in business: the *block* (sometimes called *full-block*), *traditional* (sometimes called *modified-block*), and *simplified formats*. In the modern-looking block and simplified formats, all parts of the letter are positioned flush left, but in the traditional format, several parts are indented.

The fourth format illustrated here is the *personal format* used for correspondence to family and friends. Use one of the business formats if you're writing a personal-business letter, such as a letter to your bank, or a social message, such as a thank you letter to the person in charge of a community social gathering:

Block Letter Format

March 5, 200X

Confirmation of fax mailed March 6, 200X

Ms. Jo Myrtle
Knoll Consultants, Inc.
100 Main Street
Aurora, IL 60506

Dear Ms. Myrtle:

BLOCK LETTER FORMAT

Here's an example of the clean, modern block format.

To set up this letter, position the principal parts flush left.
Single-space the body, and leave a blank space between
paragraphs and most basic parts.

If you have any questions, Ms. Myrtle, do let me know.
We appreciate your interest.

Sincerely,

Milton Hatch
Manager

jt

Myrtle.ltr

Traditional Letter Format

March 5, 200X

Knoll Consultants, Inc.
Attention Jo Myrtle
100 Main Street
Aurora, IL 60506

Ladies and Gentlemen:

TRADITIONAL LETTER FORMAT

As you can see, this letter differs from the block style in that paragraphs and various other parts are indented. Notice also that the date, complimentary close, and signature are positioned slightly right of the page center.

Although many writers like a more modern-looking format, such as the block or simplified format, the traditional format is popular among conservative writers and organizations.

Sincerely,

Milton Hatch
Manager

jt

Enclosure: List of Guidelines

By fax

Simplified Letter Format

March 5, 200X

Attention Ms. Jo Myrtle
Knoll Consultants, Inc.
100 Main Street
Aurora, IL 60506

SIMPLIFIED LETTER FORMAT

The simplified format, Ms. Myrtle, is easier to use than
any other style. The modern appearance also appeals to
many persons.

Notice that this format does not use a salutation or a
complimentary close. Therefore, to avoid an impersonal
tone, Ms. Myrtle, we suggest that you mention the
addressee's name in the opening and closing paragraphs.

Milton Hatch
Manager

jt

c: Lenore Orchard

P.S. For a free copy of our booklet on formats, send your
request to my attention at the letterhead address. MH

Personal Letter Format

March 5, 200X

Dear Jo,

I thought you might like to have this copy of the personal letter format that our word processing class is using.

It's really the same thing you and I have always used, with a comma after the salutation and no inside address, attention line, or subject line; no typed signature line; and none of those endless concluding notations that you see in business letters. Except for all those missing parts, it looks like the traditional business format, don't you think?

Guess we're up to date, Jo, so if you were worried about it (kidding), you can relax!

Seriously, though, I'm learning a lot in this word processing class. Wish you were taking it too. Have you thought about signing up next semester? It's going to be offered in the evenings, if that would help. Think about it. I know you'd really like it. So if you're interested, let me know, and I'll send a new schedule.

As always,

Memo Formats

I won't even try to guess how many memo formats are available—lots. Three of the most common formats used in business are illustrated here. The first example is a simple *note format.* You've all seen this one and probably use it every day. It's most familiar as the commercial "From the Desk of" or "Memo from" notepaper (usually about half the size of regular letterhead).

The second example is a *standard memo format.* It has introductory guide words—as many as desired—such as *Date, To, From,* and *Subject,* and the sender fills in the appropriate information after each word. No inside address, salutation, complimentary close, or typed signature line is used in a memo, although the same concluding notations used in a letter may be included. Also, if the memo is to go to a group of people, a distribution list may be added two lines below the reference initials. Although memos are not signed like a letter is, senders occasionally pen their initials after the last line of the body or after the person's name following the guide word *From.*

The third example, the *e-mail format,* is almost a duplicate of the standard memo format used for paper mail. However, e-mail software programs have templates consisting of an established heading with the familiar guide words *To, From, Date,* and any others that you might want to add. After those words, though, you would type not only the usual names, date, and so on but also the person's e-mail address. (The e-mail software needs to have this address to know where to transmit the message.) The rest of the memo—body, concluding notations, and so on—is composed the same as a standard memo.

The length of an e-mail message is of greater concern than that of a conventional memo. For example, to make it easier for people to read messages on screen, you should try to limit each message to one principal topic and a single page that will fit on one computer screen. Paper memos, however, may be any length desired:

Note Memo Format

MEMO

from Milton Hatch

March 5, 200X

Jo, the simplest memo format is the small note. Often printed and bound in notepads, this format is popular for brief, informal, sometimes handwritten messages to coworkers and outside business associates.

A wide variety of note formats is available in office-supply stores or can be ordered from printers. However, some companies prefer to design and produce their own supply for employees.

MH

Standard Memo Format

TO: Jo Myrtle   **FROM:** Milton Hatch

SUBJ: Standard Memo **DATE:**   May 5, 200X

Although memo styles vary greatly, Jo, many
formats almost look like a regular letter, except for
the heading.

Paragraphs resemble those in a business letter, and
frequently, they're positioned flush left. Although no
signature line is included, you may write your initials
beneath the last line of the body or after your name
following the "From" guide word. Notations, such as
"Enc.," are positioned at the end, the same as in a letter.

The memo, Jo, was once used only in-house, but
now it's also used for outside correspondence to close
working associates, for transmitting material and
placing orders, and, especially, for e-mail messages.

jt

Distribution:

B. Aztec
G. Carstairs
M. Lincoln

myrtle.memo

E-Mail Memo Format

DATE: March 5, 200X

TO: Jo Myrtle<jmyrtle@jiffy.com>

FROM: Milton Hatch<mhatch@techworld.com>

SUBJECT: E-Mail Memo

Although memo styles vary greatly, Jo, many of the
formats almost look like a regular letter, except for the
heading.

Paragraphs resemble those in a business letter, and
frequently, they're positioned flush left. Although no
signature line is included, you may add your initials
beneath the last line of the message. In personal correspondence, some writers type their first names about
two lines below the last line of the body. Notations, such
as "Enc.," are positioned at the end of the e-mail memo,
the same as in a letter.

The memo, Jo, was once used only in-house, but now
it's also used for outside correspondence to close
working associates, for placing orders and transmitting
material, and, especially, for e-mail messages.

jt

myrtle.doc

c: Dennis Flag

Envelope Formats

Envelope formats don't vary as much as letter or memo formats, perhaps of necessity. The U.S. Postal Service doesn't appreciate strange layouts of data. The *traditional envelope format* is still popular for social correspondence, especially handwritten material, such as a formal invitation. But in business, the *optical-character-reader (OCR) format* is becoming dominant. This format is designed for machine sorting and reading by U.S. Postal Service equipment.

For an OCR format, type the address with normal capitalization and punctuation or in all capital letters without punctuation. Leave a bottom margin of at least ⅝ inch and left and right margins of at least 1 inch. Most recent word processing software used to address envelopes will automatically place the address in the correct location. But if you have any questions, consult your local post office:

Traditional Envelope Format

H. U. Murakami
14 Ocean Avenue
Honolulu, HI 96814

<u>Special Delivery</u>

Ms. Ellen Cornville
400 Central Boulevard
Rockville, MD 20850

OCR Envelope Format

H. U. Murakami
14 Ocean Avenue
Honolulu, HI 96814

JRT 2916-4-32
THE RIGHT CO
ATTN JC RIGHT
14 W 62 ST RM 400
BUFFALO NY 14200

Parts of a Letter

A letter may have as many as fifteen main parts—sixteen if you count the continuation page heading—but it's not likely that you'll use all of them in a single letter.

Date. The date that a letter is composed or dictated (but not necessarily typed). Place the date at the top of the page, two or more lines beneath the letterhead. The traditional business and social style is *August 5, 200X*. The military and, occasionally, some nonmilitary organizations use the style *5 August 200X*.

Personal or confidential notation. An indication that the letter is to be opened and read only by the addressee. Place the notation flush left two lines below the date and about two to four lines above the inside address. (On the envelope, position the notation, in all capital letters, to the left of and two lines above the address block.)

Attention line. Used primarily to ensure that someone will read and act on a letter. Therefore, the letter may be addressed to the firm, but the person in the attention line will read the letter if he or she is there. However, since the letter is addressed to the firm, someone else will read it if the person in the attention line isn't there. You may also address a letter to a specific person, rather than to the firm, and name another person in an attention line. If the addressee is absent, the person named in the attention line will open the letter. Omit titles, such as *Ms.*, in the attention line, and place the line flush left in the inside address, either on the first line of a letter addressed to a firm generally or immediately after the addressee's name in a letter addressed to a specific person:

Attention Rhonda Eastman
Knoll Consultants, Inc.
100 Main Street
Aurora, IL 60506

Ladies and Gentlemen:

Mr. James Short
Attention Jo Myrtle
Knoll Consultants, Inc.
100 Main Street
Aurora, IL 60506

Dear Mr. Short:

Inside address. The name and address of the person to whom the letter is being written. Place the inside address flush left two or more lines below the date. When the addressee's name is unknown, use a job title such as *Manager*:

Director of Research
Dome Institute
1515 North Boulevard
Philadelphia, PA 19100

Ms. Donna Cartwheel
9 Windward Shores
Ottawa ON Canada
K1A 0B1

Mr. Jeb Magnolia
1000 Lantern Road
London WIP 6HQ
ENGLAND

Salutation. A greeting to the recipient, such as *Dear Dr. Wells*. Place the salutation two lines below the inside address flush left. In the simplified style, however, omit it. See **Letter Salutations** for examples.

Subject line. Identifies the topic of the letter. Place the subject two lines below the salutation in the block and traditional formats or three lines beneath the inside address in the simplified format. Although attorneys use the words *In re* or *Re,* other writers in general business use the word *Subject* or follow the contemporary practice of omitting any such introductory word. Do not underline the subject, although you should capitalize the important words or write the line in all capital letters:

Diskette Security

DISKETTE SECURITY

Body. Message portion of a letter beginning two lines below the salutation or subject line in the block and traditional formats and three lines below the inside address or subject line in the simplified format. Single-space the paragraphs and leave a blank line space between them. Type the paragraphs flush left or indent them, depending on the format used.

Complimentary close. A sign-off line, such as *Sincerely,* placed two lines below the last line of the last paragraph in the letter body. But omit the close in the simplified format. See **Complimentary Closes** for examples.

Signature. The name and sometimes the title of the person writing the letter. Place the typed signature four lines below and aligned beneath the complimentary close in the block and traditional formats or five lines below the body in the simplified format. See **Signature Lines** for examples.

Reference initials. Indicates who signed, dictated, and typed the letter. Although reference initials are not required in many offices, if they're used, place them flush left two lines below the typed signature line. You may omit the signer's or dictator's initials when his or her name appears in the typed signature. When all initials are given, though, place those of the person signing the letter first, followed by those of the dictator (if different), and then those of the typist. Use all capital letters for the signer's or dictator's initials: *FRJ:SM:ag.*

Enclosure notation. Indicates material enclosed. Place the notation at the bottom of the letter two lines beneath the reference initials. You may choose from various styles, such as *Enclosure; Enc.; Enclosures; Encs.; Enclosures: Brochure; Under separate cover—Book*:

mk

Enclosures 3

Filename notation. A designation of file or order numbers placed two lines below the reference initials and enclosure notation. You may also put the recipient's number immediately below your own reference. In that case, add the words *Our ref.* (or *Reference*) and *Your ref.* (or *Reference*) for clarity:

mk

Enc.

Our ref.: myrtle.ltr

Your ref.: davis.doc

If you use only your own filename, omit those introductory words:

mk

Enc.

myrtle.ltr

Delivery notation. Instruction for special class or treatment of mail or transmission. Place notations such as *By fax* two lines below the reference initials, enclosure notation, and filename notation:

mk

Enc.

myrtle.ltr

By Federal Express

If your letter is a confirmation copy of a fax sent earlier, rather than a new letter, place a notation to that effect two lines below the date:

August 30, 200X

Confirmation of fax sent August 29, 200X

Copy notation. Indicates where copies are being sent. Put a *regular copy notation* (*c* or *copy*) on the original and all copies. Or instead of using *c* or *copy* for all types of copies, you may use *c* or *copy* for the original printout or typed copy, *fc* for a fax copy, and *pc* for a photocopy. Place a *blind-copy notation* (*bc*) only on the copy going to the designated person and on the office file copy but not on the original going to the addressee. You would use a *bc* when you don't want the addressee to know that the other person is getting a copy. Place copy notations flush left two lines below the reference initials, enclosure notation, and filename notation:

mk

Enclosure—map

myrtle.ltr

c: Ben Hill
   Dee Lake

Postscript. Used for comments unrelated to the subject of the main message but *not* for remarks that you neglected to include in the body. Place it two lines beneath the last notation and place the sender's initials immediately after the last word of the postscript:

mk

Encs.

myrtle.ltr

By UPS

P.S. I thought you might like to see the enclosed booklet on rising medical costs in the United States. RLC

Continuation page. Any page after the first page of a letter. (But do not put the word *continued* or the abbreviation *cont.* at the bottom of the first page.) The heading on a continuation page consists of the addressee's name, the date, and the page number. You may place those facts across the top of the page on one line or stack them, with each line flush left. If the continuation page has a return address or other information printed at the top, begin the typed facts two or three lines below it:

Richard Dice, May 13, 200X, page 2

Richard Dice
May 13, 200X
Page 2

Parts of a Memo

A memo has nine main parts—ten if you count the continuation page heading. As with a letter, you probably won't use all of the parts, especially the many concluding notations, in a single memo.

Heading. Guide words preceding the body. E-mail software has a template that includes these words (and, usually, you can add others, such as *Order No.*, if you like), and paper memo letterhead may have guide words printed at the top of the page beneath the letterhead address: *Date, To, From, Subject,* and so on. You would then fill in the appropriate information after each guide word:

DATE: February 4, 200X

TO: Neil Crow

FROM: Nora Raven

SUBJECT: Annual Meeting

Body. The message of the memo. Prepare the memo body like the body of a letter (see **Parts of a Letter**), with paragraphs indented or flush left, as desired. Since a memo has no salutation, begin the first paragraph two or more lines below the last row of guide words.

Notations. Miscellaneous reference material at the end of the message. Place the notations—reference initials, enclosure notation, filename notation, delivery notation, copy notation, and postscript—in the same position as those in a traditional letter, as described in **Parts of a Letter**.

Continuation page. Follow the guidelines described in **Parts of a Letter**.

Forms of Address

Should you say *Dear Mrs. Forest* in the salutation or *Dear Ms. Forest*? Should you address the letter to *The Honorable Carl Crow* or *Ambassador Carl Crow*? How do you address a letter if you not only don't know a person's name but you also don't know the person's gender? Questions like this can drive you crazy, so I hope that the next long, long list will help you ward off total nail-biting, hair-pulling insanity at least another day or two.

The list gives the proper forms of inside address, salutation, and complimentary close for men and women in general social and business circumstances and for men and women in an official capacity. Although local usage may differ and your office or profession may have other exceptions, the suggested salutation and complimentary close for each person or official in the list is suitable for most social and business correspondence. When a different salutation or close should be used for business and social situations, both are given. See **Letter Saluta-tions** and **Complimentary Closes** for more examples.

The titles that are suggested in the list for women are generally suitable for social and business usage. Some common exceptions are mentioned in the list, but individual women may prefer still a different form of usage than that suggested here. If so, always respect the woman's wishes and use the name and title that she prefers.

Esquire is rarely used in the United States, except occasionally by attorneys. When it's used, omit the personal or professional title before the name: *Edna Antler, Esq.* and *George Swan, Esq.* But don't use *Esq.* in addressing a married couple: *Mr. and Mrs. Joel North* (not *Mr. and Mrs. Joel North, Esq.*).

When an address is included in the list, it's usually a business or office address. However, except when office and home are the same, as with the president of the United States, you would obviously send social correspondence to a person's home address. You would also include the person's spouse in the inside address and salutation if the correspondence involves both of them: *The Right Reverend Dr. and Mrs. Julian Spring; Professor and Mrs. Andrew Holstein.*

Examples of both men and women officials are included in the list, but the only significant difference is in the use of the titles *Ms., Mrs.,* or *Madam* for women and *Mr.* for men. In all cases, when an individual has a professional title such as *Dr., Ambassador,* or *Reverend,* you should substitute it for the personal title:

Men

Business and social. Use *Mr.,* unless the man has a professional title such as *Dr.*:

Mr./Dr. Alfred H. Peace
The True Corporation
Sales Department
[Address]

Dear Mr./Dr. Peace:
Sincerely,

Single Women

Business and social. Use *Ms.*, unless the woman has a professional title such as *Dr.* (use *Miss* on formal social invitations only if the woman prefers that title over *Ms.*):

Ms./Dr. Cecilia Q. Peace
The True Corporation
Sales Department
[Address]

Dear Ms./Dr. Peace:
Sincerely,

Married or Widowed Women

Business. Use *Ms.* or *Mrs.* with the woman's first name and her married last name, maiden name, or a maiden-married combination, as she prefers. (*Note:* Some authorities discourage the use of *Mrs.* with a married or widowed woman's own first name since that form is also used to indicate that a woman is divorced.) If you don't know the person's preference, use *Ms.* with the woman's first name and married last name. In all cases, though, if the woman has a professional title such as *Dr.*, use it:

Ms./Mrs./Dr. Cecilia Q. Peace/Tyler/Tyler-Peace
The True Corporation
Sales Department
[Address]

Dear Ms./Mrs./Dr. Peace/Tyler/Tyler-Peace:
Sincerely,

Social. For strictly formal social material, such as a formal invitation, use *Mrs.* with the woman's married last name and her husband's first name. Some widowed women, though, may prefer to use their own first name with *Ms.* For informal social correspondence sent to the woman alone, use *Ms.* or *Mrs.* with the woman's first

name and her married last name or maiden-married
combination, as she prefers. (Again, some authorities believe that *Mrs.* should be used with a woman's own first
name only if she is divorced.) But if the woman has a
professional title such as *Dr.*, use it:

Mrs. Alfred H. Peace (*formal social*)
[Address]

Dear Mrs. Peace:
Sincerely,

Dr. Cecilia Q. Peace (*alternative formal social*)
[Address]

Dear Dr. Peace:
Sincerely,

Ms./Mrs./Dr. Cecilia Q. Peace/Tyler-Peace (*informal
    social*)
[Address]

Dear Ms./Mrs./Dr. Peace/Tyler-Peace:
Sincerely,

Divorced Women

Business. Use *Ms.* with the woman's first name and her
married last name, maiden name, or maiden-married
names combined, as she prefers. If the woman has a
professional title such as *Dr.,* use it:

Ms./Dr. Cecilia Q. Peace/Tyler/Tyler-Peace
The True Corporation
Sales Department
[Address]

Dear Ms./Dr. Peace/Tyler/Tyler-Peace:
Sincerely,

Social. Use one of two main options: (1) the title *Mrs.*
with the woman's first name and her married last name
or maiden-married names combined, as she prefers; or
(2) the title *Ms.* with the woman's first name and maiden
name, married name, or maiden-married names combined, as she prefers. (On formal social invitations, use
Miss only if she prefers that title.) If the woman has a
professional title such as *Dr.,* use it:

Mrs./Dr. Cecilia Q. Tyler/Tyler-Peace
[Address]

Dear Mrs./Dr. Tyler/Tyler-Peace:
Sincerely,

Ms./Dr. Cecilia Q. Peace/Tyler/Tyler-Peace
[Address]

Dear Ms./Dr. Peace/Tyler/Tyler-Peace
Sincerely,

Couples

Business. Use the names preferred by the individual
persons, and write them in one line as *Mr. Alfred H.
Peace and Ms. Cecilia Q. Peace* or stack the two
names. Use *Mrs.* if the woman prefers. (But see the
previous discussion of using *Mrs.* with a woman's first
name in *Married or Widowed Women.*) If either person has a professional title, however, use it. In that
case, place the titled or highest-ranking person first
(list names alphabetically if both titles are the same
rank). If a married woman prefers to use a different
last name, observe her preference. If the couple are
not married, use their respective names and the title
Ms. (or a professional title) for the woman:

Mr. Alfred H. Peace
Ms./Mrs. Cecilia Q. Peace

The True Corporation
Sales Department
[Address]

Dear Mr. Peace and Ms./Mrs. Peace:
Sincerely,

Mr. Alfred H. Peace and Ms./Mrs. Cecilia Q. Peace
The True Corporation
Sales Department
[Address]

Dear Mr. Peace and Ms./Mrs. Peace:
Sincerely,

Dr. Cecilia Q. Peace and Dr. Alfred H. Peace
The True Corporation
Sales Department
[Address]

Dear Drs. Peace:
Sincerely,

Social. For strictly formal social correspondence, such
as a formal invitation, use *Mrs.* for a married woman
with her husband's full name. Informally, when writing
to a woman alone, use *Ms.* or *Mrs.,* as she prefers, and
her own first name. (But see the previous caution about
using *Mrs.* with her first name in *Married and Widowed
Women.*) If either one of the couple has a professional
title such as *Dr.,* use it:

Mr. and Mrs. Alfred H. Peace
[Address]

Dear Mr. and Mrs. Peace:
Sincerely,

Dr. and Mrs. Alfred H. Peace
[Address]

Dear Dr. and Mrs. Peace:
Sincerely,

Drs. Alfred H. and Cecilia Q. Peace
[Address]

Dear Drs. Peace:
Sincerely,

Dr. Cecilia Q. and Mr. Alfred H. Peace
[Address]

Dear Dr. and Mr. Peace:
Sincerely,

Man or Woman: Gender or Name Unknown

Gender unknown. Socially, you should determine the gender of the person before writing. In business, if you don't know, use the person's first name instead of a title:

A. H. Peace
The True Corporation
Sales Department
[Address]

Dear A. H. Peace:
Sincerely,

Name unknown. If you don't know the name but do know the person's job title, use it. If you know neither, address the letter generally to the firm (or a department):

Manager
The True Corporation
Sales Department
[Address]

Dear Manager:
Sincerely,

Companies

Use *Ladies and Gentlemen* when writing to a firm consisting of both men and women. Use one or the other if you're certain that the firm consists only of men or only of women:

The True Corporation
Sales Department
[Address]

Ladies and Gentlemen:
Sincerely,

U.S. Government

The president

The President
The White House
1600 Pennsylvania Avenue
Washington, DC 20500

Dear Mr. President:
Respectfully yours,/Yours very truly,

Former president

The Honorable Alfred H. Peace
[Address]

Dear Mr. Peace:
Sincerely yours,

The vice president

The Vice President
United States Senate
Old Executive Office Building
Washington, DC 20510

Dear Mr. Vice President:
Respectfully yours,/Yours very truly,

The chief justice, U.S. Supreme Court

The Chief Justice of the United States
The Supreme Court
One First Street NE
Washington, DC 20543

Dear Mr. Chief Justice:/Dear Chief Justice Peace:
Very truly yours,/Sincerely yours,

Associate justice, U.S. Supreme Court

Justice Peace
The Supreme Court
One First Street NE
Washington, DC 20543

Dear Madam Justice:/Dear Justice Peace:
Sincerely yours,

Retired justice, U.S. Supreme Court

The Honorable Alfred H. Peace
[Address]

Dear Justice Peace:
Sincerely yours,

Speaker, House of Representatives

The Honorable Cecilia Q. Peace
The Speaker of the House of Representatives
Washington, DC 20515

Dear Madam Speaker:
Sincerely yours,

Former speaker, House of Representatives

The Honorable Alfred H. Peace
[Address]

Dear Mr. Peace:
Sincerely yours,

Cabinet officers: secretary

The Honorable Cecilia Q. Peace
The Secretary of [Department]
[Address]

Dear Madam Secretary:
Sincerely yours,

Former cabinet officer

The Honorable Alfred H. Peace
[Address]

Dear Mr. Peace:
Sincerely yours,

The attorney general

The Honorable Cecilia Q. Peace
The Attorney General of the United States

The Department of Justice
Washington, DC 20503

Dear Madam Attorney General:
Sincerely yours,

Under secretary of a department

The Honorable Alfred H. Peace
The Under Secretary of [Department]
[Address]

Dear Mr. Under Secretary:
Sincerely yours,

Senator

The Honorable Cecilia Q. Peace
United States Senate
Washington, DC 20510

Dear Senator Peace:
Sincerely yours,

Former senator

The Honorable Alfred H. Peace
[Address]

Dear Mr. Peace:
Sincerely yours,

Senator-elect

The Honorable Cecilia Q. Peace
Senator-elect
United States Senate
Washington, DC 20510

Dear Ms. Peace:
Sincerely yours,

Committee or subcommittee chairman

The Honorable Alfred H. Peace
Chairman
[Committee Name]
United States Senate
Washington, DC 20510

Dear Senator Peace:
Sincerely yours,

U.S. representative or congressman, congresswoman

The Honorable Cecilia Q. Peace
United States House of Representatives
House Office Building
Washington, DC 20515

Dear Ms. Peace:
Sincerely yours,

Former representative

The Honorable Alfred H. Peace
[Address]

Dear Mr. Peace:
Sincerely yours,

Territorial delegate

The Honorable Cecilia Q. Peace
Delegate of [Territory]
[Address]

Dear Ms. Peace:
Sincerely yours,

Resident commissioner

The Honorable Alfred H. Peace
Resident Commissioner of [Territory]
United States House of Representatives
Washington, DC 20515

Dear Mr. Peace:
Sincerely yours,

Heads of independent federal offices, agencies, commissions, and other organizations

The Honorable Cecilia Q. Peace
Director
[Organization]
[Address]

Dear Ms. Peace:
Sincerely yours,

Other high officials of the United States (comptroller general, public printer, and so on)

The Honorable Alfred H. Peace
[Official Name]
[Address]

Dear Mr. Peace:
Sincerely yours,

Secretary to the president

Ms. Cecilia Q. Peace
Secretary to the President

The White House
1600 Pennsylvania Avenue
Washington, DC 20500

Dear Ms. Peace:
Sincerely yours,

Press secretary to the president

Mr. Alfred H. Peace
Press Secretary to the President
The White House
1600 Pennsylvania Avenue
Washington, DC 20500

Dear Mr. Peace:
Sincerely yours,

State and Local Government Officials

Governor. The form of address for governors used in
the next examples is common in most states. *His/Her
Excellency, the Governor of [State],* is the form required by law in Massachusetts and by courtesy in
some other states.

The Honorable Cecilia Q. Peace
Governor of [State]
[Address]

Dear Governor Peace:
Sincerely yours,

Acting governor

The Honorable Alfred H. Peace
Acting Governor of [State]
[Address]

Dear Mr. Peace:
Sincerely yours,

Lieutenant governor

The Honorable Cecilia Q. Peace
Lieutenant Governor of [State]
[Address]

Dear Ms. Peace:
Sincerely yours,

Secretary of state

The Honorable Alfred H. Peace
Secretary of the State of [State]
[Address]

Dear Mr. Peace:
Sincerely yours,

State attorney general

The Honorable Cecilia Q. Peace
Attorney General of [State]
[Address]

Dear Madam Attorney General:
Sincerely yours,

President of a state senate

The Honorable Alfred H. Peace
President of the Senate of the State of [State]
[Address]

Dear Mr. Peace:
Sincerely yours,

Speaker of a state assembly or house of representatives.
In New York, California, Wisconsin, and Nevada, the
legislative body is called the *Assembly*. In Maryland,
Virginia, and West Virginia, it is known as the *House
of Delegates*. In New Jersey, it is called the *House of
General Assembly.*

The Honorable Cecilia Q. Peace
Speaker of the Assembly of the State of [State]
[Address]

Dear Ms. Peace:
Sincerely yours,

State treasurer, auditor, comptroller

The Honorable Alfred H. Peace
Treasurer of the State of [State]
[Address]

Dear Mr. Peace:
Sincerely yours,

State senator

The Honorable Cecilia Q. Peace
Senate of the State of [State]
[Address]

Dear Ms. Peace:
Sincerely yours,

State representative, assemblyman, delegate

The Honorable Alfred H. Peace
House of Delegates of the State of [State]
[Address]

Dear Mr. Peace:
Sincerely yours,

District attorney

The Honorable Cecilia Q. Peace
District Attorney, [County Name] County
County Courthouse
[Address]

Dear Ms. Peace:
Sincerely yours,

Mayor

The Honorable Alfred H. Peace
Mayor of [City]
[Address]

Dear Mayor Peace:/Dear Mr. Mayor:
Sincerely yours,

President of a board of commissioners

The Honorable Cecilia Q. Peace
President, Board of Commissioners
City of [City]
[Address]

Dear Ms. Peace:
Sincerely yours,

City attorney, city counsel, corporation counsel

The Honorable Alfred H. Peace
City Attorney
City of [City]
[Address]

Dear Mr. Peace:
Sincerely yours,

Alderman

Alderman Cecilia Q. Peace
City Hall
[Address]

Dear Ms. Peace:
Sincerely yours,

Court Officials

Chief justice, chief judge, of a state supreme court

The Honorable Alfred H. Peace
Chief Justice
The Supreme Court of the State of [State]
[Address]

Dear Mr. Chief Justice:
Sincerely yours,

Associate justice of the highest court of a state

The Honorable Cecilia Q. Peace
Associate Justice
The Supreme Court of the State of [State]
[Address]

Dear Justice Peace:
Sincerely yours,

Presiding justice

The Honorable Alfred H. Peace

Presiding Justice, Appellate Division
The Supreme Court of the State of [State]
[Address]

Dear Justice Peace:
Sincerely yours,

Judge. Not applicable to the U.S. Supreme Court,
listed earlier.

The Honorable Cecilia Q. Peace
Judge of the [Name of Court and, if applicable,
    District]
[Address]

Dear Judge Peace:
Sincerely yours,

Clerk of a court. When the title *Esq.* is used (for both
men and women), no other title precedes the name.

Alfred H. Peace, Esq.
Clerk of the [Name of Court]
[Address]

Dear Mr. Peace:
Sincerely yours,

U.S. Diplomatic Representatives

American ambassador. Add the name of the country
in which an ambassador or minister is based when the
individual is not at his or her post: *The Honorable
Alfred H. Peace, The Ambassador of the United States
to Sweden.* If the person holds military rank, the diplomatic complimentary title *The Honorable* is omitted,
as in *General Alfred H. Peace.* To avoid confusion,

especially with ministers and ambassadors to Central and South American countries, always use *The Ambassador/Minister of the United States* instead of *American Ambassador/Minister.*

> The Honorable Alfred H. Peace
> The Ambassador of the United States
> American Embassy, [Country]
> [Address]
>
> Dear Mr. Ambassador:
> Sincerely yours,

American minister

> The Honorable Cecilia Q. Peace
> The Minister of the United States
> American Legation, [City and Country]
> [Address]
>
> Dear Madam Minister:
> Sincerely yours,

American chargé d'affaires, consul general, consul, vice consul

> Mr. Alfred H. Peace
> American consul, [City and Country]
> [Address]
>
> Dear Mr. Peace:
> Sincerely yours,

High commissioner

> The Honorable Cecilia Q. Peace
> United States High Commissioner to [Country]
> [Address]

Dear Ms. Peace:
Sincerely yours,

Foreign Officials and Representatives

Foreign ambassador in the United States. Official titles vary from country to country. Therefore, you should contact the Office of Protocol in the State Department or the appropriate embassy to confirm the correct form of address in a specific country. British representatives, for example, are referred to in speech as *British Ambassador* or *British Minister,* and one should use the following form of address when the representative is British or a member of the British Commonwealth: *The Right Honorable* and *The Honorable,* in addition to *His/Her Excellency* wherever appropriate.

Her Excellency Olga M. Peace
The Ambassador of [Country]
[Address]

Excellency:/Dear Madam Ambassador:
Sincerely yours,

Foreign minister in the United States. A diplomatic title would be omitted if an individual had a royal title such as *His/Her Highness* or *Prince.* Otherwise, *His* or *Her Excellency* or *The Honorable* (or both) is a common title.

The Honorable Petre B. Peace
The Minister of [Country]
[Address]

Dear Mr. Minister:
Sincerely yours,

Foreign diplomatic representative with a personal title.
Titles of special courtesy in Spanish-speaking countries, such as *Dr., Señor,* or *Dom,* may be used with the diplomatic title *His/Her Excellency* or *The Honorable.*

His Excellency Count Michele R. Peace
The Ambassador of [Country]
[Address]

Excellency:/Dear Mr. Ambassador:
Sincerely yours,

Prime Minister

His Excellency Masura H. Peace
Prime Minister of [Country]
[Address]

Dear Mr. Prime Minister:
Sincerely yours,

British prime minister

The Right Honorable Harold J. Peace, M.P.
Prime Minister of Great Britain
[Address]

Bus.: Dear Sir:/Dear Mr. Prime Minister:/Dear Prime Minister:
Yours very truly,

Soc.: Dear Prime Minister:/My Dear Prime Minister:
Yours sincerely,

Canadian prime minister

The Right Honorable Jeanne A. Peace, P.C., M.P.
Prime Minister of Canada
[Address]

Bus.: Dear Madam:/Dear Madam Prime Minister:/
Dear Prime Minister:
Yours very truly,

Soc.: Dear Prime Minister:/My Dear Prime Minister:
Yours sincerely,

President of a republic

His Excellency Joaquim Peace
President of [Republic]
[Address]

Excellency:/Dear Mr. President:
Sincerely yours,

Premier

Her Excellency Marie J. Peace
Premier of [Country]
[Address]

Excellency:/Dear Madam Premier:
Sincerely yours,

Foreign chargé d'affaires (de missi) in the United States

Mr. Anders V. Peace
Chargé d'Affaires of [Country]
[Address]

Dear Mr. Peace:
Sincerely yours,

Foreign chargé d'affaires ad interim in the United States

Mr. Sean A. Peace
Chargé d'Affaires ad interim of [Country]
[Address]

Dear Mr. Peace:
Sincerely yours,

The Armed Forces:
Army, Air Force, Marine Corps

Traditionally, civilian writers spell out the rank for all branches of the service, but abbreviations are used by military writers, for example, *CPT* for *captain* and *1LT* for *first lieutenant.* The full rank is stated on the envelope and inside address (*Lieutenant Colonel Alfred H. Peace*) but not in the salutation (*Dear Colonel Peace:*). Titles in the air force and the Marine Corps are the same as those in the army, except that the top rank in the Marine Corps is *commandant.* In the army, regular service is signified by *USA,* and the reserve is indicated by *USAR.* The regular air force uses *USAF* and *USAFR,* and the Marine Corps, *USMC* and *USMCR.*

General, lieutenant general, major general, brigadier general

Lieutenant General Alfred H. Peace, USA
[Address]

Dear General Peace:
Sincerely yours,

Colonel, lieutenant colonel

Lieutenant Colonel Cecilia Q. Peace, USA
[Address]

Dear Colonel Peace:
Sincerely yours,

Major

Major Alfred H. Peace, USA
[Address]

Dear Major Peace:
Sincerely yours,

Captain

Captain Cecilia Q. Peace, USA
[Address]

Dear Captain Peace:
Sincerely yours,

First lieutenant, second lieutenant

Second Lieutenant Alfred H. Peace, USA
[Address]

Dear Lieutenant Peace:
Sincerely yours,

Chaplain. Officially, a chaplain is usually addressed by military rank but informally may be called chaplain, father, or rabbi. The title *chaplain* may be used in correspondence to Roman Catholic chaplains and some Anglican priests, but the individual is referred to by the religious title *father*.

Captain Alfred H. Peace
Chaplain, USA
[Address]

Bus.: Dear Captain Peace:
    Sincerely yours,

Soc.: Dear Father Peace:
    Sincerely yours,

Chief warrant officer, warrant officer

Chief Warrant Officer Cecilia Q. Peace, USA
[Address]

Dear Ms. Peace:
Sincerely yours,

Noncommissioned officer

Private First Class Alfred H. Peace, USA
[Address]

Bus.: Dear Private Peace:
    Sincerely yours,

Soc.: Dear Mr. Peace:
    Sincerely yours,

Cadet

Cadet Cecilia Q. Peace, USA
[Address]

Bus.: Dear Cadet Peace:
    Sincerely yours,

Soc.: Dear Ms. Peace:
    Sincerely yours,

The Armed Forces: Navy, Coast Guard

Titles in the Coast Guard are the same as those in the navy, except that the top rank is *admiral.* In the navy, regular service is indicated by *USN* and the reserve by *USNR.* In the Coast Guard, it is *USCG* and *USCGR.*

Admiral, vice admiral, rear admiral

Rear Admiral Alfred H. Peace, USN
[Address]

Dear Admiral Peace:
Sincerely yours,

Commodore, captain, commander, lieutenant commander

Lieutenant Commander Cecilia Q. Peace, USN
[Address]

Dear Commander Peace:
Sincerely yours,

Junior officers: Lieutenant, lieutenant junior grade, ensign

Ensign Alfred H. Peace, USN
[Address]

Bus.: Dear Ensign Peace:
    Sincerely yours,

Soc.: Dear Mr. Peace:
Sincerely yours,

Chaplain

Captain Alfred H. Peace
Chaplain, USN
[Address]

Bus.: Dear Captain Peace:
      Sincerely yours,

Soc.: Dear Rabbi Peace:
      Sincerely yours,

Chief warrant officer, warrant officer

Chief Warrant Officer Cecilia Q. Peace, USN
[Address]

Dear Mrs./Ms. Peace:
Sincerely yours,

Noncommissioned officer

Chief Petty Officer Alfred H. Peace, USN
[Address]

Bus.: Dear Petty Officer Peace:
      Sincerely yours,

Soc.: Dear Mr. Peace:
      Sincerely yours,

Naval midshipman, Coast Guard cadet

Midshipman Alfred H. Peace, USN
[Address]

Bus.: Dear Midshipman Peace:
      Sincerely yours,

Soc.: Dear Mr. Peace:
Sincerely yours,

Catholic Faith

Observe the local custom and the preferences of the individuals in the use of full names and titles. For example, in addresses, some brothers, sisters, and other persons religious prefer the use of the first name only, the last name only, or both the first and last names. Also, in some religious bodies, the use of the prefix *The* preceding *Reverend* is not required or observed in contemporary usage. Consult the *Official Catholic Directory* for additional information about names, titles, and other forms.

The pope

His Holiness, Pope [Name]/His Holiness the Pope
Vatican City
[Address]

Your Holiness:/Most Holy Father:
Respectfully yours,

Apostolic delegate

The Most Reverend Alfred H. Peace
Archbishop of [Place]
The Apostolic Delegate
[Address]

Most Reverend Sir:/Dear Archbishop Peace:
Respectfully,

Cardinal in the United States

His Eminence Alfred Cardinal Peace/His Eminence
   Cardinal Alfred Peace
Archbishop of [Place] [if he's also an archbishop]
[Address]

Your Eminence:/Dear Cardinal Peace:
Respectfully,

Archbishop in the United States

The Most Reverend Alfred H. Peace, D.D.
Archbishop of [Place]
[Address]

Your Excellency:/Most Reverend Sir:/Dear Archbishop
   Peace:
Respectfully,

Roman Catholic bishop in the United States

The Most Reverend Alfred H. Peace, D.D.
Bishop of [Place]
[Address]

Your Excellency:/Most Reverend Sir:/Dear Bishop
   Peace:
Respectfully,

Monsignor

The Right Reverend Monsignor Peace
[Address]

Right Reverend Monsignor:/Dear Monsignor Peace:
Respectfully,

Abbot

The Right Reverend Alfred H. Peace [initials of order, if used]
Abbot of [Place]
[Address]

Right Reverend Abbot:/Dear Father Abbot:
Sincerely yours,

Superior of a brotherhood and priest. Consult the *Official Catholic Directory* for the address of the superior of a brotherhood, since this depends on whether or not he is a priest or has a title other than *superior*.

The Very Reverend Alfred H. Peace [initials of order, if used]
Director
[Address]

Dear Father Peace:
Sincerely yours,

Priest

The Reverend Alfred H. Peace [initials of order, if [used]
[Address]

Reverend Father:/Dear Father Peace:
Sincerely yours,

Brother

Brother Alfred H. Peace [initials of order, if used]
[Address]

Dear Brother:/Dear Brother Alfred:/Dear Brother
   Peace:
Sincerely yours,

Mother superior of a sisterhood. Many religious con-
gregations, both Catholic and Protestant, no longer
use the title *superior*. The head of the congregation is
known instead by another title, such as *president*.

Mother Cecilia Q. Peace [initials of order, if used]
[Address]

Dear Mother Peace:
Sincerely yours,

Sister superior. Consult the *Official Catholic Directory*
for the address of the superior of a sisterhood. This
depends on the order to which she belongs, and the
initials of the order are not always used.

Sister Cecilia Q. Peace [initials of order, if used]
[Address]

Dear Sister Peace:
Sincerely yours,

Sister

Sister Cecilia Q. Peace [initials of order, if used]
[Address]

Dear Sister:/Dear Sister Cecilia:/Dear Sister Peace:
Sincerely yours,

Jewish Faith

Rabbi

Rabbi Alfred Peace Goldberg, D.D./Rabbi Alfred Peace Goldberg [without a doctorate]
[Address]

Dear Rabbi Goldberg:/Dear Dr. Goldberg:/Dear Rabbi:
Sincerely yours,

Protestant Faith

Anglican archbishop

The Most Reverend Alfred H. Peace
The Lord Archbishop of [Place]
[Address]

Your Grace:/Dear Archbishop Peace:
Respectfully,

Protestant Episcopal bishop. The presiding bishop would be addressed as *The Most Reverend.* Otherwise use *The Right Reverend.*

The Right Reverend Alfred H. Peace, D.D., LL.D.
Bishop of [Place]
[Address]

Right Reverend Sir:/Dear Bishop Peace:
Respectfully,

Anglican bishop

The Right Reverend Alfred H. Peace
The Lord Bishop of [Place]
[Address]

Right Reverend Sir:/Dear Bishop Peace:
Respectfully,/Sincerely yours,

Methodist bishop

The Reverend Alfred H. Peace, D.D.
Methodist Bishop
[Address]

Reverend Sir:/Dear Bishop Peace:
Respectfully,/Sincerely yours,

Archdeacon

The Venerable Alfred H. Peace
Archdeacon of [Place]
[Address]

Venerable Sir:/Dear Archdeacon Peace:
Respectfully,/Sincerely yours,

Dean. This applies only to the head of a cathedral or theological seminary.

The Very Reverend Alfred H. Peace, D.D.
Dean of [Place]
[Address]

Very Reverend Sir:/Dear Dean Peace:
Respectfully,/Sincerely yours,

Minister

The Reverend Alfred H. Peace, D.D., Litt.D./The Reverend Dr. Alfred H. Peace/The Reverend Alfred H. Peace [without doctorate]
[Address]

Dear Dr. Peace: Dear Mr. Peace:
Sincerely yours,

Episcopal priest, high church

The Reverend Alfred H. Peace, D.D., Litt.D./The Reverend Dr. Alfred H. Peace/The Reverend Alfred H. Peace [without doctorate]
[Address]

Dear Dr. Peace:/Dear Mr. Peace:
Sincerely yours,

College and University Officials

President of a college or university

Dr. Alfred H. Peace/Mr. Alfred H. Peace [without doctorate]
President
[Institution]
[Address]

Dear Dr. Peace:/Dear Mr. Peace:
Sincerely yours,

University chancellor

Dr. Alfred H. Peace/Mr. Alfred H. Peace [without doctorate]
Chancellor
[Institution]
[Address]

Dear Dr. Peace:/Dear Mr. Peace:
Sincerely yours,

Dean, assistant dean, of college or graduate school

Dr. Cecilia Q. Peace/Dean Cecilia Q. Peace [without doctorate]
[Institution]
[Address]

Dear Dean Peace:/Dear Dr. Peace:
Sincerely yours,

Professor

Dr. Alfred H. Peace/Professor Alfred H. Peace [without doctorate]
[Institution]
[Address]

Dear Dr. Peace:/Dear Professor Peace:
Sincerely yours,

Associate, assistant professor

Dr. Cecilia Q. Peace/Professor Cecilia Q. Peace [without doctorate]
[Institution]
[Address]

Dear Dr. Peace:/Dear Professor Peace:
Sincerely yours,

Instructor

Dr. Alfred H. Peace/Mr. Alfred H. Peace [without doctorate]
[Institution]
[Address]

Dear Dr. Peace:/Dear Mr. Peace:
Sincerely yours,

United Nations Officials

The United Nations has six branches: The General Assembly, The Security Council, The Economic and Social Council, The Trusteeship Council, The International Court of Justice, and The Secretariat.

Secretary general. An American citizen is never addressed as *Excellency,* although certain officials from other countries are addressed by that title.

His Excellency Alfred H. Peace
Secretary General of the United Nations
[Address]

Excellency:/Dear Mr. Secretary General:/Dear Mr. Peace:
Yours very truly,/Sincerely yours,

Under secretary

The Honorable Alfred H. Peace
Under Secretary of the United Nations
The Secretariat
United Nations
[Address]

Dear Mr. Under Secretary:/Dear Mr. Peace:
Sincerely yours,

Foreign representative with ambassadorial rank

His Excellency Maximilian B. Peace
Representative of [Country] to the United Nations
[Address]

Excellency:/Dear Mr. Ambassador:
Sincerely yours,

U.S. representative with ambassadorial rank

The Honorable Alfred H. Peace
United States Representative to the United Nations
[Address]

Dear Mr. Ambassador:
Sincerely yours,

Letter Salutations

In the previous list of address forms, you just saw a huge variety of letter salutations ranging from the usual *Dear so and so* to the very formal *Your Eminence*. With most salutations used in ordinary business, social, and personal correspondence, you should follow the guidelines given here.

Capitalization. Capitalize the first word in a salutation and the addressee's name and title:

Dear Mrs. Marina:
Dear Rabbi Goldberg:

Punctuation. Put a colon after the salutation in business, personal-business, and social-business letters and after strictly social letters to persons you don't know well. Use a comma after personal letters to friends and family and after social letters to neighbors and other acquaintances:

Dear Mr. Hall:
Dear Mom and Dad,
Dear Ellie,

Titles. Use abbreviations for personal and professional titles such as *Mr., Ms., Mrs.,* and *Dr.:*

Dear Mrs. Palm:
Dear Messrs. Bagel and Cloque:

Spell out religious, military, and most professional titles such as *Father, Major,* and *Professor*:

Dear Sister Mary:
Dear Colonel Dish:

Men and women. For more than one woman, use professional titles, such as *Dr.,* or individually preferred titles, if known. Otherwise, use *Mss.* (sometimes spelled *Mses.*) with their last names, *Ladies*, or *Mesdames* (very formal):

Dear Dr. Fitchet, Ms. Nub, and Mrs. Quick:
Dear Ms. Fitchet, Ms. Nub, and Mrs. Quick:
Dear Mss. Fitchet, Nub, and Quick:
•Ladies:

For more than one man, repeat *Mr., Dr.,* or other title with each name; use *Messrs.* (very formal) in front of the names; or use *Gentlemen* without any names:

Dear Dr. Rustic and Mr. Dent:
Dear Mr. Rustic and Mr. Dent:
Dear Messrs. Rustic and Dent:
Gentlemen:

For men and women, each addressed by name, use professional titles or *Mr.* and *Ms.* or *Mrs.*:

Dear Dr. Potter and Sister Ship:
Dear Mr. Ferry and Ms. Hackle:
Dear Mr. Nail and Mrs. Rent:

Name and gender unknown. When the gender of the addressee is unknown, use the person's full name:

Dear M. J. Shell:
Dear Leslie Gown:

When the name is unknown or both the name *and* gender are unknown, use a professional title such as *Director*. When the title is unknown, use *Sir, Madam,* or *Sir or Madam*:

Dear Editor:
Dear Sir:
Dear Sir or Madam:

Companies and groups. Use *Ladies and Gentlemen.* Use *Gentlemen* or *Messrs.* only when a group or organization is composed entirely of men and *Ladies* or *Mesdames* only when it's composed entirely of women:

Ladies and Gentlemen:
Gentlemen:
Ladies:

In letters to groups of persons, use a collective term:

Dear Friends:
Dear Employees:

Formal greetings. Use greetings such as *Sir* or *Excellency* only for certain high officials from other countries (never from the United States) or for certain persons religious, such as a cardinal or archbishop, in official or very formal correspondence. Also, use *Sir* and *Madam* only when you want to show your respect to persons of higher rank, age, or status. In other words, the person using the term is indicating that he or she holds an inferior position in some respect and that the person being called *Sir* or *Madam* holds a superior position:

Your Eminence:
Most Reverend Sir:

Complimentary Closes

One thing is the same with both salutations and complimentary closes—the degree of formality that you need to use. For example, if you think that you should use a very formal salutation, you should also use a very formal close and vice versa.

Informal closes are used in personal correspondence; social correspondence to friends and acquaintances, especially those who are peers; and a wide range of business correspondence among employees, customers and clients, associates, and so on.

Formal closes are used in legal, official, and other formal correspondence and in a variety of social and business correspondence to persons of higher rank, to individuals one does not know, to international readers who expect more reserve and formality, and so on.

Certain closes, such as *Respectfully* or *Respectfully yours,* convey especially high regard for the addressee. You might, therefore, use this type of close in correspondence to a high church official, such as a bishop, or to a high governmental official, such as the president of a republic. But you wouldn't use it in correspondence to a college instructor or the personnel manager in a business corporation.

Use this general rule to help you decide how formal to be: You always convey your high regard to someone of *higher* rank. Therefore, a person of higher rank would not use a close associated with higher rank when writing to someone of lower rank. For example, an ordinary citizen might use *Respectfully* when writing to the president of a republic, but the president wouldn't use that close when answering the citizen's letter.

The most common informal social and business close is *Sincerely,* followed by the slightly more formal sounding *Sincerely yours.* The nice thing about *Sincerely yours* is that it can be safely used in a variety of social and business situations to both peers and to persons of higher *or* lower rank. The closes *Yours truly* and *Yours very truly* (the latter preferred by some authorities over

Very truly yours), used in both official and general business correspondence, sound somewhat more formal than *Sincerely yours.*

Placing the word *Very* before *Sincerely* (*Very sincerely yours*) or *Cordially* (*Very cordially yours*) changes each to a more formal close. Also, the word *Cordially* alone or with *Very* conveys a slightly warmer, friendlier tone and is less formal than *Sincerely* alone or with *Very.*

In general, select a friendlier, warmer close, such as *Cordially* or *Best regards,* for close friends and business associates, especially in informal situations. When a slightly more formal or less familiar sounding close is desired, select one such as *Yours very truly* or *Sincerely yours.* Either of those is less likely to be interpreted by the reader as being inappropriately familiar. The following closes in each column are generally arranged from the most formal or least casual to the least formal or most casual. Even among the closes in the second column that you can use for informal situations, *Sincerely* sounds less informal than *Warmest regards:*

Formal	*Informal*
Respectfully,	Sincerely yours,
Respectfully yours,	Cordially yours,
Yours truly,	Sincerely,
Yours very truly,	Regards,
Very sincerely yours,	Best regards,
Very cordially yours,	Warmest regards,
Sincerely yours,	Best wishes,

If you want something more personal than any of the formal or informal choices, say whatever you're feeling: *Love, As ever, As always, Yours, Affectionately, Fondly,* or anything else. Note, however, that the last two—*Affectionately* and *Fondly*—rub some people the wrong way. To some, they seem to say: "I like you, but get it through your head that I don't *love* you even as a friend; I only tell my *good* friends that I *love* them, and you don't qualify for that." If you think someone might be a bit irked by those closes, use something safer like *Yours.*

Signature Lines

Signature lines don't seem to worry people as much as salutations or complimentary closes. But as you'll see, a few rules apply. Mostly you'll be concerned about business signatures. In personal correspondence, you don't use a typed signature line; you simply sign your name beneath the complimentary close.

Company. Accountants and certain other individuals may want the company rather than the individual to be emphasized. In such cases, place the company name in all capital letters (as it appears on the letterhead) two lines below the complimentary close. Place the signer's name four lines below the firm name:

Sincerely yours,

A. C. PYRE, INC.

Horace Pinesap

Horace Pinesap, CPA
Auditor

Man. Write the man's name exactly as he signs it. *Mr.* is placed in parentheses before the name *only* when it would not otherwise be clear that the signer is a man:

Sincerely yours,

David Filch

David Filch, CFA
Financial Adviser

Sincerely yours,

D. R. Filch

(Mr.) D. R. Filch, CFA
Financial Adviser

Single woman. Do not use *Ms.* in the signature line except in international correspondence or unless it would not otherwise be clear that the signer is a woman. Short job titles may be placed on the same line or on the next line, as preferred:

Sincerely yours,

Maxine Lugo

Maxine Lugo, Designer

Sincerely yours,

M. J. Lugo

(Ms.) M. J. Lugo
Designer

Married or widowed woman. Do not use *Ms.* in the signature line except in international correspondence or unless it would not otherwise be clear that the signer is a woman. However, you may use *Mrs.* in parentheses before the name if you want to signal that you prefer to be addressed as *Mrs.* rather than *Ms.*:

Sincerely yours,

Wilma C. Lance

Wilma C. Lance
Director, Public Relations

Sincerely yours,

Wilma C. Lance

(Mrs.) Wilma C. Lance
Director, Public Relations

Divorced woman. Do not use *Ms.* in the signature line except in international correspondence or unless it would not otherwise be clear that the signer is a woman. Although it is uncommon for a divorced woman to use *Mrs.*, you would place *Mrs.* in parentheses before the name to signal that you prefer to be addressed as *Mrs.* rather than *Ms.*:

Sincerely yours,

Marcia Quill

Marcia Quill
President

Signing for another. When signing your own name to a letter naming someone else in the signature line, omit the person's first name after the words *Secretary to* or *Assistant to* (unless another person in the firm has the same last name). When you sign the other person's name rather than your own name, put your initials in parentheses after the person's name or immediately under it:

Sincerely yours,

Deanne Moraine

Deanne Moraine
Assistant to Mr. Hem

Sincerely yours,

Roger Long (dm)

Roger Long
General Manager

See also the placement of complimentary closes and signature lines illustrated in **Letter Formats** and the description of the complimentary close and signature line in **Parts of a Letter**.

INDEX